Lecture Notes in Computer Science 8450

Commenced Publication in 1973
Founding and Former Series Editors:
Gerhard Goos, Juris Hartmanis, and Jan van Leeuwen

T0212809

Bart Preneel   Demosthenes Ikonomou (Eds.)

Privacy Technologies and Policy

Second Annual Privacy Forum, APF 2014
Athens, Greece, May 20-21, 2014
Proceedings

 Springer

Volume Editors

Bart Preneel
KU Leuven and iMinds
Department of Electrical Engineering (ESAT)
Kasteelpark Arenberg 10, Bus 2452, 3001 Leuven, Belgium
E-mail: bart.preneel@esat.kuleuven.be

Demosthenes Ikonomou
ENISA, Information Security and Data Protection Unit
1 Vasilissis Sofias, Marousi, 15124 Athens, Greece
E-mail: demosthenes.ikonomou@enisa.europa.eu

ISSN 0302-9743   e-ISSN 1611-3349
ISBN 978-3-319-06748-3   e-ISBN 978-3-319-06749-0
DOI 10.1007/978-3-319-06749-0
Springer Cham Heidelberg New York Dordrecht London

Library of Congress Control Number: Applied for

LNCS Sublibrary: SL 4 – Security and Cryptology

Typesetting: Camera-ready by author, data conversion by Scientific Publishing Services, Chennai, India

Printed on acid-free paper

Springer is part of Springer Science+Business Media (www.springer.com)

Preface

The Second Annual Privacy Forum (APF 2014) was held in Athens, Greece, during May 20-21, 2014. The forum was co-organized by the European Union Agency for Network and Information Security (ENISA) and the European Commission Directorate General for Communications Networks, Content and Technology (DG CONNECT), with the support of the Systems Security Laboratory (SSL) of the University of Piraeus. APF 2014 took place during the the Greek Presidency of the Council of the European Union.

We are witnessing the fast development of technologies that play an ever more central role in our lives; the most notable developments are the wide deployment of cloud computing, the explosion of social networks, the development of "big data" solutions, and the emerging Internet of Things. While these developments improve the quality of our lives, they also transform society and raise increasing concerns related to privacy.

Privacy is an abstract and subjective concept, which depends on context and cultural issues, and that evolves over time. Moreover, several stakeholders interact to resolve ever more complex privacy issues. The revelations by Snowden, which started in the middle of 2013, have brought the privacy risks related to mass surveillance to the forefront of the international community. In the context of big data, companies are collecting an increasing amount of information in order to offer improved and customized services and to reduce fraud and abuse. The developments in social networks show that users have a joint responsbility for protecting each other's privacy online. As it is clear that this complex societal issue can only be addressed by a combination of technical and legal means, the European institutions are developing a new Privacy Regulation, whose goal is to update and improve the important 1995 EU Data Protection Directive.

The aim of APF 2014 was to close the loop from research to policy by bringing together scientists and key decision-makers, thereby complementing scientific events dedicated to privacy and privacy technologies. The program of APF 2014 mixed contributed papers that had undergone a scientific review process with invited speakers and panels. But in contrast to most scientific events, researchers were encouraged to submit position papers or overview papers that offered a broader perspective on their research.

As a result of the Call for Papers, 21 papers were submitted; after a thorough review by the members of the scientific Program Committee, in which each paper received at least four reviews, 12 papers were accepted for presentation at APF 2014 and for inclusion in these proceedings. One of these accepted papers is a merged version of two related submissions. Four of the accepted papers have undergone an additional step of reviewing with the help of a shepherd from the Program Committee.

The themes explored by the forum include: the concept and implementation of "privacy by design," with applications to encrypted databases; the study of video surveillance architectures and new networking concepts; and innovative solutions for identity management. The presentations addressed the technical, legal, and economic aspects of these problems.

Several people have contributed to the success of APF 2014. First, we would like to thank all the presenters, as well as the authors who submitted their work. We sincerely thank all the Program Committee members, who volunteered to review the papers and contributed to an intensive discussion phase. APF 2014 would not have been such a success without the continuous contribution of the staff of ENISA. We would also like to thank Dr. Paul Timmers and his colleagues at the European Commission DG CONNECT as well as Prof. Sokratis Katsikas and his team at the Systems Security Laboratory (SSL) of the University of Piraeus. Our gratitude is also extended to the Greek Presidency of the EU Council. Finally we want to express our gratitude to ISACA and INTRALOT, and in particular to Mr. Dimitriadis Christos for his support.

We hope that this forum can continue to stimulate the European and international privacy community — offering a forum for the exchange of views and ideas between policymakers, research communities, and industry.

March 2014   Demosthenes Ikonomou
                                                                     Bart Preneel

APF 2014

Annual Privacy Forum
Athens, Greece, May 20-21, 2014

Organized by

*European Union Agency for Network and Information Security
(ENISA)*

*European Commission Directorate General for Communications
Networks, Content and Technology (DG CONNECT)*

Systems Security Laboratory (SSL), University of Piraeus

General Co-chairs

Paul Timmers	European Commission, EC DG CONNECT
Sokratis Katsikas	University of Piraeus
Demosthenes Ikonomou	ENISA

Organizing Committee

Aimilia Bantouna	University of Piraeus
Rosa Barcelo	EC DG CONNECT
Daria Catalui	ENISA
Stefan Schiffner	ENISA

Program Chair

Bart Preneel	KU Leuven and iMinds, Belgium

Program Committee

External Reviewers

Gergely Acs
Andreas Albers
Kovila Coopamootoo

Aliaksandr Lazouski
Lukasz Olejnik

Table of Contents

Privacy by Design:
From Technologies to Architectures
(Position Paper)

Thibaud Antignac and Daniel Le Métayer

Inria, Université de Lyon
{thibaud.antignac,daniel.le-metayer}@inria.fr

Abstract. Existing work on privacy by design mostly focus on technologies rather than methodologies and on components rather than architectures. In this paper, we advocate the idea that privacy by design
should also be addressed at the architectural level and be associated with
suitable methodologies. Among other benefits, architectural descriptions
enable a more systematic exploration of the design space. In addition,
because privacy is intrinsically a complex notion that can be in tension
with other requirements, we believe that formal methods should play a
key role in this area. After presenting our position, we provide some hints
on how our approach can turn into practice based on ongoing work on a
privacy by design environment.

1 Introduction

Privacy by design is often held up as a necessary step to improve privacy protection in the digital society [32,50]. It will even become a legal obligation in the
European Community[1] if the current draft of Data Protection Regulation [15]
eventually gets adopted. The fact that future regulatory frameworks promote
or impose privacy by design is definitely a positive step but their adoption will
take time, they are unlikely to be applicable in all regions of the world and
the interpretation of the principle itself may vary greatly[2] among jurisdictions.
Therefore, the possible adoption of privacy by design laws should obviously not
be seen as the end of the story: the extent to which a true privacy by design will
actually turn to reality will also depend on other factors such as social demand,
economic conditions and of course the availability of technical solutions. Even
though all these dimensions are essential and all possible means should be used
to foster the adoption of privacy by design, we choose to focus on the technical
issues in this paper.

---

[1] And also "a prerequisite for public procurement tenders according to the Directive
of the European Parliament and of the Council on public procurement as well as
according to the Directive of the European Parliament and of the Council on procurement by entities operating in the water, energy, transport and postal services
sector."

[2] And it is obviously out of question to define it very precisely in a legal document.

B. Preneel and D. Ikonomou (Eds.): APF 2014, LNCS 8450, pp. 1–17, 2014.

As discussed by several authors [12,21,28,19], a range of privacy enhancing technologies (PETs) are now available, which can provide strong privacy guarantees in a variety of contexts. Even if more research on PETs will always be needed, a question that arises at this stage is how to favor the uptake of these technologies. The position that we want to promote and bring forward for discussion in this paper is threefold:

1. Existing work in this area mostly focus on technologies rather than methodologies and on components rather than architectures. We advocate the idea that privacy by design should also be addressed at the architectural level and be associated with suitable methodologies. Among other benefits, architectural descriptions enable a more systematic exploration of the design space.
2. Because privacy is intrinsically a complex notion, which, in addition, often turns out to be (or seems to be) in tension with other requirements, formal methods should play a key role in this area. Among other benefits, formal descriptions make it possible to define precisely the concepts at hand and the guarantees provided by a solution, to reason about the design choices and ultimately to justify them rigorously, hence contributing also to accountability.
3. Because designers are generally not experts in formal methods, dedicated frameworks and user-friendly interfaces should be designed to hide the complexities of the models and make them usable in this context. Such frameworks should allow designers to express their requirements and to interact with the system to refine or adapt them until a satisfactory architecture is obtained.

The paper is organized as follows: We present our position and discuss it in more detail in Section 2. In order to illustrate this position, we proceed in Section 3 with an example of formal privacy logic which is applied in Section 4 to the design of smart metering systems. Section 5 discusses related work and Section 6 outlines directions for further research.

2   Position

A wide array of techniques have been proposed or applied to the definition of new PETs during the last decades [11,18,28,52], including zero-knowledge proofs, secure multi-party computation, homomorphic encryption, commitments, private information retrieval (PIR), anonymous credentials, anonymous communication channels, or trusted platform modules (TPM). These PETs have been used to provide strong privacy guarantees in a variety of contexts such as smart metering [17,33,53], electronic traffic pricing [4,27,49]), ubiquitous computing [32] or location based services [9,29,30]. Even if more techniques will always be needed to defeat new attacks in this eternal game between cops and robbers, there is now a need for serious thinking about the conditions for the adoption of existing PETs by industry. This reflection has started with convincing cases for the development of appropriate methodologies [12,21,58] or development tools [28] for privacy by design. In this paper, we pursue this line of thought in arguing that privacy by design should also (and firstly) be considered at the architecture level and should be supported by appropriate reasoning tools relying on formal models.

Let us consider the case for architectures first. Many definitions of architectures have been proposed in the literature. In this paper, we will adopt a definition inspired by [6][3]: *The architecture of a system is the set of structures needed to reason about the system, which comprise software and hardware elements, relations among them and properties of both.* The atomic components of an architecture are coarse-grain entities such as modules, components or connectors. In the context of privacy, as suggested in Section 3, the components are typically the PETs themselves and the purpose of the architecture is their combination to achieve the privacy requirements of the system. Therefore, an architecture is foremost an abstraction and "this abstraction is essential to taming the complexity of a system – we simply cannot, and do not want to, deal with all the complexity all the time" [6].

Most of the reasons identified in [6] to explain why architectures matter are very relevant for privacy by design:

- The architecture is a carrier of the earliest and hence most fundamental hardest-to-change design decisions: overlooking architectural choices may thus seriously hamper the integration of privacy requirements in the design of a system.
- Architectures channel the creativity of developers, reducing design and system complexity: because they make it possible to abstract away unnecessary details and to focus on critical issues, architectures can help privacy designers reason about privacy requirements and the combination of PETs which could be used to meet them.
- A documented architecture enhances communication among stakeholders: documenting the design choices is especially important in the context of privacy to meet the obligations arising from Privacy Impact Assessments (PIA) and accountability (which are emphasized in the Data Protection Regulation draft [15]).
- An architecture can be created as a transferable, reusable model: architectures can therefore play a key role to increase the reusability of privacy friendly solutions, which could lead to significant cost reductions and better dissemination of knowledge and expertise among developers. Being able to go beyond case-by-case strategies and to factorize efforts is a key step for privacy by design to move from craft to industry.

If the choice is made to work at the architectural level, the next question to be answered is: "how to define, represent and use architectures ?" In practice, architectures are often described in a pictorial way, using different kinds of graphs with legends defining the meaning of nodes and vertices, or semi-formal

---

[3] This definition is a generalization (to system architectures) of the definition of software architectures proposed in [6].

representations such as UML diagrams (class diagrams, use case diagrams, sequence diagrams, communication diagrams, etc.). The second point we want to make here is that, even though such pictorial representations can be very useful (especially when their use is standardized), reasoning about privacy requirements is such a subtle and complex issue that the architecture language used for this purpose must be defined in a formal way. By formal, we mean that the properties of the architectures must be defined in a mathematical logic and reasoning about these properties must be supported by a formal proof or verification system. Reasoning about privacy is complex for different reasons: first, it is a multi-faceted notion stemming from a variety of principles which are not defined very precisely. It is therefore of prime importance to circumscribe the problem, to define precisely the aspects of privacy which are taken into account and how they are interpreted in the design choices. The fact that not all aspects of privacy are susceptible to formalization is not a daunting obstacle to the use of formal methods in this context: the key point is to build appropriate models for the aspects of privacy (such as data minimization) which are prone to formalization and involve complex reasoning. Another source of complexity in this context is the fact that privacy often seems to conflict with other requirements such as guarantees of authenticity or correctness, efficiency, usability, etc. To summarize, formal methods should:

- Make it possible to define precisely the concepts at hand (requirements, assumptions, guarantees, etc.).
- Help designers to explore the design space and to reason about the possible choices. Indeed, privacy by design is often a matter of choice [36]: multiple options are generally available to achieve a given set of functionalities, some of them being privacy friendly, others less, and a major challenge for the designer is to understand all these options, their strengths and weaknesses.
- Provide a documented and rigorous justification of the design choices, which would be a significant contribution to the accountability requirement. Accountability is defined in Article 22 of the current draft of the future Data Protection Regulation [15] as the following obligation for data collectors: "The controller shall adopt appropriate policies and implement appropriate and demonstrable technical and organizational measures to ensure and be able to demonstrate in a transparent manner that the processing of personal data is performed in compliance with this Regulation..."

It should be clear however, that designers are generally not experts in formal methods and appropriate tools and user-friendly interfaces have to be made available to hide the complexities of the models. Such frameworks should allow designers to express their requirements, to get understandable representations (or views) of the architectural options, to navigate in these views, and to refine or adapt them until a satisfactory architecture is obtained.

Considering all these requirements, it should be clear that specific, dedicated formal frameworks have to be devised to support privacy by design. To make the discussion more concrete, we provide in the following sections some hints about such a framework and its application to a real case study.

3 Example of Formal Model

As an illustration of the position advocated in the previous section, we present now a subset of a privacy logic to reason about two key properties: the minimization (of the collection of personal data) and the accuracy (of the computations) . Indeed, the tension between data minimization and accuracy is one of the delicate issues to be solved in many systems involving personal data. For example, electronic traffic payment systems [4,27,49] have to guarantee both the correctness of the computation of the fee and the limitation of the collection of location data; smart metering systems [17,33,53] have also to ensure the correct computations of the fees and to limit the collection of consumption data; recommendation systems [42] need to achieve both the accuracy of the recommendations while minimizing the disclosure of personal preferences; electric vehicle charging systems [22] also need to guarantee the accuracy of the bills and the protection of the location information of the vehicles.

3.1 Excerpt of a Privacy Epistemic Logic

Because privacy is closely connected with the notion of knowledge, epistemic logics form an ideal basis to reason about privacy properties. Epistemic logics [16] are a family of modal logics using a knowledge modality usually denoted by $K_i(\phi)$ to express the fact that agent i knows the property ϕ. However standard epistemic logics based on possible worlds semantics suffer from a weakness which makes them unsuitable in the context of privacy: this problem is often referred to as "logical omniscience" [20]. It stems from the fact that agents know all the logical consequences of their knowledge (because these consequences hold in all possible worlds). An undesirable outcome of logical omniscience would be that, for example, an agent knowing the commitment $C(v)$ (or hash) of a value v would also know v (or the possible values of v). This is obviously not the intent in a formal model of privacy where commitments are precisely used to hide the original values to the recipients. This issue is related to the fact that standard epistemic logics do not account for limitations of computational power.

Therefore it is necessary to define dedicated epistemic logics to deal with different aspects of privacy and to model the variety of notions and techniques at hand (e.g. knowledge, zero-knowledge proof, trust, etc.). Let us consider for the sake of illustration the following excerpt of a privacy epistemic logic:

$$\phi ::= \phi_0 \tag{1}$$
$$|\; \neg\phi \tag{2}$$
$$|\; \phi \wedge \phi' \tag{3}$$
$$|\; K_i(\phi_0) \tag{4}$$
$$|\; X_i(\phi_0) \tag{5}$$

$$\phi_0 ::= \text{receive}_{i,j}(x) \tag{6}$$
$$| \text{ receive}_{i,j}(prim) \tag{7}$$
$$| \text{ trust}_{i,j} \tag{8}$$
$$| \text{ compute}_i(x = t) \tag{9}$$
$$| \text{ check}_i(eq) \tag{10}$$
$$| \text{ has}_i(x) \tag{11}$$
$$| \text{ prim } | \ p \ | \ \phi_0 \wedge \phi_0' \tag{12}$$

$$prim ::= \text{proof}_{i,j}(p) \ | \ att \ | \ prim \wedge prim' \tag{13}$$
$$p ::= att \ | \ eq \ | \ p \wedge p' \tag{14}$$
$$att ::= \text{attest}_i(eq) \tag{15}$$
$$eq ::= t \ rel \ t' \tag{16}$$
$$rel ::= \ = \ | < | > | \le | \ge \tag{17}$$
$$t ::= c \ | \ x \ | \ \text{F}(t_1, \dots, t_n) \tag{18}$$

This logic involves only two modalities: the usual knowledge operator K_i and the "algorithmic knowledge" [16,51] denoted by X_i, which represents the knowledge that an agent i can actually build. Properties ϕ_0 include both the basic properties p on variables of the system and properties used to characterize the architecture itself. More precisely, receive$_{i,j}(x)$ means that agent j can send the variable x to agent i, receive$_{i,j}(prim)$ means that agent j can send the property $prim$ to agent i where $prim$ can be a combination of (non interactive) zero-knowledge proofs and attestations. An attestation attest$_i(eq)$ is a simple declaration by agent i that property eq holds. This declaration is of no use to agent j unless j trusts i, which is expressed by trust$_{j,i}$. The primitive proof$_{i,j}(p)$ means that agent i can make a proof of property p which can be checked by agent j[4]. The properties compute$_i(x = t)$ and check$_i(p)$ are used to express the fact that an agent i can respectively compute a variable x defined by the equation $x = t$ or check a property p. Symbol F stands for the available basic operations (e.g. hash, homomorphic hash, encryption, random value generation, arithmetic operations, etc.), c stands for constants, and x for variables. Last but not least, has$_i(x)$ is the property that agent i can get the value of variable x (which does not, in itself, provide any guarantee about the correctness of this value).

3.2   Semantics and Axiomatization

The semantics of this logic can be defined using an augmented Kripke model $M = (Arch, \pi, \mathcal{D}_1, \dots, \mathcal{D}_n)$ where:

- *Arch* is a set of possible architectures (generally called worlds) of the system under consideration. In our setting, an architecture is defined as a property ϕ_0 which characterizes all the operations available to the agents.

---

[4] In general a proof could be checked by several agents, which could be expressed using a set of agents names as second index.

- π is an interpretation for the primitives *prim* and the relations *eq*.
- $\mathcal{D}_1, \ldots, \mathcal{D}_n$ are the deductive systems associated with agents $1, \ldots, n$.

The deductive system associated with an agent i makes it possible to define the semantics of the X_i operator (knowledge built by agent i). In other words, each agent i can apply rules $\rhd_i$ to derive new knowledge. Typical rules of deductive systems include:

- $\text{receive}_{i,j}\,(prim) \rhd_i prim$
- $\text{attest}_j\,(eq)\,, \text{trust}_{i,j} \rhd_i eq$
- $\text{proof}_{j,i}\,(p) \rhd_i p$
- $\text{check}_i\,(eq) \rhd_i p$
- $\text{compute}_i\,(x = t) \rhd_i x = t$
- $\text{hash}\,(x_1) = \text{hash}\,(x_2) \rhd_i x_1 = x_2$
- $\text{hhash}\,(x) = \text{hhash}\,(x_1) \otimes \text{hhash}\,(x_2) \rhd_i x = x_1 + x_2$
- $\text{receive}_{i,j}\,(x) \rhd_i \text{has}_i\,(x)$
- $\text{compute}_i\,(x = t) \rhd_i \text{has}_i\,(x)$
- $\text{has}_i\,(x_1)\,, \ldots, \text{has}_i\,(x_m)\,, \text{dep}\,(x, \{x_1, \ldots, x_m\}) \rhd_i \text{has}_i\,(x)$
  with $\text{dep}\,(x, \{x_1, \ldots, x_m\})$ a dependence relationship known by i stating that x can be derived from $x_1, \ldots, x_m$.

In order to reason about architectures, we can use an axiomatization in the style of previous work on deductive algorithmic knowledge [16,51]. Typical examples of axioms and inference rules include:

$$\textbf{TAUT}: \text{All instances of propositional tautologies.} \tag{19}$$

$$\textbf{MP}: \text{From } \phi \text{ and } \phi \to \psi \text{ infer } \psi \tag{20}$$

$$\textbf{Gen}: \text{From } \phi \text{ infer } K_i\,(\phi) \tag{21}$$

$$\textbf{K}: K_i\,(\phi \to \psi) \to (K_i\,(\phi) \to K_i\,(\psi)) \tag{22}$$

$$\textbf{T}: K_i\,(\phi) \to \phi \tag{23}$$

$$\textbf{KC}: K_i\,(\phi \wedge \psi) \to (K_i\,(\phi) \wedge K_i\,(\psi)) \tag{24}$$

$$\textbf{XD}: \text{From } X_i(\phi_1), \ldots, X_i(\phi_n) \text{ and } \phi_1, \ldots, \phi_n \rhd_i \phi \text{ infer } X_i(\phi) \tag{25}$$

$$\textbf{XT}: X_i\,(\phi) \to \phi \tag{26}$$

$$\textbf{XC}: X_i\,(\phi \wedge \psi) \to (X_i\,(\phi) \wedge X_i\,(\psi)) \tag{27}$$

A key difference between the properties of K_i and X_i is the lack of counterpart of axioms **Gen** and **K** for X_i, which makes it possible to avoid the omniscience problem. In contrast, the knowledge built by an agent i depends on the associated deductive system $\rhd_i$ as expressed by rule **XD**. Rules **T** and **XT** express the fact that an agent cannot derive false properties.

The axiomatization outlined in this section forms the basis for an inference algorithm which makes it possible to prove properties of architectures (expressed as ϕ_0 properties) as discussed in the next subsection.

3.3   Use of the Formal Model

The first functionality of a design environment is to make it possible for the designer to express the requirements that apply to the system and, optionally, the design choices which have already been made (or which are imposed by the environment or the client) as well as the possible trust assumptions.

Formally speaking, the requirements are made of three components:

- Functional requirements: the purpose of the system, which is expressed as a set of equations $x = t$.
- Privacy and knowledge requirements: values that should not (respectively should) be known by certain actors, which is expressed by properties $\neg \mathrm{has}_i (x)$ (respectively $\mathrm{has}_i (x)$).
- Correctness (integrity) requirements: the possibility for certain actors to ensure that certain values are correct, which is expressed as $X_i (eq)$.

Generally speaking, other non-functional requirements could also be considered but the combination of privacy and correctness already provides a degree of complexity which is sufficient to illustrate the approach.

The design choices, which add further requirements on the architecture, can be defined as ϕ_0 properties. They can express, for example, the fact that communication links are (or are not) available between specific components or certain computations (zero-knowledge, homomorphic hash, etc.) can (or cannot) be performed by certain components.

Several situations are possible when the designer has entered this first batch of information:

1. The requirements may be contradictory, for example because privacy requirements conflict with knowledge or architectural requirements or because architectural requirements themselves are not consistent (operations computed by components which cannot get access to the necessary parameters, checks which cannot be carried out because some values are not available to the component, etc.). The system returns the identified contradictions, which may provide some hints to the designer to modify his initial input.
2. The requirements may be consistent but not precise enough to characterize a unique architecture. In this case, the system can use a library of existing PETs to provide suggestions to the user. The user can then decide to apply a given PET (which is expressed formally by the addition of a new assumption, e.g. $\mathrm{receive}_{i,j} \left(\mathrm{proof}_{j,i} (p) \right)$ for a zero-knowledge proof of property p sent by agent j to agent i.
3. The requirements may be precise enough to specify a unique (and correct architecture).

The first two cases lead to a new iteration of the procedure. In the last case, the designer has obtained a satisfactory architecture (which does not prevent him from performing a new iteration with different assumptions to further explore the design space).

4   Example of Application

Let us now illustrate the framework outlined in the previous section with a small smart metering case study. Privacy friendly smart grids and smart metering systems have been studied extensively [17,25,26,53]. Our purpose here is neither to present a new solution nor to provide a comprehensive study of smart-metering systems but to show how a formal framework can help a designer to find his way among the possible options. We focus here on the billing functionality and the potential tensions between the privacy requirements of the clients and the need for the operator to ensure the correctness of the computation of the fee.

Let us assume in the first instance that the system is made of three components: the back-end system of the operator o, the computer of the user (customer) u and the meter m. The requirements for this case study are the following:

– Functional requirements: the purpose of the system is the computation of the fee which is expressed as the equation $Fee = \sum_{i=1}^{n}(P(C_i))$ where C_i are the actual consumption values for the considered period of time ($i \in [1, n]$) and P is the cost function.
– Privacy and knowledge requirements: $\neg has_o(C_i)$ and $has_o(Fee)$ respectively, to express the fact that the operator o should not obtain the individual consumption values C_i but should get the fee.
– Correctness (integrity) requirements: the operator must be sure that the fee is correct: $X_o(Fee = \sum_{i=1}^{n}(P(C_i)))$.

Let us assume in a first scenario that the designer considered a direct communication link between the meter and the operator, which means that the architecture would include the property $receive_{o,m}(C_i)$. This possibility would obviously conflict with the privacy requirement since $receive_{o,m}(C_i) \rhd_i has_o(C_i)$. Two communication links are therefore necessary: from m to u and from u to o.

The next question is where the computation of P should take place: generally speaking, this could be at the back-office of the operator, on the meter, or on the computer of the user. Depending on his initial ideas about the architecture and the constraints imposed by the hardware, the designer can either enter directly the appropriate $compute_o$, $compute_m$ or $compute_u$ property. Otherwise these options would be suggested in turn by the system.

– The first option turns out to conflict with the privacy requirements (because the operator would need the input values C_i to compute Fee) unless homomorphic encryption can be used to allow the operator to compute Fee on encrypted values.
– The second option can be further explored if it does not incur inacceptable additional costs on the meters. However, the system would then identify a trust requirement (which may or may not have been foreseen by the designer): the operator must trust the meter ($trust_{o,m}$) because the only information received by the operator would be an attestation of the meter ($attest_m(Fee = \sum_{i=1}^{n}(P(C_i)))$) and an attestation can turn into a true guarantee only in conjunction with a trust assumption (as expressed by the rule $attest_j(eq), trust_{i,j} \rhd_i eq$).

– The third option will be more appealing if the role of the meters has to be confined to the delivery of the consumption measures. But this choice leads to another requirement: either the user can be trusted by the operator (which is excluded by assumption) or he has to be able to provide to the operator a proof of correctness of the computation of the fee [53] $(receive_{o,u} \left(\text{proof}_{u,o} \left(Fee = \sum_{i=1}^{n} (P(C_i))\right)\right))$.

If none of these options is available, further actors need to be considered and involved in the computation of the fee. In general, these actors can either be pairs or trusted third parties. In both cases, further requirements would arise: a secure multi-party computation scheme would be necessary to ensure that the pairs do not learn each other's consumptions and trust assumptions would be necessary to ensure that computations can be delegated to the third party.

As discussed in Section 2, designers are usually not experts in formal methods. As a result, a design environment should provide alternative modes of interaction hiding the complexities of the formal model. Considering that designers are used to graphical notations, we have chosen to represent the different views of the architecture as annotated graphs. The interested reader can find in Annex 1 the "location views" showing, for the two successful scenarios described above, the architectures obtained at the end of the interaction process.

5 Related Work

This position paper stands at the crossroads of at least three different areas: software architectures, formal models for privacy and engineering of privacy by design.

Software architectures have been an active research topic for several decades [54] but they are usually defined using purely graphical, informal means [6] or within semi-formal [8] frameworks. Formal frameworks have been proposed to define software architectures [2,23,34,48] but they are usually based on process algebras or graph grammars and they are not designed to express privacy properties. One exception is the framework introduced in [37] which defines the meaning of the available operations in a (trace-based) operational semantics and proposes an inference system to derive properties of the architectures. The inference system is applied to the proof of properties related to the use of spot checks in electronic traffic pricing systems. Even though the goal of [37] is to deal with architectures, it remains at a lower level of abstraction than the framework sketched here (because of its operational underpinning, which contrasts with the epistemic logic used here) and can hardly be extended to other privacy mechanisms.

On the other hand, dedicated languages have been proposed to specify privacy properties [3,5,7,24,35,38,45,59] but the policies expressed in these languages are usually more fine-grained than the properties considered here because they are not intended to be used at the architectural level. Similarly, process calculi such as the applied pi-calculus [1] have been applied to define privacy protocols [10]. Because process calculi are general frameworks to model concurrent systems, they are more powerful than dedicated frameworks. The downside is that protocols in these languages are expressed at a lower level and the tasks of specifying a protocol and its expected properties are more complex. Again, the main departure of the approach advocated in this paper with respect to this trend of work is that we reason at the level of architectures, providing ways to express properties without entering into the details of specific protocols.

Notions such as k-anonymity [39,56], l-diversity [40] or ϵ-differential privacy [13,14] have also been proposed as ways to measure the level of privacy provided by an algorithm. Differential privacy provides strong privacy guarantees independently of the background knowledge of the adversary: the main idea behind ϵ-differential privacy is that the presence (or the absence) of an item in a database (such as the record of a particular individual) should not change in a significant way the probability of obtaining a certain answer for a given query. Methods [14,41,43] have been proposed to design algorithms achieving privacy metrics or to verify that a system achieves a given level of privacy [57]. These contributions on privacy metrics are complementary to the work described in this paper. We follow a logical (or qualitative) approach here, proving that a given privacy property is met (or not) by an architecture. As suggested in the next section, an avenue for further research would be to cope with quantitative reasoning as well, using inference systems to derive properties expressed in terms of privacy metrics.

As far as the engineering of privacy is concerned, several authors [12,21,28,46,55] have already pointed out the complexity of problem as well as the "richness of the data space"[12], calling for the development of more general and systematic methodologies for privacy by design. [21] has used design patterns to define eight privacy strategies[5] called respectively: Minimise, Hide, Separate, Aggregate, Inform, Control, Enforce and Demonstrate. As far as privacy mechanisms are concerned, [28] points out the complexity of their implementation and the large number of options that designers have to face. To address this issue and favor the adoption of these tools, [28] proposes a number of guidelines for the design of compilers for secure computation and zero-knowledge proofs. In a different context (designing information systems for the cloud), [44] also proposes implementation techniques to make it easier for developers to take into account privacy and security requirements. In the same spirit, [47] proposes a decision support tool based on design patterns to help software engineers to take into account privacy guidelines in the early stage of development.

A recent proposal ([31]) also points out the importance of architectures for privacy by design. [31] proposes a design methodology for privacy (inspired by [6]) based on tactics for privacy quality attributes (such as minimization, enforcement or accountability) and privacy patterns (such as data confinement, isolation or Hippocratic management). The work described in [31] is complementary to the approach presented here: [31] does not consider formal aspects while this paper does not address the tactics for privacy by design.

---

[5] Strategies are defined as follows in [21]: "A design strategy describes a fundamental approach to achieve a certain design goal. It has certain properties that allow it to be distinguished from other (fundamental) approaches that achieve the same goal."

Finally, even though we decided to focus on one (important) aspect of privacy by design here, namely data minimization, other aspects also deserve more attention, in particular the design of appropriate interfaces to allow users to take more informed decisions about their personal data [46].

6   Directions for Further Work

The basic idea put forward in this paper is that privacy by design should be addressed at the architecture level and this should be done, at least for critical aspects such as minimization, in a formal way. As stated in Section 1, some aspects of privacy (such as proportionality or purpose) may be more difficult to formalize or impossible to formalize entirely. This should not be an obstacle to the use of formal methods for other aspects of privacy. Generally speaking, architectures are made of different views [6]: some of them can be described informally or in a purely pictorial way while others are based on a formal model. In any case, working at the architectural level is a key success factor for privacy by design because architectures carry "the earliest and hence most fundamental hardest-to-change design decisions"[6]. They should also play a key role to support accountability requirements because they can provide evidence that appropriate decisions have been taken and the reasons for taking them.

Obviously the design of an architecture meeting all privacy requirements is not the end of the story: because an architecture is set, by definition, at a fairly high level of abstraction, the remaining task is to use or devise appropriate mechanisms to implement it. In some sense, the architecture defines precise requirements on the techniques (PETs) to be used in the implementation. The approach presented here is therefore complementary to the work done on the improvement of the implementation of privacy mechanisms [28]. It is also complementary to the ongoing work on the conception of new PETs. In practice, a design environment should include a library of available PETs with their associated guarantees (in the privacy logic) and this library should follow the progress of the technologies. One challenge to this respect will be to ensure that the logical framework is general and versatile enough to allow the description of future mechanisms. We believe that epistemic logics provide a well-established and suitable framework to this aim but this claim has to be confirmed in practice.

As far as the formal framework itself is concerned, we have suggested a "logical" (or qualitative) approach in this paper. An avenue for further research in this area would be to study the integration of quantitative measures of privacy (such as differential privacy) into the framework. This extension would be required to deal with the (numerous) situations in which data cannot be classified into two categories (can or cannot be disclosed) but can be disclosed provided a sufficiently robust sanitization algorithm is applied. Further work on this issue will benefit from existing results [14,41,43] on the design of mechanisms achieving differential privacy.

In this paper we provided some hints on how our approach can turn into practice based on ongoing work on a privacy by design environment. Needless to say, more work has to be done on the HCI front, to improve the interactions with designers. As suggested in Section 3, graphical means can be used to convey the essence of the properties in the logic and the architecture under construction, for example to picture data flows, the locations of the computations and the trust relationships. A key concept to this respect is the notion of view in software architectures. More experience is needed, however, to understand what will be the most useful views for a designer.

Last but not least, another interesting avenue for further research would be to apply this approach to other aspects of privacy (using combinations of formal and semi-formal methods) and to establish a link with the coarse-grain strategies defined in [21] to drive the interactions with the system.

Acknowledgement. This work was partially funded by the European project PRIPARE / FP7-ICT-2013-1.5, the ANR project BIOPRIV, and the Inria Project Lab CAPPRIS (Collaborative Action on the Protection of Privacy Rights in the Information Society.)

References

1. Abadi, M., Fournet, C.: Mobile Values, New Names, and Secure Communication. In: Proceedings of the 28th ACM SIGPLAN-SIGACT Symposium on Principles of Programming Languages, pp. 104–115 (2001)
2. Allen, R., Garlan, D.: Formalizing Architectural Connection. In: Proc. 16th Int'l Conf. Software Eng. pp. 71–80 (May 1994)
3. Backes, M., Dürmuth, M., Karjoth, G.: Unification in privacy policy evaluation - translating EPAL into Prolog. In: POLICY, pp. 185–188 (2004)
4. Balasch, J., Rial, A., Troncoso, C., Preneel, B., Verbauwhede, I., Geuens, C.: PrETP: Privacy-preserving electronic toll pricing. In: USENIX Security Symposium, pp. 63–78 (2010)
5. Barth, A., Datta, A., Mitchell, J.C., Nissenbaum, H.: Privacy and contextual integrity: Framework and applications. In: IEEE Symposium on Security and Privacy, pp. 184–198 (2006)
6. Bass, L., Clements, P., Kazman, R.: Software architecture in practice, 3rd edn. SEI Series in Software Engineering. Addison-Wesley (2013)
7. Becker, M.Y., Malkis, A., Bussard, L.: A practical generic privacy language. In: Jha, S., Mathuria, A. (eds.) ICISS 2010. LNCS, vol. 6503, pp. 125–139. Springer, Heidelberg (2010)
8. Booch, G., Jacobson, I., Rumbaugh, J.: The Unified Modeling Language Reference Manual, 2nd edn. Addison Wesley Professional (2004)
9. Damiani, M.L., Bertino, E., Silvestri, C.: The probe framework for the personalized cloaking of private locations. Transactions on Data Privacy 3(2), 123–148 (2010)
10. Delaune, S., Kremer, S., Ryan, M.D.: Verifying Privacy-type Properties of Electronic Voting Protocols. Journal of Computer Security 17(4), 435–487 (2009)
11. Deswarte, Y., Melchor, C.A.: Current and future privacy enhancing technologies for the internet. Annals of Telecommunications 61(3), 399–417 (2006)
12. Gürses, S.F., Troncoso, C., Diaz, C.: Engineering privacy by design. In: Computers, Privacy & Data Protection (2011)

13. Dwork, C.: Differential privacy. In: Bugliesi, M., Preneel, B., Sassone, V., Wegener, I. (eds.) ICALP 2006. Part II, LNCS, vol. 4052, pp. 1–12. Springer, Heidelberg (2006)

14. Dwork, C.: A firm foundation for private data analysis. Commun. ACM 54(1), 86–95 (2011)

15. E.C. European Commission. Regulation of the European Parliament and of the Council on the protection of individuals with regard to the processing of personal data and on the free movement of such data (General Data Protection Regulation). inofficial consolidated version after LIBE Commitee vote provided by the rapporteur (October 22, 2013)

16. Fagin, R., Halpern, J.Y., Moses, Y., Vardi, M.: Reasoning About Knowledge. A Bradford Book (January 9, 2004); 1st MIT Press Paperback edition

17. Garcia, F.D., Jacobs, B.: Privacy-friendly energy-metering via homomorphic encryption. In: Cuellar, J., Lopez, J., Barthe, G., Pretschner, A. (eds.) STM 2010. LNCS, vol. 6710, pp. 226–238. Springer, Heidelberg (2011)

18. Goldberg, I.: Privacy-enhancing technologies for the internet III: ten years later. In: Digital Privacy: Theory, Technologies, and Practices, pp. 84–89. TeX Users Group (December 2007)

19. Hafiz, M.: A Pattern Language for Developing Privacy Enhancing Technologies. Foftware Practice and Experience 43(7), 769–787 (2013)

20. Halpern, J.Y., Pucella, R.: Dealing with logical omniscience: Expressiveness and pragmatics. Artif. Intell. 175(1), 220–235 (2011)

21. Hoepman, J.-H.: Privacy Design Strategies. CoRR (2013)

22. Höfer, C., Petit, J., Schmidt, R., Kargl, F.: POPCORN: Privacy-preserving charging for e-mobility. In: Proceedings of the 2013 ACM Workshop on Security, Privacy & Dependability for Cyber Vehicles (CyCAR 2013), pp. 37–48. ACM, New York (2013)

23. Inverardi, P., Wolf, A.: Formal specification and analysis of software architectures using the chemical abstract machine model. IEEE Transactions on Software Engineering, Special Issue on Software Architectures 21(4), 373–386 (1995)

24. Jafari, M., Fong, P.W.L., Safavi-Naini, R., Barker, K., Sheppard, N.P.: Towards defining semantic foundations for purpose-based privacy policies. In: CODASPY, pp. 213–224 (2011)

25. Jawurek, M., Johns, M., Kerschbaum, F.: Plug-In Privacy for Smart Metering Billing. In: Fischer-Hübner, S., Hopper, N. (eds.) PETS 2011. LNCS, vol. 6794, pp. 192–210. Springer, Heidelberg (2011)

26. Jawurek, M., Kerschbaum, F., Danezis, G.: Privacy Technologies for Smart Grids - A Survey of Options. MSR-TR-2012-119 (November 2012)

27. de Jonge, W., Jacobs, B.: Privacy-friendly electronic traffic pricing via commits. In: Degano, P., Guttman, J., Martinelli, F. (eds.) FAST 2008. LNCS, vol. 5491, pp. 143–161. Springer, Heidelberg (2009)

28. Kerschbaum, F.: Privacy-preserving computation. In: Preneel, B., Ikonomou, D. (eds.) APF 2012. LNCS, vol. 8319, pp. 41–54. Springer, Heidelberg (2014)

29. Kosta, E., Zibuschka, J., Scherner, T., Dumortier, J.: Legal considerations on privacy-enhancing location based services using PRIME technology. Computer Law and Security Report 4, 139–146 (2008)

30. Krumm, J.: A survey of computational location privacy. Pers. Ubiquit. Comput. 13, 391–399 (2008)

31. Kung, A.: PEARs: Privacy enhancing aRchitectures. In: Preneel, B., Ikonomou, D. (eds.) APF 2014. LNCS, vol. 8450, pp. 18–30. Springer, Heidelberg (2014)

32. Langheinrich, M.: Privacy by design - principles of privacy-aware ubiquitous systems. In: Abowd, G.D., Brumitt, B., Shafer, S. (eds.) UbiComp 2001. LNCS, vol. 2201, pp. 273–291. Springer, Heidelberg (2001)
33. LeMay, M., Gross, G., Gunter, C.A., Garg, S.: Unified architecture for large-scale attested metering. In: HICSS, pp. 115–124 (2007)
34. Le Métayer, D.: Software Architecture Styles As Graph Grammars. ACM SIGSOFT Software Eng. Notes (November 1996)
35. Le Métayer, D.: A formal privacy management framework. In: Degano, P., Guttman, J., Martinelli, F. (eds.) FAST 2008. LNCS, vol. 5491, pp. 162–176. Springer, Heidelberg (2009)
36. Le Métayer, D.: Privacy by design: A matter of choice. In: Data Protection in a Profiled World, pp. 323–334. Springer (2010)
37. Le Métayer, D.: Privacy by design: a formal framework for the analysis of architectural choices. In: CODASPY 2013, pp. 95–104 (2013)
38. Li, N., Yu, T., Antón, A.I.: A semantics based approach to privacy languages. Comput. Syst. Sci. Eng. 21(5) (2006)
39. Li, N., Qardaji, W.H., Su, D.: Provably private data anonymization: Or, k-anonymity meets differential privacy. CoRR, abs/1101.2604 (2011)
40. Machanavajjhala, A., Gehrke, J., Kifer, D., Venkitasubramaniam, M.: l-diversity: Privacy beyond k-anonymity. ACM Trans. Knowl. Discov. Data 1(1), Article 3 (March 2007)
41. McSherry, F.: Privacy integrated queries: an extensible platform for privacy-preserving data analysis. Commun. ACM 53(9), 89–97 (2010)
42. McSherry, F., Mironov, I.: Differentially private recommender systems: building privacy into the net. In: Proceedings of the 15th ACM SIGKDD International Conference on Knowledge Discovery and Data Mining (KDD 2009), pp. 627–636. ACM, New York (2009)
43. McSherry, F., Talwar, K.: Mechanism design via differential privacy. In: FOCS, pp. 94–103 (2007)
44. Manousakis, V., Kalloniatis, C., Kavakli, E., Gritzalis, S.: Privacy in the Cloud: Bridging the Gap between Design and Implementation. In: Franch, X., Soffer, P. (eds.) CAiSE Workshops 2013. LNBIP, vol. 148, pp. 455–465. Springer, Heidelberg (2013)
45. May, M.J., Gunter, C.A., Lee, I.: Privacy APIs: Access control techniques to analyze and verify legal privacy policies. In: CSFW, pp. 85–97 (2006)
46. Mulligan, D.K., King, J.: Bridging the Gap between Privacy and Design. University of Pennsylvania Journal of Constitutional Law 4(14) (2012)
47. Pearson, S., Benameur, A.: A Decision Support System for Design for Privacy. Privacy and Identity, IFIP AICT 352, 283–296 (2011)
48. Perry, D.E., Wolf, A.L.: Foundations for the study of software architecture. ACM SIGSOFT Software Eng. Notes (October 1992)
49. Popa, R.A., Balakrishnan, H., Blumberg, A.J.: Vpriv: Protecting privacy in location-based vehicular services. In: USENIX Security Symposium, pp. 335–350 (2009)
50. Poullet, Y.: About the e-privacy directive, towards a third generation of data protection legislations. In: Data Protection in a Profile World, pp. 3–29. Springer (2010)
51. Pucella, R.: Deductive Algorithmic Knowledge. Journal of Logic and Computation 16(2), 287–309 (2006)
52. Rezgui, A., Bouguettaya, A., Eltoweissy, M.Y.: Privacy on the web: facts, challenges, and solutions. In: IEEE Security and Privacy, pp. 40–49 (2003)

53. Rial, A., Danezis, G.: Privacy-preserving smart metering. In: Proceedings of the 2011 ACM Workshop on Privacy in the Electronic Society, WPES 2011. ACM (2011)
54. Shaw, M., Clements, P.: The Golden Age of Software Architecture: A Comprehensive Survey. In: Research Report CMU-ISRI-06-101. Carnegie Mellon University (2006)
55. Spiekermann, S., Cranor, L.F.: Engineering Privacy. IEEE Transactions on Software Engineering 35(1) (2009)
56. Sweeney, L.: k-anonymity: A model for protecting privacy. International Journal of Uncertainty, Fuzziness and Knowledge-Based Systems 10(5), 557–570 (2002)
57. Tschantz, M.C., Kaynar, D.K., Datta, A.: Formal verification of differential privacy for interactive systems. CoRR, abs/1101.2819 (2011)
58. Tschantz, M.C., Wing, J.M.: Formal methods for privacy. In: Cavalcanti, A., Dams, D.R. (eds.) FM 2009. LNCS, vol. 5850, pp. 1–15. Springer, Heidelberg (2009)
59. Yu, T., Li, N., Antón, A.I.: A formal semantics for P3P. In: In Proceedings of the 2004 Workshop on Secure Web Service (SWS 2004), pp. 1–8 (2004)

Annex 1

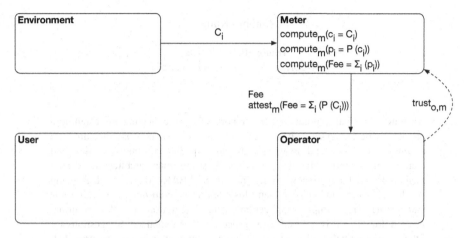

Fig. 1. Option 2 of Section 4: The meter computes the fee and has just to be trusted by the operator. C_i are the actual consumptions and c_i the values actually used by the meter.

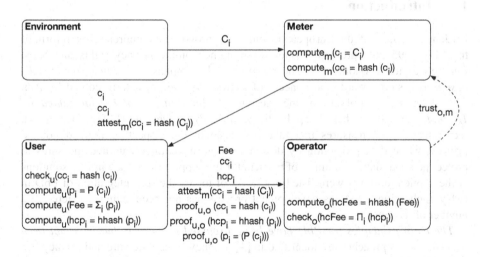

Fig. 2. Option 3 of Section 4: The user computes the fee and the operator has to trust the meter (for using the right value c_i). hhash is a homomorphic hash function which allows the operator to check that the hash of the global fee Fee is consistent with the hashes hcp_i of individual fees p_i. This architecture is an abstraction of the solution proposed by [53].

PEARs: Privacy Enhancing ARchitectures

Antonio Kung

Trialog, Paris, France
antonio.kung@trialog.com

Abstract. This paper points out the importance of architecture in designing a privacy-by-design system. It provides an overview on how architectures are designed, analysed and evaluated, through quality attributes, tactics and architecture patterns. It then specifies a straw man architecture design methodology for privacy. The resulting PEAR (Privacy Enhancing ARchitecture) methodology is then illustrated through an *Intelligent Transport systems* (ITS) example application. The integration of the resulting methodology in a Privacy-by-Design process is then explained. Suggestions for future work that will lead to an agreed engineering practice are finally provided.

Keywords: Architecture, Quality attributes, Tactics, Privacy Patterns, PEAR, PET, Privacy-by-Design.

1 Introduction

On January 25, 2012, the European Commission proposed a comprehensive reform of the EU's 1995 data protection rules to strengthen online privacy rights and boost Europe's digital economy [1]. The reform put the emphasis on *data protection by design* as a step towards the concept of *Privacy-by-Design*, a term coined by Ann Cavoukian [2]. Applied to the design of *Information and Communication Technologies* (ICT) based applications, Privacy-by-Design (PbD) focuses on requirements and measures that take into account the respect of the individuals' privacy, while data protection by design focuses on requirements and measures to protect personal data. A number of barriers for the support of privacy in ICT solutions at the application level were listed in [3]. As of today, the full integration of PbD in today applications, systems development process has not been achieved. Here are a number of reasons:

The main principles for PbD have been discussed extensively but have not been agreed. Two approaches are identified in [4]: privacy-by-architecture and privacy-by-policy. The former focuses on data minimization while the latter focuses on enforcing policies in data processing. The position that data minimization should be the foundational principle is taken in [5]. Three principles are defined in [6], minimisation, enforcement and transparency.

The integration of privacy in a development processes includes many dimensions that need guidelines. Some guidelines for instance have been made available recently, for example for the assessment or the requirement dimension.

B. Preneel and D. Ikonomou (Eds.): APF 2014, LNCS 8450, pp. 18–29, 2014.

Concerning assessment, PbD is generally associated with Privacy Impact Assessments (PIAs) [7]. A PIA is defined as a systematic process for evaluating the potential effects on privacy of a project, initiative or proposed system or scheme and finding ways to mitigate or avoid any adverse effects [8]. The relationship between assessment and risk analysis was addressed recently by CNIL, the French data protection authority. It published a risk management methodology that can be used for the analysis of privacy risks [9]. This methodology is derived from the more general French security risk analysis methodology called EBIOS [10].

Concerning requirements, the relationship between privacy requirements and development requirements was addressed by the standardisation body OASIS [11], which published in July 2013 PMRM (Privacy Management Reference Model and Methodology) [12]. PMRM explains how privacy principles and practices, privacy laws and policies, privacy control statements leading to policy and business requirements are mapped onto operational requirements on privacy and security services. Three categories of privacy services are identified: the core policy services (agreement, control), the privacy assurance services (validation, audit, certification, enforcement), and the presentation and lifecycle services (interaction, usage, agent, access).

The architectural dimension is not well addressed at the methodology level. The architectural dimension of Privacy-by-Design is currently not well highlighted. Yet almost all privacy preserving solutions devised today have a profound impact on architecture:

Pay-As-You-Drive is a vehicle insurance scheme whereby customers are charged depending on where and when they drive. Many implementations involved the collecting of location data by insurers. PriPAYD [13] proposes a system where premium calculation is carried out locally in vehicle while only aggregated data are made available to the insurers.

Electronic Toll Pricing (ETP) is a similar scheme whereby customers are charged according to the roads they use and to parameters such as the kind of road, the time of usage and other parameters such as traffic. PrETP [14] proposes a privacy-preserving ETP system where the vehicle computes fees locally, proves to the service provider in charge of billing the vehicle that they carry out correct computations while revealing the minimum amount of location data.

Smart metering privacy has been addressed by [15] to cope with the conflict between privacy and the need for fine grained billing by using an architecture involving the meter, the provider and a user agent. The user agent performs and proves the correctness of computations based on readings on their own metre devices, without disclosing any fine grained consumption to the provider.

These research contributions focus on security mechanisms and provide evidence on correctness and feasibility. They also explain the resulting architectures in terms of data location and granularity. But they do not provide guidelines on how these architectures can be designed.

This paper addresses the architecture design and its associated methodology dimension. It first provides an overview on how architectures are designed, analysed and evaluated, through quality attributes, tactics and architecture patterns. It then specifies a straw man architecture design methodology for privacy. We call this methodology the Privacy Enhancing Architecture or the PEAR methodology.

The PEAR methodology is then illustrated through an Intelligent Transport Systems (ITS) example application. The integration of the PEAR in a Privacy-by-Design process is then explained. Suggestions for future work that will lead to an agreed engineering practice are finally provided.

2   Todays Practice of Architecture Design

ICT architecture design is a well-known but specialised and specific activity which depends on the domain sector. Different methodologies are used in the automotive, telecommunication, smart grid, railways, or aeronautics domain. Global standards for architecture design are wanting. For instance [16] focuses on the description of an architecture not are still with different standards. As a result, Rather than presenting several different practices, we propose to present today practice through a representative architecture design methodology, the software architecture methodology from Carnegie Mellon. It is the result of a nearly 15-year research work, and extensive literature is available [18].

2.1   Quality Attributes

The CMU software architecture methodology is organised around the concept of *quality attributes* (often called non-functional requirements) as opposed to functional requirements. Functional requirements express what a system does (e.g. a location oriented service), while quality attributes express how well a system does it. Quality attributes can cover execution qualities (such as security, usability, dependability), evolution qualities (such as testability, maintainability, scalability), business qualities (time-to-market, cost) and so forth.

While the architecture design phase starts when functional requirements, quality attributes and constraints (i.e. design decision that are already taken) are available, quality attributes are often considered as the requirements that have the most important impact on architecture decisions. In other words, quality attributes are satisfied by structures and behaviors of the architecture.

The approach to specify quality attributes requirements is to specify scenarios. The elements of a scenario are showed in Fig. 1: the *stimulus*, a condition which requires a response when it arrives at a system; the *source* of a stimulus; the *environment* where the system is; the *artifact* being stimulated; the *response* or the activity undertaken as the result of the arrival of the stimulus; and the *response measure*.

Fig. 1. Abstract Model of a Quality Attribute Scenario

Here is an example: Alice accesses a corporate data base storing health records. She wants to read Bob's record. But the request is made without the right authorization. Access is consequently denied. In this case, Alice is the *source*, the request is the *stimulus*, the *artifact* is the data base, the *environment* is the corporate data base in operation, the *response* is rejection. The response measure is 0% (percentage of non-authorized access).

While quality attribute scenario models seem deceptively simple, they allow for proper focus on important aspects. In particular the measurability of responses necessitate the identification of metrics (e.g. response time), which can then be transformed into an operational requirement (e.g. less than 5 seconds response time). Further quality attributes can often be associated with models of functions to predict the response measures given a stimulus for a particular architecture. There are two known approaches for such models: analytic models which support quantitative analysis (e.g. Markov models for hardware availability, scheduling theory for predictability), or check lists/guidelines which support scales (e.g. common criteria level, safety integrity level or SIL).

2.2 Architecture Tactics

The whole design process can be described as involving three steps. First scenarios are identified and specified. Then appropriate architecture techniques influencing the response measures of the scenarios are selected. These measures are called architecture tactics. Finally the impact of such tactics on response measures is verified. Figure 3 shows how architecture tactics are displayed in a scenario model.

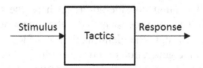

Fig. 2. Architecture Tactic

A wealth of tactics for availability, interoperability, modifiability, performance, security, testability, usability quality attributes are available in [18]. Figure 3 shows an example for security tactics. In general tactics are displayed in a structured way but the intention is to act as a practical cheat sheet not as a definitive taxonomy.

2.3 Patterns for Re-use

In order to ease re-use, architecture tactics are often described through patterns. More than 40 security patterns (including some privacy patterns) are identified by [19]. While patterns are often described informally (see [20] for a list of privacy patterns), it is often more effective to describe them through abstract models. In [21] security and dependability models are stored digitally so that they can be directly integrated into application design models.

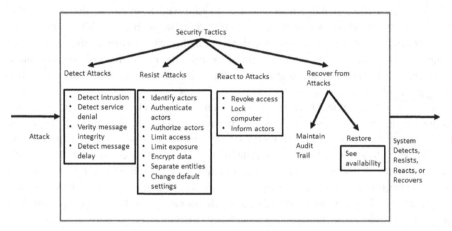

Fig. 3. Security Tactics

2.4   Architecture Analysis and Evaluation

One important part of an architecture design process is its analysis and evaluation. SARA or Software Architecture Review of Assessment [17] is an example. [18] describes an analysis method called ATAM (Architecture Tradeoff Analysis method) and an evaluation method called CBAM (Cost Benefit Analysis Method).

ATAM allows for the elicitation of ASR or Architecturally Significant Requirements). For instance the performance quality attribute could focus on throughput with a requirement such *as at peak load, system is able to complete 150 transactions per second*. The analysis will contain considerations such as the business value and the impact on architecture. An iteration process includes the following steps: The selection of the element of the system to design; the identification of ASR (architecturally significant requirements) for that part; the generation of a design solution; an inventory of remaining requirements and selection of input for the next iterations. ATAM includes 9 steps: presentation of ATAM; presentation of business drivers; presentation of architecture; identification of architectural approaches; generation of utility trees (with ASR); analysis of architectural approaches; brainstorming and prioritisation of scenarios; final analysis of approach; final presentation.

CBAM takes place after ATAM. The approach is to "measure" the utility of a tactic in a scenario. For instance a scenario with 99.999 percent availability could have an utility value of 100 while a 99.99 percent availability could have a value of 90. The CBAM include 9 steps: collate scenario; refine scenario; prioritise scenario; assign utility measure; identify architectural strategies and associated scenarios; determine overall utility; calculate benefit from an architectural strategy; select architectural strategy; compare and confirm result with intuition.

3   A Straw Man Architecture Design Methodology for Privacy

This section explains how a comprehensive architecture design methodology can be defined for PbD. In a nutshell, this Privacy Enhancing Architecture or PEAR methodology considers privacy functional requirements as well as quality attribute functional requirements, it makes use of four categories of tactics related to minimisation, enforcement, accountability and modifiability, it uses a wealth of privacy architecture patterns (possibly with associated PETs) and finally it uses an evaluation scheme based on risk analysis.

3.1   Functional vs Non Functional Requirements

We suggest that a distinction be made between functional privacy requirements and quality attribute privacy requirements as follows.

Function privacy requirements cover the *what* part (i.e. what the system does). It therefore include elements such as purpose limitation, purpose specification, collection, use, disclosure and retention limit.

Quality attribute requirements cover the *how* part (i.e. how the system does it). It therefore includes attributes that will influence architecture such as minimisation, enforcement, accountability and modifiability.

3.2   Tactics for Privacy by Design

No privacy tactics "cheat sheet" is provided in [18]. We therefore make a proposal in Fig. 4.

Minimisation tactics focus on the minimization of disclosed information. They include anonymous credentials tactics which allow users to authenticate themselves without revealing their identity. But they also include tactics which make sure that computing is restricted to a given perimeter (for instance the computation is kept in the user client device).

Enforcement tactics include data protection policies enforcement (for instance of access rights), or processing protection (for instance computing sandboxes).

Accountability tactics include logging of relevant events (for instance the removal of data according to retention policies could be logged) and protection of logging (the logging data must be unforgeable).

Modifiability tactics are needed to cope with evolution needs. They include policy change (e.g. the user changes its policies, or the data controller changes its protection policies), crypto change (e.g. for better minimization) and protection change (e.g. a security system is getting obsolete).

Tactics are associated with architecture patterns and technologies. Applied to privacy tactics, the result of selecting tactics in the design phase is a resulting architecture specification which integrates a set of relevant architecture patterns and privacy enhancing technologies (PETs). The art of selecting the right tactics depends on the state of the art in technology and the cost effectiveness. They correspond to the concept of BAT (best available technique) used by EDPS[1].

---

[1] The EDPS web site glossary provides the following definition: Best Available Techniques refer to the most effective and advanced stage in the development of activities and their methods of operation, which indicate the practical suitability of particular techniques for providing in principle the basis for complying with the EU data protection framework. They are designed to prevent or mitigate risks on privacy and security.

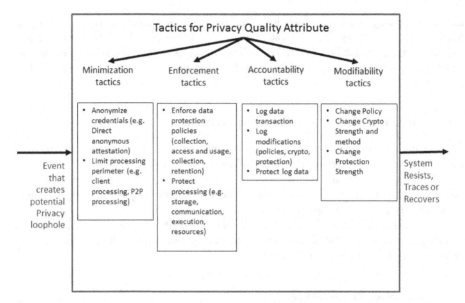

Fig. 4. Tactics for Privacy Quality Attribute

3.3   Example of Patterns

We present below three examples of patterns, the user data confinement pattern, the hippocratic management pattern and the isolation pattern.

The use data confinement pattern is depicted in Fig. 5. The objective is to collect and process personal data in a location that is physically controlled by the user. It necessitates the availability of security mechanisms (PET) to control what is revealed to other stakeholders involved in the operation of the application.

Examples of research contributions using this pattern are the application mentioned in section 2 (Pay per use, Electronic Toll pricing, Smart meter) or the personal health record management approach from [22], which is further extended to secure personal data servers [23].

It is worth mentioning that this pattern is an instance of the *location granularity pattern* in the recent initiative [24] to provide practical advice on PbD by creating a repository of privacy patterns (privacy patterns are design solutions to common privacy problems).

Fig. 5. User Data Confinement Pattern

The Hippocratic management pattern is depicted in Fig. 6. The objective is to enforce the collecting and processing of data in a predefined confinement area (which could be a user controlled location, or an engineer defined distributed location). The rationale for the enforcement principle is to prevent accidental or malicious leaking of personal data. For instance careless management of a web server that collects customer data would increase the risk that employees access such data without authorisation. Agrawal [25] coined the term Hippocratic database (after the Hippocratic Oath), and suggested that the implementation of a data management capability should follow the principles for data protection (purpose specification, consent, limited collection-use-disclosure-retention, accuracy, safety, openness, and compliance). The resulting architecture associates data with metadata describing protection policies, e.g. who can have access to data, or retention parameters. Data can only be accessed through a well-defined interface (e.g. based on a query language). Finally the data management takes proactive moves for enforcing policies (e.g. data is deleted after the retention limit).

The Hippocratic pattern was used the PRECIOSA FP7 project [26] to implement data-centric approach for protecting personal data in a cooperative ITS environment, resulting in an architecture called PeRA (Privacy enforcing Run-time Architecture) PeRA supports distributed protection perimeters [27, 28].

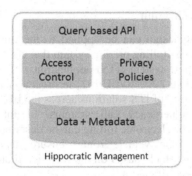

Fig. 6. Hippocratic Management Pattern

The isolation pattern is depicted in Fig. 7. It provides isolation between independent applications which run on the same platform. The rationale is to prevent the risk for other applications to accidentally or maliciously access computing resources and data associated with another application. The isolation pattern is based on the concepts of partitions which are created by a virtualisation layer.

Virtualisation can be used to allocate virtual resources (e.g. CPU, memory, disk space) to a given partition. Virtualisation is achieved through technology bricks called hypervisors [29]. The isolation PEAR is used in the OVERSEE FP7 project [30] to implement a secure open platform for ITS. OVERSEE is based on the XTratum hypervisor [31].

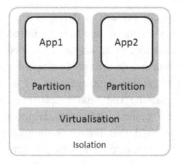

Fig. 7. Isolation Pattern

3.4   Privacy Architecture Analysis and Evaluation

ATAM and CBAM can be used for privacy architecture analysis and evaluation by integrating a proper risk management analysis such as [9]. The analysis uses two scales, the severity scale and the likelihood scale. Risks with a high severity and likelihood must absolutely be avoided. Risks with a high severity but a low likelihood must be avoided. Risks with a low severity and a high likelihood must be reduced. Risks with a low severity and likelihood may be taken.

3.5   Example of an Application

We show how privacy-by-design can be applied to the implementation of a more globally preserving electronic tolling pricing system that could be integrated in the set of future intelligent transport system (ITS) applications. The European Commission adopted in 2010 the directive 2010/40/EU [32] in order to address the compatibility, interoperability and continuity of ITS solutions across the EU, for areas such as traffic and travel information, emergency call systems, or intelligent truck parking. Application requirements for electronic tolling can be described as follows: constantly record information about the vehicle route; ensure accuracy of the recorded information; bill the driver/vehicle based on the recorded route information; and keep the information for invoice verification.

A privacy-preserving solution supports the following non-functional requirements:

User control of data by keeping the driven route private from road toll collectors, and keep route specific information only during the invoice litigation period. The result is a minimized data set consisting of the customer identification which is required to associate a vehicle with a customer account and billing information, the proof data of the driven route, and the associated cost. Associated data transformation could be based on the optimistic payment protocol as described in [14]. Policies associated with manipulated data are as follows: detailed data concerning the vehicle route are kept and processed only inside the On-Board Equipment (OBE) of the vehicle; proof about the route driven is stored by the OBE only for a limited time that is needed for invoice verification; data sent outside the OBE only contain the customer ID and the cost for the distance that vehicle has driven the area operated by a toll charger. This data should not allow inferring data about a driver's travel. Finally this aggregated data is signed by the OBE to prevent tampering. This requirement is met with the user data confinement pattern and the optimistic payment PET.

Protection of data within confinement area. The management of data in the OBE should be enforced so that accidental or malicious access is not possible. This requirement is met with the hippocratic management pattern. Deployed within an OBE, it ensures that recorded route information is only processed inside the protected perimeter within the OBE according to given privacy policies, i.e. raw position data is accessed only by a cost calculation application running only inside the perimeter. The application calculates the aggregated cost values that are then reported outside the perimeter and transmitted to the toll service provider. Applications running in an OBE outside the perimeter have no access to the raw data inside.

Isolation against other applications. The OBE could be used to run electronic tolling applications in parallel (e.g. an automotive diagnostic application, an emergency call system). This requirement is met with the isolation pattern. It ensures that another application cannot have access to the data processed by the application.

An overall architecture analysis and risk analysis can then be carried out. The risk analysis and the resulting decisions will form the basis for the production of privacy assessment impact (PIA) documents. The PIA is the concluding PbD artefact.

The table below summarises the privacy-by-design artefacts that are involved in the development of the example application.

Application	PEAR methodology output	Privacy-by-Design Artefacts
Electronic Tolling Pricing	Tactic for user control of data in order to reduce risk of data leak	User data confinement architecture pattern
		Optimistic payment protocol PET
	Tactic for protection of data within confinement area in order to reduce risk of accidental access to data	Hippocratic management architecture pattern
	Tactic for isolation against other applications in order to reduce risk of access from them.	Isolation pattern
	Architecture evaluation based on privacy risk management	Privacy Impact Assessment

4   Integration of PEAR in the PbD Process

Figure 8 shows how the straw man architecture design methodology can be integrated in an overall PbD process:

In the first phase, privacy functional requirements are identified. Then privacy quality attribute requirements are identified. Then architecture tactics and PET can be selected. Because an architecture tactic and PET can have an impact on the data to be collected, i.e. more data can be minimised, there is a back loop allowing for the revisiting of privacy functional requirements. Architecture decisions are then analysed and evaluated following a privacy risk analysis methodology. When the analysis yields satisfactory risks then documentation artifacts for privacy impact assessment documents can be provided.

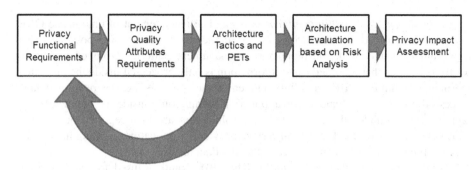

Fig. 8. A PbD Process Integrating Architecture Design

5   Conclusions

This paper has focused on the importance of an architecture design methodology and has specified a straw man PEAR methodology, based on quality attributes, tactics, PETs and risk management.

In the future some further work needs to be undertaken: the definition of a more holistic PbD methodology integrating PEAR; an agreement by the community on the concepts of privacy requirements and of privacy quality attribute requirements; and last but not least a standardisation of the methodology.

The straw man methodology will be an input to the PRIPARE FP7 project [33]. PRIPARE (Preparing Industry to PbD by supporting its Application in Research) is a support action that will contribute to the definition of a more holistic PbD methodology integrating PEAR.

We acknowledge the support of the European Commission in the following FP7 projects: PRECIOSA, PRESERVE, PRIPARE.

References

1. http://eur-lex.europa.eu/LexUriServ/
   LexUriServ.do?uri=COM:2012:0011:FIN:EN:PDF
2. Privacy-by-Design,
   http://www.ipc.on.ca/english/Privacy/Introduction-to-PbD/
3. Kung, A.: ICT and Privacy: Barriers. In: Annual Privacy Forum, Limassol, Cyprus, October 10-11(2012)
4. Spiekermann, S., Cranor, L.: Privacy Engineering. IEEE Transactions on Software Engineering 35(1), 67–82 (2009)
5. Gürses, S.F., Troncoso, C., Diaz, C.: Engineering Privacy-by-Design. Computers, Privacy & Data Protection (2011)
6. Kung, A., Freytag, J., Kargl, F.: Privacy-by-design in ITS applications. In: 2nd IEEE International Workshop on Data Security and Privacy in Wireless Networks, Lucca, Italy (June 20, 2011)
7. Wright, D., de Hert, P. (eds.): Privacy Impact Assessment. Series: Law, Governance and Technology Series, vol. 6. Springer (2012)
8. PIAF: Privacy Impact Assessment Framework, http://www.piafproject.eu

9. CNIL methodology for privacy risk management, `http://www.cnil.fr/fileadmin/documents/en/CNIL-ManagingPrivacyRisks-Methodology.pdf`
10. EBIOS. Expression des Besoins et Identification des Objectifs de Sécurité, `http://www.ssi.gouv.fr/IMG/pdf/EBIOS-1-GuideMethodologique-2010-01-25.pdf`
11. OASIS. Organization for the Advancement of Structured Information, `https://www.oasis-open.org/`
12. OASIS Privacy Management Reference Model (PMRM) Technical Committee, `https://www.oasis-open.org/committees/pmrm/charter.php`
13. Troncoso, C., Danezis, G., Kosta, E., Balasch, J., Preneel, B.: PriPAYD: Privacy-Friendly Pay-As-You-Drive Insurance. IEEE Transactions on Dependable and Secure Computing 8(5), 742–755 (2011)
14. Balasch, J., Rial, A., Troncoso, C., Geuens, C., Preneel, B., Verbauwhede, I.: PrETP: Privacy-Preserving Electronic Toll Pricing (extended version). In: 19th USENIX Security Symposium
15. Rial, A., Danezis, G.: Privacy-Preserving Smart Metering. In: Proceedings of the 2011 ACM Workshop on Privacy in the Electronic Society, WPES 2011, USA (October 17, 2011)
16. ISO/IEC/IEEE 42010:2011, Systems and software engineering — Architecture description
17. Software Architecture Review and Assessment (SARA) Report, version 1.0, `http://kruchten.com/philippe/architecture/SARAv1.pdf` (February 2002)
18. Software Architecture in Practice (3rd Edition), Len Bass, Paul Clementz, Rick Kazman. Addison-Wesley (2012)
19. Chung, E., Hong, J., et al.: Development and Evaluation of Emerging Design Patterns for Ubiquitous Computing. Patterns C1-C15, DIS2004 (2004)
20. `http://www.privacypatterns.org`
21. `http://www.teresa-project.org`
22. Anciaux, N., Benzine, M., Bouganim, L., Jacquemin, K., Pucheral, P., Yin, S.: Restoring the Patient Control over her Medical History. In: Proc. of the 21th IEEE International Symposium on Computer-Based Medical Systems (CBMS), Jyväskylä, Finland, pp. 132–137 (June 2008)
23. Allard, T., Anciaux, N., Bouganim, L., Guo, Y., Le Folgoc, L., Nguyen, B., Pucheral, P., Ray, I., Ray, I., Yin, S.: Secure Personal Data Servers: A Vision Paper. In: Proc. of the 36th International Conference on Very Large Data Bases (VLDB), Singapore, PVLDB 3(1), 25–35 (September 2010)
24. `http://privacypatterns.org/`, `http://privacypatterns.org/patterns/Location-granularity`
25. Agrawal, R., Kiernan, J., Srikant, R., Xu, Y.: Hippocratic Databases. In: 28th International Conference on Very Large Data Bases, Hong Kong (August 2002)
26. PRECIOSA, `http://www.preciosa-project.org/`
27. Kargl, F., Schaub, F., Dietzel, S.: Mandatory Enforcement of Privacy Policies Using Trusted Computing Principles. Intelligent Information Privacy Management Symposium, Stanford University (AAAI 2010 Spring Symposia) (March 2010)
28. V2X Privacy Verifiable Architecture. Deliverable D7. Preciosa FP7 Project, `http://www.preciosa-project.org/` (November 2009)
29. Goldberg, R.: Architectural Principles for Virtual Computer Systems. PhD thesis, National Technical Information Service (February 1973)
30. OVERSEE, `https://www.oversee-project.com/`
31. `http://www.xtratum.org/`
32. `http://eur-lex.europa.eu/LexUriServ/LexUriServ.do?uri=OJ:L:2010:207:FULL:EN:PDF`
33. `http://pripare.eu/`

Privacy-Preserving Statistical Data Analysis on Federated Databases

Dan Bogdanov[1], Liina Kamm[1,2], Sven Laur[2], Pille Pruulmann-Vengerfeldt[3], Riivo Talviste[1,2], and Jan Willemson[1,4]

[1] Cybernetica, Mäealuse 2/1, 12618 Tallinn, Estonia
{dan,liina,riivo,janwil}@cyber.ee
[2] University of Tartu, Institute of Computer Science, Liivi 2, 50409 Tartu, Estonia
swen@ut.ee
[3] University of Tartu, Institute of Journalism, Communication and Information Studies, Lossi 36, 51003 Tartu, Estonia
pille.vengerfeldt@ut.ee
[4] ELIKO Competence Centre in Electronics-, Info- and Communication Technologies, Mäealuse 2/1, Tallinn, Estonia

Abstract. The quality of empirical statistical studies is tightly related to the quality and amount of source data available. However, it is often hard to collect data from several sources due to privacy requirements or a lack of trust. In this paper, we propose a novel way to combine secure multi-party computation technology with federated database systems to preserve privacy in statistical studies that combine and analyse data from multiple databases. We describe an implementation on two real-world platforms—the SHAREMIND secure multi-party computation and the X-Road database federation platform. Our solution enables the privacy-preserving linking and analysis of databases belonging to different institutions. Indeed, a preliminary analysis from the Estonian Data Protection Inspectorate suggests that the correct implementation of our solution ensures that no personally identifiable information is processed in such studies. Therefore, our proposed solution can potentially reduce the costs of conducting statistical studies on shared data.

Keywords: secure multi-party computation, federated database infrastructures, linking sensitive data, privacy-preserving statistical analysis.

1 Introduction

During the last decade we have witnessed a rapid growth of e-government technology adoption, e.g. online services for citizens based on federated state databases. The Estonian X-Road system is one of the more successful platforms. It is operational since 2001 and mediates the vast majority of the governmental data exchange requests of today. State agencies maintain their individual databases and queries are made over the X-Road as needed. The distribution of data between several owners also prevents the creation of "superdatabases",

B. Preneel and D. Ikonomou (Eds.): APF 2014, LNCS 8450, pp. 30–55, 2014.

that contain an extensive amount of information on a single person or company. However, there are analytical tasks that require the linking of one or more databases. For example, the government needs to combine tax records with educational records to analyse the efficiency of educational investments.

However, every such database combination is a privacy risk for citizens. Even if the databases are pseudonymised or anonymised, records become larger in the joined databases. This, in turn, gives the attackers the ability to use additional information available from public sources like social networks to restore the identities. Potential attackers vary from malicious hackers to misbehaving officials. The latter class of attackers is the most complicated one to handle, as the official may have a completely legal access to the raw datasets, and just use them to gain more information than is necessary for completion of legitimate tasks.

Our goal is to perform all the required computations without revealing any microdata to the computing entities and mitigate the privacy risk. This paper proposes a novel extension of federated database systems that adds the feature of privacy-preserving data analysis using secure multi-party computation.

Secure multi-party computation (SMC) has been researched and developed for several decades. For years, SMC was rightfully considered too inefficient for practical use. However, in recent years, several fast implementations have been developed [9,17]. Still, SMC has not yet become popular in practice, as people have managed without such a technology for a long time and have replaced it with social solutions like non-disclosure agreements and hope that their partners protect the data being shared.

In this paper, we describe a joint architecture combining federated database environments with SMC. We describe a concrete solution based on the Estonian X-Road federated database platform and the SHAREMIND [7] secure multi-party computation system. However, our idea is general enough to be applied to other database environments and secure computation technologies.

The paper is organised as follows. First, Section 2 illustrates the benefits of combining data in a federated database setting, describes the X-Road platform and discusses candidate microdata protection mechanisms. Section 3 explains secure multi-party computation, gives a privacy definition for SMC applications and explains how to satisfy it in data analysis algorithms. Section 4 discusses how to combine a federated database environment like the X-Road with SMC to provide a secure data analysis environment. In Section 5, we validate the need of the proposed solution through a set of interviews with potential end users.

We then focus on the practical implementation of the solution. Section 6 describes our first pilot project where we apply the proposed technology. Section 7 describes our implementation of secure multi-party statistical analysis algorithms and Section 8 analyses their performance with a set of benchmarks.

Related Work. There have been efforts to implement statistical analysis using SMC. Cryptographic primitives for evaluating statistical functions like mean, variance, frequency analysis and regression were proposed in [14,18,19]. Early implementations of filtered sums and scalar products are described in [47,52]. Solutions based on secret sharing include a protocol for mean value [34,33].

A protocol for calculating weighted sums over homomorphically encrypted sensitive data is given in [27].

In 2004, Feigenbaum *et al.* proposed to use SMC for analysing faculty incomes in the annual Taulbee Survey [21]. The protocols designed for this study can be found in [1]. In 2011, Bogdanov *et al.* deployed SMC for financial data analysis for the Estonian Association of Information Technology and Telecommunications [10]. Kamm *et al.* have shown how to conduct secure genome-wide association studies using secure multi-party computation [31].

Our Contribution. We provide a novel privacy definition for data analysis using SMC and give guidance on how to achieve it. We propose a privacy-preserving data sharing solution in federated database environments based on SMC. We validate the proposed solution by analysing interviews conducted with potential end-users of the technology. We analyse the responses of our interviewees and identify their expectations towards an SMC-based solution. We illustrate the use of the solution by describing a first pilot project following its design.

We then describe the most complete secure multi-party statistics implementation made to date, supporting the calculation of mean, variance, standard deviation, frequency tables and quantiles. We show how to clean the data and apply custom filters. We give descriptions of privacy-preserving hypothesis testing using standard and paired t-tests, Wilcoxon tests and the χ^2-test. We report on our experimental validation of the proposed algorithms on the SHAREMIND SMC platform and provide performance results proving their feasibility.

2   Data Sharing in Federated State Databases

2.1   Benefits of Openness in State Databases

There exist several initiatives that promote access to and usage of open data to provide enhanced services and greater public transparency to the citizens; the Open Data Foundation[1], ePSI platform[2] and Open Access to scholarly research results [46] just to name a few.

Lane, Heus and Mulcahy [35] discuss the role of publicly accessible sources in research, and identify four essential arguments to support data openness.

1. **Data utility:** data are useful only when they are being used.
2. **Replicability:** original data sources for a scientific result need to be published so that independent scholars could verify the work.
3. **Communication:** research results are always subject to interpretation, and results relying on closed sources are more prone to be misinterpreted.
4. **Efficiency:** data collection is a time-consuming and costly process, hence it makes sense to open it to bring down the social cost of research.

---

[1] http://www.opendatafoundation.org
[2] http://www.epsiplatform.eu

They also acknowledge the need for data protection and discuss four levels of it – technological, statistical, operational and legal protection. In 2008 when the paper [35] was published, the authors saw VPN and Citrix-like thin-client approach as the main technical protection mechanisms. Whereas these solution mitigate the risks caused by the need to have a copy of the dataset available for the research, they still assume direct access to the data. Our paper can be seen as extension of [35], enriching the pool of available data processing tools with secure multi-party computations tools.

Privacy-preserving technologies like secure multi-party computation support the cause of the open data movement by providing a platform for linking and aggregating confidential data sources into less sensitive, publishable streams. For example, if we securely link two personalised databases and aggregate the individual records into demographic groups, we can publish the resulting groups. This is especially useful when the source databases are confidential and should not be openly linked as is the case for many government databases.

2.2   The X-Road Secure Data Exchange Infrastructure

By early 2000s, the level of computerisation in the Estonian state databases had reached both the level of sufficient technical maturity and a certain critical volume so that the need for a unified secure access mechanism was clear. The development activities on the modernisation of national databases started in the beginning of 2001 [30,28]. The first version of the developed X-Road infrastructure was launched on December 17th 2001. The number of queries and replies mediated through the infrastructure per year exceeded 240 million in 2011 [29].

One of the more significant benefits of X-Road is the reduction of data duplication and the ability to combine data from many national databases. Furthermore, all communication is bilaterally authenticated and encrypted, meaning that parties on the X-Road can always prove the source of a request or a data item. Today, already the fifth generation of the X-Road is in operation and the sixth generation is under development, adding new features as high-performance qualified digital signatures [3] and increased availability under cyber threats [4]. Detailed technical descriptions of the whole system can be found in [2,51].

2.3   Privacy Protection Mechanisms for Data Sharing

The Use of Pseudonymisation in X-Road and Its Shortcomings. Since the beginning of 2011, X-Road provides a solution for joining different databases without revealing the identities of the persons included [50]. In order to protect these identities, but still facilitate connecting the data items corresponding to the same individuals, *pseudonymisation* is used. On the technical level, the pseudonyms are computed by encrypting the ID codes of the individuals by a common symmetric AES key distributed via offline means.

Even though this solution offers some protection against curious data analysts, it is not sufficient to resist more determined and targeted attacks. As the data fields of the records are not encrypted, it is possible to breach the privacy by comparing these fields to other datasets, e.g. publicly available data on the person's gender, age, education, home town. Thus it is practically impossible to give any kind of security guarantee to a pseudonymisation-based solution.

Other Candidates for Microdata Protection Mechanisms. Several microdata protection mechanisms have been proposed such as k-anonymity [44,48] and ℓ-diversity [42]. The main idea on k-anonymity is to ensure that each record in a dataset is indistinguishable from at least $k-1$ other records with respect to so-called quasi-identifiers, i.e. certain sets of attributes that can be used to identify at least one person uniquely. Machanavajjhala *et al.* [42] showed that k-anonymity approach has several practical weaknesses. For example, the k-anonymity approach does not take into account a possible background knowledge of attackers. The ℓ-diversity approach [42] was designed to overcome the weaknesses of k-anonymity, but it has also been shown to have limitations [40].

3   Secure Multi-party Computation as a Privacy-Enhancing Technology

Secret sharing [45] is a concept of hiding a secret value by splitting it into random parts and distributing these parts, called shares, to different parties so that each party has only one share. Depending on the secret sharing scheme used, all or a known threshold of shares are needed to reconstruct the original secret value.

Secure multi-party computation allows to compute functions of secret shared values so that each party learns only the corresponding function output value and no inputs of other parties. For example, given a secret value x that is split into n shares so that party P_i has x_i, all parties can collaboratively compute

$$y_1, \ldots, y_n = f(x_1, \ldots, x_n)$$

so that party P_i learns only the output value y_i.

There are a lot of SMC implementations with various features. Most of them are academic research implementations that solve a problem in a very specific setting and are thus not easily usable together with other solutions. More mature implementations with programmable protocol suites include VIFF [16], SEPIA [13], FairplayMP [6] and SHAREMIND [7].

The SHAREMIND application server is a practical implementation of secure multi-party computation technology that allows privacy-preserving computation on secret shared data. It is an SMC implementation powering several real-world applications [10,15]. Its applications are developed using the SecreC programming language [8]. At the time of writing this paper, SHAREMIND is a secure multi-party computation platform with the largest selection of practical features. Therefore, we have chosen it as the platform of choice for this paper.

3.1   Modelling SMC Deployments

We define three fundamental roles in an SMC system—the input party $\mathcal{I}$, the computation party $\mathcal{C}$ and the result party $\mathcal{R}$. Input parties collect and send data to the SMC system. The SMC system itself is hosted by computation parties who carry out the SMC protocols on the inputs and send results to result parties in response to queries.

We use the following notation for modelling SMC applications. Let $\mathcal{I}^k = (\mathcal{I}_1, \ldots, \mathcal{I}_k)$ be the list of input parties, $\mathcal{C}^m = (\mathcal{C}_1, \ldots, \mathcal{C}_m)$ be the list of computing parties and $\mathcal{R}^n = (\mathcal{R}_1, \ldots, \mathcal{R}_n)$ be the list of result parties. Let Π be an SMC protocol for performing a specific task.

In the following, $\mathcal{ICR}$ refers to a party that fills all three roles, similarly, $\mathcal{IC}$ refers to a party with roles $\mathcal{I}$ and $\mathcal{C}$. We use superscripts ($k, m, n \geq 1$) to denote that there are several parties with the same role combination in the system.

Real world parties can have more than one of these roles assigned to them. The set $\{\mathcal{I}, \mathcal{C}, \mathcal{R}\}$ has 7 non-empty subsets and there are 2^7 possibilities to combine them. However, we want to look only at cases where all three roles are present. This leaves us with $128 - 16 = 112$ possible combinations. Not all of these make sense in a real-world setting, but we claim that all deployments of SMC can be expressed using these 112 combinations.

3.2 Privacy Expectations and Definitions

We are mainly interested in the privacy-preserving properties of SMC. Therefore, we want the private inputs of the input parties remain hidden from the computing parties and the result parties.

While it is tempting to define privacy so that the computing parties and result parties learn nothing about the values of the input parties, such a definition would be rather impractical. First, we would need to hide the sizes of all inputs from the computing parties. There are several techniques for hiding the input size (e.g. [23,41]), but no generic solution exists and practical protocols often leak the upper bound of the size.

Second, we would need to hide all branching decisions based on the private inputs. While this can be done by always executing both branches and obliviously choosing the right result, we can significantly save resources when we perform some branching decisions based on published values. However, such behaviour can partially or fully leak the inputs to the computing parties (and also to the result parties, should they measure the running time of Π).

This directs us to a relaxed privacy definition, that allows the computing parties to learn the sizes of inputs and make limited branching decisions based on published values that do not directly leak private inputs. Finally, to support practical statistical analysis tasks, we also allow the result parties to learn certain aggregate values based on the inputs (e.g. percentiles). In a real-world setting, we prevent the abuse of such queries using query auditing techniques, that reject queries or query combinations that are extracting many private inputs.

Definition 1 (Relaxed Privacy of a Multi-party Computation Procedure). *A multi-party computation procedure Π evaluated by parties $\mathcal{I}^k$, $\mathcal{C}^m$, $\mathcal{R}^n$ preserves the privacy of the input parties if the following conditions hold:*

Source Privacy. *During the evaluation of Π, computing parties cannot associate a particular computation result with the input of a certain input party.*

Cryptographic Privacy. *During the evaluation of Π, computing parties learn nothing about the intermediate values used to compute results, including the individual values in the inputs of input parties, unless any of these values are among the allowed output values of Π. As an additional exception, if a computing party is also an input party, it may learn the individual values in the input of only that one input party.*

Restricted Outputs. *During the evaluation of Π, the result parties learn nothing about the intermediate values used to compute results, including the individual values in the inputs of input parties, unless any of these values are among the allowed outputs of Π. Additionally, if a result party is also an input party, it may learn the input of only that one input party.*

Output Privacy. *The outputs of Π do not leak significant parts of the private inputs.*

3.3 Adapting Private Data Analysis Procedures for SMC

We now describe general guidelines for designing privacy-preserving algorithms that satisfy Definition 1. For source privacy, we require that computing parties cannot associate an intermediate value with an individual input party that contributed to this value. For instance, we may learn the smallest value among the private inputs, but we will not know which input party provided it. This can be achieved by starting the protocol by *obliviously shuffling* the data [38].

Cryptographic privacy is achieved by using SMC protocols that collect and store inputs in a protected (e.g. encrypted, secret-shared) form. This prevents the computing parties from recovering private inputs on their own. Furthermore, the protection mechanism must be maintained for private values throughout the algorithm execution. The computing parties must not remove the protection mechanism to perform computations. Examples of suitable techniques include homomorphic secret sharing, homomorphic encryption and garbled circuits.

Restricting outputs is quite straightforward. First, the computing parties must publish to other parties only the result values that Π allows to publish. Everything else must remain protected. Trivially, it follows that the computing parties must run only the procedures to which the computational parties have agreed. Furthermore, the computing parties must reject all queries from the result parties that the computing parties have not agreed to among themselves. In practice, all computation nodes audit their copy of the code and if they do not agree with the operations it wants to perform on the data, they can reject the code. This effectively halts the computation process, as the code needs to be executed in parallel by all of the involved parties for the computation to work.

Output privacy is the most complex privacy goal, requiring a more creative approach. The most complex part in algorithm design is to control the leakage of input value bits through published outputs. There are many measures for this leakage, including input entropy estimation and differential privacy [20]. Regardless of the approach, the algorithm designer must analyse the potential impact of publishing the results of certain computations. In some cases, such an analysis is straightforward. For example, publishing the results of aggregations like sum and mean is a negligible leak unless there are only a few values.

Typically, directly publishing a value from the private inputs should not be allowed. However, there are exceptions to this rule. For example, descriptive values, such as the minimal value in a private input, are used by statisticians to evaluate data quality. The main concern of data analysts in our interviews was that if we take away their access to individual data values, we need to give them a way to get an overview of the data in return. That is the reason why our privacy model allows the publishing of descriptive statistics.

4 Using SMC for Secure Data Sharing and Analysis

4.1 Solution Architecture

We propose a way how secure multi-party computation can be used among federated databases to process sensitive data. We will model the solution after SHAREMIND and the Estonian X-Road as two practical implementations. First, we need to deploy secure multi-party computation nodes within the X-Road infrastructure. These nodes must be coupled with X-Road security servers or they can be standalone computation servers with high network bandwidth. The only restriction for the SHAREMIND nodes is that they must be operated by independent parties to avoid collusion. If the SHAREMIND computation nodes are operated by the same institutions as X-Road security servers belonging to separate government institutions, then secure multi-party computation protocols working in the honest-but-curious model are sufficient as government institutions have no incentive to collude. Furthermore, collusion requires some level of co-operation between the institutions and it is enough for a host to reject suggestions for collusion to defeat the institutional attacker. In the case of an outside attacker, the theft of a single SHAREMIND node does not leak the sensitive data. Should an attack occur, the privacy-preserving *resharing* procedure will ensure that stealing other parts of the secret-shared database will not compromise the sensitive information.

Upon receiving a query that spans databases of multiple service providers, the service consumer contacts the security servers of involved X-Road service providers as usual. These security servers request the needed database from their internal network, perform secret sharing on its contents and distribute the shares among previously chosen SHAREMIND computation nodes. This data sharing step may also be completed before the actual computation request.

The service consumer issuing the request then asks the involved SHAREMIND computation nodes to perform the actual computation on the secret-shared data. Once the secure multi-party computation is finished, the computation nodes send output shares back to the X-Road service consumer who can then reconstruct the final answer for the request. This workflow is shown on Figure 1.

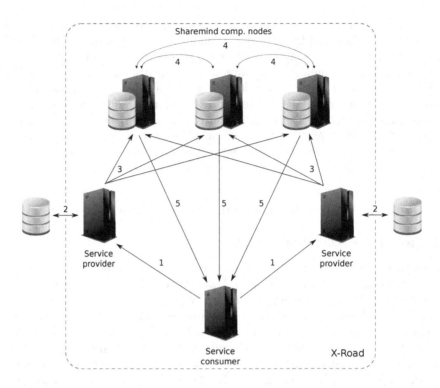

Fig. 1. A step-by-step workflow of using SHAREMIND together with X-Road

4.2   Choosing Computing Nodes

For each computation request, the input data has to be shared and distributed between the same computation nodes. Hence, choosing these nodes has to be coordinated, and this turns out to be a non-trivial task. Consider a situation where X-Road service providers have a preference list of computation nodes to whom they are willing to entrust their secret-shared data. Such a list may be based on a reputation system as described in [5]. Then, upon receiving the computation request from a service consumer, the service providers involved in that request must communicate to agree on a common set of trusted computation nodes to use in the following secure computation. It may happen that such an intersection with a sufficient size does not exist.

Alternatively, we can state that all the deployed SHAREMIND computation nodes are equally trustworthy. Then the task becomes easier as the service consumer issuing the request can itself dictate which nodes to use and just informs the security servers of the involved service providers about its decision.

If a participating X-Road service provider requires more control over the computation process, it can host a SHAREMIND computation node. This gives the service provider an opportunity to halt the secure multi-party data processing if it suspects that anything is wrong. When choosing the computation nodes, this possible limitation has to be taken into account.

5   Validating the Solution with Potential End Users

One of the goals of our work on SMC was to validate the real-world need for secure multi-party computation solutions. For this, we performed and analysed a number of interviews with stakeholders from a variety of fields to find out whether data holders see a need for this technology.

As previous research has indicated, a serious obstacle in user-driven innovation and involving users in the early stages of development work is the problem of explaining such a complex technology to the end-user who is rarely an expert [25,39]. Therefore, we first devised a way to explain the emerging technology to potential end users.

5.1   Using Visualization to Explain SMC to Non-specialists

As our goal was to validate the need for privacy-preserving data sharing, we discussed SMC with people from different areas and asked them if they had had problems with sharing data in their field. We assumed that the interviewees did not have a background in computer science so approaching them with the usual SMC descriptions was out of the question.

We planned to visualise typical SMC applications to make the idea understandable. Fortunately, our role-based model translates easily into illustrative diagrams. See Table 1 for examples of deployment models inspired by published research on SMC applications.

We prepared for the interviews by designing 12 deployment models, some of which were based on existing SMC applications and some were hypothetical. We designed large colourful and easily readable figures to help us describe SMC to stakeholders during the interviews. On these figures we did not use the $\mathcal{ICR}$ syntax, but rather real-world roles that the interviewee could relate to. The description of each model included the security and trust guarantees that SMC provides for the parties. We could not include the figures here due to size constraints, but they can be found in [43].

5.2   Interview Process and Results

Our sample of 25 people was designed with the aim to get as much diversity as possible. The recruitment was based on the fields which, according to previous literature, were considered potentially interested in using SMC applications and also the snowballing technique for furthering the sample. The interviewees were always given a possibility to propose additional fields outside of their own where this kind of technology could be beneficial. Not all of our interviewees could be considered potential users, some could rather be described as stakeholders

Table 1. SMC deployment models and example applications

Basic deployment model	Example applications
$\mathcal{ICR}^k \rightleftarrows$ (SMC)	**The classic millionaires' problem [53]** *Parties:* Two—Alice and Bob (both $\mathcal{ICR}$) *Overview:* Millionaires Alice and Bob use SMC to determine who is richer. **Joint genome studies [31]** *Parties:* Any number of biobanks (all $\mathcal{ICR}$) *Overview:* The biobanks use SMC to create a joint genome database and study a larger population.
$\mathcal{IC}^k \rightleftarrows$ (SMC) $\rightarrow \mathcal{R}^m$	**Studies on linked databases (this paper)** *Parties:* Ministry of Education, Tax Board, Population Register (all $\mathcal{IC}$) and Statistics Bureau ($\mathcal{R}$). *Overview:* Databases from several government agencies are linked to perform statistical analyses and tests.
$\mathcal{IR}^k \rightleftarrows$ (SMC) $\leftarrow \mathcal{C}^m$	**Outsourcing computation to the cloud [22]** *Parties:* Cloud customer ($\mathcal{IR}$) and cloud service providers (all $\mathcal{C}$). *Overview:* The customer deploys SMC on one or more cloud servers to process her/his data.
$\mathcal{ICR}^k \rightleftarrows$ (SMC) $\rightleftarrows \mathcal{IR}^m$	**Collaborative network anomaly detection [13]** *Parties:* Network administrators (all $\mathcal{IR}$) a subset of whom is running computing servers (all $\mathcal{ICR}$). *Overview:* A group of network administrators uses SMC to find anomalies in their traffic.
$\mathcal{I}^k \rightarrow$ (SMC) $\rightleftarrows \mathcal{CR}^n$ $\uparrow$ $\mathcal{C}^m$	**The sugar beet auction [11]** *Parties:* Sugar beet growers (all $\mathcal{I}$), Danisco and DKS (both $\mathcal{CR}$) and the SIMAP project ($\mathcal{C}$). *Overview:* The association of sugar beet growers and their main customer use SMC to agree on a price for buying contracts.
$\mathcal{I}^k \rightarrow$ (SMC) $\rightarrow \mathcal{R}^n$ $\uparrow$ $\mathcal{C}^m$	**The Taulbee survey [21]** *Parties:* Universities in CRA (all $\mathcal{I}$), universities with computing servers (all $\mathcal{IC}$) and the CRA ($\mathcal{R}$). *Overview:* The CRA uses SMC to compute a report of faculty salaries among CRA members. **Financial reporting in a consortium [10]** *Parties:* Members of the ITL (all $\mathcal{I}$), Cybernetica, Microlink and Zone Media (all $\mathcal{IC}$) and the ITL board ($\mathcal{R}$). *Overview:* The ITL consortium uses SMC to compute a financial health report of its members.

with knowledge of potential social barriers. For instance, among others, we interviewed a lawyer and an ethics specialist in order to understand the larger societal implications. As we aimed for the maximum diversity, our interviewees originated from six different countries, came from academia, from both public and private sector organisations, from small and medium sized enterprises to large multinational corporations, from local government to state level. The people we interviewed included representatives from the financial sector, agriculture, retail, security, mobile technologies, statistics companies and IT in general.

We sent the materials to the interviewees beforehand to let them prepare for the interview. We also used the figures during the interview process to trigger conversation and to assist in understanding the principles of the technology. During the interviews, we asked whether our interviewees recognised situations in their field of expertise where they need to share protected data with others.

Our interviewees outlined a number of different potential uses, some more realistic and closer to actual implementation, others brought examples of ideas where the concept of privacy-preserving computing might be useful or beneficial. While the interviewees struggled with identifying concrete applications, their conceptualisation of the technological framework identified several fields of inquiry. Of all the possible cases brought out in the deployment models, the cases concerning the use of databases from different data sources for performing statistical analysis were most discussed. It seems that the benefits of merging different databases for statistical analysis were easily comprehensible for the interviewees. On one hand, the interviewees had many concerns, such as SMC conflicting with the traditional ways of doing things and problems related to the existing legal and regulatory framework. At times, the interviewees could not distinguish between anonymisation and SMC, or understand the operational challenges of using this kind of solution in practice. On the other hand, the interviewees also saw many potential benefits of the possible applications of SMC.

Several interviewees brought out examples how SMC could be advantageous in their professional field, and pointed out that at the moment, the state collects information that is necessary for its purposes, but the public use and benefit of the same data suffers. With secret sharing, information given for general statistical purposes could support a wider range of goals. A researcher from the biomedicine field has an example of this kind of thinking:

"For example, if I as a researcher get the data about the number of abortions but I also want to know how much all kind of associated complications cost, I need to get data from the national Health Insurance Fund. But I only get data from the Health Insurance Fund if I have the data from the abortion registry with names and national identification numbers and then I ask the medical cost records of those people. What I think is actually a really big security risk. If it would be possible to link them differently, so I would receive impersonalised data, that would be really good." (Interview 11, Academic sector, Biomedicine)

In addition to identifying data use possibilities directly relevant to their field of work, interviewees also pointed out how SMC could be used on a more general level. The idea of using different state databases for statistical analysis was seen as highly beneficial. The potential benefit was seen not only for the members of public getting data, but also with the potential of more efficient state systems or use of public funding. For instance, an official working in a state institution that coordinates the work of the national information system stated that making more data and information available for public use is a relevant problem.

"After the presentation I thought that the state data should be made available for people this way: for researches, statisticians, universities. Publishing these data has always been a topic in the state, all the data have to be public, we should put them on the cloud or somewhere else. But do it in a secure way, I haven't thought about it before, but it seemed to me that there were no good solutions." (Interview 8, Public sector, IT security)

People are concerned about the privacy and personal integrity of the individuals whose data could be shared in such way. The legal barriers protecting individuals have a limited understanding or awareness of SMC capabilities and use of such application is hence seen possible only in distant future. At the same time, several interviewees see that state information systems using such applications could set the standard and help to develop trust. Alternatively, an EU regulation can help to overcome some implementation barriers as then different state systems will have to implement these data use regulations.

Interestingly, interviewees whose work involves data processing remained somewhat critical, mostly because of the practical issues. Although an interviewee working in biomedicine saw the benefits of using different databases in scientific research, he also foresaw possible issues that could hinder their work. The main concern could be expressed as the necessity to "see" the data.

"But in the context of genetics, the researcher who does the calculations, he has to see the data. He has to understand the data, because there the future work will be combined. You never take just means, but when you are already calculating genotypes and their frequencies, then you have to take into account some other factors all the time. Adjust them according to age, height, weight. And you need to see these data. Without understanding the data, you cannot analyse them." (Interview 11, Academic sector, Biomedicine)

This obviously raises the question as to what is actually meant by "seeing" and "understanding" the data. The visibility of the data seems to be crucial, but it does not necessarily mean that no alternative solutions or procedures are possible. The interviewees remarked that it would be possible to do scientific analysis without "seeing" the data but that it would make their work more complicated and therefore would be met with hesitation. Hence, it may be possible that the barrier here is the practiced and accepted way of doing things. Even now statistics offices often respond to data requests by disclosing sample databases that resemble the data so that researchers can script their queries.

However, the interviews also revealed that the visibility of data is necessary to guarantee their quality. This aspect was for instance stressed by an expert working in the Statistics Office. Similarly, the interviewee doing scientific research thought it possible that the quality of their work and data suffers if they do not have the full overview.

"We cannot combine different statistical works if we don't have the identifiers. To do statistics, to have good quality information, we need to have it /full overview of data/." (Interview 13, Public sector, Statistics)

This quote illustrates nicely the way new technologies are understood first and foremost in the context of existing practices and boundaries. Similarly, people considering the importance of statistical analysis with SMC can imagine the activities they do in their current framework. Hence, statistical analysis comes down to finding means, comparing samples in valid ways, finding correlations and relationships within the data. And all this preferably with a user environment that is recognisable. While, for instance, the Statistics Office employees can write their own scripts for queries, for wider usability, future SMC systems will need to be similar to existing tools.

6   An Example Application: Linking Tax and Education Data

6.1   Estimating Economic Trends in Education

Governments are often interested in knowing what the return of investment of various kinds of education is. The underlying question is, what kind of specialists are needed in order to ensure the future economic success of the country and what kind of specialist may need re-education. One possible way for estimating this is to look at the trends in the earnings of different individuals. In Estonia, this information is distributed among several government institutions—the Tax and Customs Board has information about incomes and the Education Information System has all the education records for recent years. In a common scenario, the state will contact its Statistics Bureau and ask it to conduct the analysis. The latter has to contact the Tax and Customs Board and the Education Information System and ask them for the relevant data. The compiled database has a very high risk factor due to containing both income and educational information.

The authors of this paper are participating in a project called "Privacy-preserving statistical studies on linked databases[3]" (PRIST) started in 2013. In this project, we are answering the above question without compiling a full database of people and their incomes. Instead, we are conducting the study using secure multi-party computation and, more specifically, SHAREMIND.

6.2   Deploying Secure Multi-party Computation for the Study

As SMC technology is not yet integrated into X-Road, there are several extra steps that must be taken. First, we have to find partners who are willing to act as computing parties and who have the necessary technical knowledge. In PRIST, the role of a computation node is carried out by the IT department

---

[3] Funded by the European Regional Development Fund from the sub-measure "Supporting the development of the R&D of information and communication technology" through the Archimedes Foundation.

of the Ministry of Internal Affairs (the Tax and Customs Board is part of it), Estonian Information System's Authority and Cybernetica AS. The latter also provides the secure multi-party computation technology. All of the partners have to audit the SMC platform before deploying it in their premises and have to engage in a pairwise public key exchange to establish secure channels during the computation.

The use of SMC technology requires that the secret sharing of input data is done at the data owner's premises. Therefore, we will provide a special-purpose data import program to the Tax and Customs Board and the Ministry of Education and Science. This importer takes a database (e.g. a CSV file), applies secret sharing to each of its values and distributes the shares among the computing parties over a secure channel. Both institutions create this intermediate CSV database with a query to their internal databases.

A team of statisticians fulfils the role of the result party. Their job is to initiate the secure computation process, receive the statistical results and interpret them. They are also responsible for compiling the study plan. The plan is implemented on SHAREMIND using the SecreC statistical library (see Section 7). The resulting application is distributed among the computation nodes and each one of them audits the code separately. Each computation node tracks what kind of operations are requested on the data and which results are published. Only if they agree that the program does what is expected, they compile the code and deploy it into their SHAREMIND installation so it can be executed.

We also provided a description of the study process for analysis to the Estonian Data Protection Inspectorate. Their response states that if the study is conducted according to the description, then no permit for the processing of personally identifiable information needs to be requested, as no such processing takes place[4]. This is an important result, as it significantly simplifies such studies in the future without jeopardising the privacy of citizens.

6.3   Conducting the Study

After the computation nodes have been set up, the analysis program code has been deployed and data have been imported, the actual secure multi-party computation process can be initiated by the statistical analysis team. In this project, the analysis starts by securely joining the database containing income information with the database containing education information. In SHAREMIND, the secure database join operation is similar to the one used in X-Road today (see Section 2.3) using AES block cipher to encrypt the key values and performing the actual join operation on ciphertexts [36]. However, in SHAREMIND the AES encryption works on secret shared plaintexts and with a secret shared key that no single party knows. This ensures that the sensitive inputs are not published to any person or computer during linking.

As the actual join operation also works on published (reconstructed) ciphertexts, this method leaks for each encrypted key the number of matching keys

---

[4] Official response in Estonian available at
http://adr.rik.ee/aki/dokument/2663016

in the other database. However, the key values and their positions are not revealed. More formally, if we depict the key columns of the joinable databases as bipartite graph with an edge marking matching keys, the join operation leaks its edge structure with the precision of the graph isomorphism. This information leakage is usually acceptable. Nevertheless, a slightly less efficient version of the oblivious database join operation that does not leak this information is described in [37].

After the join operation is done, the resulting table is ready for statistical analysis. In this study, we expect to perform a range of descriptive statistical analyses, statistical tests and regressions. The statistical analysis will be able to request previously agreed-to analyses and it will receive only the results of the analyses. The statistical tool receives one share of each result value from the SHAREMIND computation nodes and reconstructs the results. The statistical analysis library is prepared in a way that prevents query results that are aggregations of a single person's data.

6.4 The Benefits of Integrating Secure Multi-party Computation into X-Road

The integration of SMC into X-Road will optimise the study process as follows. First, we avoid setting up the computation nodes separately for every such project. This does not include only installing the SMC software but also the key exchange process. The public keys of SHAREMIND computation nodes can be exchanged by using signed X-Road messages.

Second, there will be no need for a separate importer application. The X-Road security server can directly access the internal database, apply secret sharing to the relevant tables according to a given task description and distribute the shares among the computation nodes. It is important to notice here that this also eliminates the need to create a database view as a data file. Getting rid of this standalone data file also eliminates the risk of leaking this file. Based on this, we are planning to combine SHAREMIND with the next generation of the X-Road core developed in the SDSB project[5].

7 Implementing Statistical Studies with Secure Multi-party Computation

7.1 Data Import and Filtering

When collecting data from several input parties, a common data model has to be agreed upon and key values for linking data from different parties have to be identified. For efficiency, it is often useful to preprocess and clean data at the input parties before sending it to computing parties. This will not compromise data privacy as the data will be processed by the input party itself. We now look at how to filter and clean data once it has been sent to the computing parties.

---

[5] Secure Distributed Service Bus—http://www.eliko.ee/secure-service-bus

In the following, let $[\![x]\!]$ denote a private value x, let $[\![a]\!]$ denote a private value vector a, and let binary operations between vectors be point-wise operations.

Encoding Missing Values. Sometimes, single values are missing from the imported dataset. There are two options for dealing with this situation: we can use a special value in the data domain for missing values; or add an extra availability mask for each attribute to store this information. Let the availability mask $[\![\mathsf{available}(a)]\!]$ of vector $[\![a]\!]$ contain 0 if the corresponding value in the attribute $[\![a]\!]$ is missing and 1 otherwise. The overall count of records in storage is public. If missing elements exist, that value does not reflect the number of available elements and it is not possible to know which elements are available by looking at the shares. The number of available elements can be computed as a sum of values in the availability mask.

Evaluating Filters and Isolating Filtered Data. To filter data based on a condition, we securely compare each element in the the private attribute vector $[\![a]\!]$ to the filter value and obtain a private vector of comparison results. This mask vector $[\![m]\!]$ contains 1 if the condition holds and 0 otherwise. If there are several conditions in a filter, the resulting mask vectors are multiplied to combine the filters. Such filters do not leak which records correspond to the conditions.

Most of our algorithms can use a provided filter automatically during calculations. However, in some cases, it is necessary to "cut" the vector—keep a subset vector containing only the filtered data. To cut the vector, we first obliviously shuffle the value and mask vectors, retaining the correspondence of the elements. Next, the mask vector is declassified and values, for which the mask vector shows a zero, are removed from the value vector. The obtained cut vector is then returned to the user.

This process leaks the number of values that correspond to the filters that the mask vector represents. This makes cutting trivially safe to use, when the number of records in the filter would be published anyway. Oblivious shuffling ensures that no other information about the private input vector and mask vector is leaked [38]. Therefore, algorithms using oblivious cut provide source privacy.

7.2   Linking Multiple Tables

After collecting input values and compiling filters for the outliers, we can link the input databases to form the final analysis database. There are various ways for linking databases in a privacy-preserving manner. As a minimum, we desire linking algorithms that do not publish private input values and only disclose the sizes of the input and output databases, as described in Section 6.3.

7.3   Data Quality Assurance and Visibility

Quantiles and Outlier Detection. Datasets often contain errors or extreme values that should be excluded from the analysis. Although there are many elaborate outlier detection algorithms like [12], outliers are often detected using quantiles. As no one method for computing quantiles has been widely agreed upon in the statistics community, we use algorithm $\mathbf{Q_7}$ from [26], because it is the default choice in our reference statistical analysis package GNU R. Let p be the percentile we want to find and let $[\![a]\!]$ be a vector of values sorted in ascending order. Then the quantile is computed using the following function:

$$\mathbf{Q_7}(p, [\![a]\!]) = (1 - \gamma) \cdot [\![a]\!][j] + \gamma \cdot [\![a]\!][j + 1] \ ,$$

where $j = \lfloor (n - 1)p \rfloor + 1$, n is the size of vector $[\![a]\!]$, and $\gamma = np - \lfloor (n - 1)p \rfloor - p$. Once we have the index of the quantile value, we can use oblivious versions of vector lookup or sorting to learn the quantile value from the input vector.

We do not need to publish the quantile to use it for outlier filtering. Let q_0 and q_1 be the 5% and 95% quantiles of an attribute $[\![a]\!]$. It is common to mark all values smaller than q_0 and larger than q_1 as outliers. The corresponding mask vector is computed by comparing all elements of $[\![a]\!]$ to $\mathbf{Q_7}(0.05, [\![a]\!])$ and $\mathbf{Q_7}(0.95, [\![a]\!])$, and then multiplying the resulting index vectors. This way, data can be filtered to exclude the outlier data from further analysis. It is possible to combine the mask vector with the availability mask $[\![\mathsf{available}(a)]\!]$ and cache it as an updated availability mask to reduce the filtering load. Later, this mask can be used with the data attributes as they are passed to the statistical functions.

Descriptive Statistics. As discussed in Section 5.2, one of the data analysts' main concerns was that they will lose the ability to see individual values. We claim that data quality can be ensured without compromising the privacy of individual data owners by providing access to aggregate values and enabling outlier filtering. While the aggregate value of an attribute leaks information about the inputs, the leakage is small and determined by the aggregate function.

A common aggregate is the five-number summary—a combination of the minimum, lower quartile, median, upper quartile and maximum of an attribute. We can compute the five-number summary using the quantile formula and use the published result to draw box-plots that give a visual overview of the data and effectively draw attention to outliers.

It is also important to analyse the distribution of a data attribute. For categorical attributes, this can be done by computing the frequency of the occurrences of different values. For numerical attributes, we must split the range into bins specified by breaks and compute the corresponding frequencies. The resulting frequency table can be visualised as a histogram. This publishes the number of bins and the number of values in each bin.

7.4   Statistical Testing

The Principles of Statistical Testing. Many statistical analysis tasks conclude with the comparison of different populations. For instance, we might want to know whether the average income of graduates of a particular university is significantly higher than that of other universities. In such cases, we first extract two groups—the case and control populations. In our example, the case population corresponds to graduates of the particular university in question and the control group is formed of persons from other universities. Note that a simple comparison of corresponding means is sufficient as the variability of income in the subpopulations might be much higher than the difference between means.

Statistical tests are specific algorithms, which formally quantify the significance of the difference between means. These test algorithms return the test statistic value that has to be combined with the sizes of the compared populations to determine the significance of the difference. While we could also implement a privacy-preserving lookup to determine this significand and prevent the publication of the statistic value, statisticians are used to including the statistic values and group sizes in their reports.

The Construction of Case and Control Populations. We first need to privately form case and control groups before starting the tests. One option is to select the subjects into one group and assume all the rest are in group two, e.g. students who go to city schools and everyone else. Alternatively, we can choose subjects into both groups, e.g. men who are older than 35 and went to a city school and men who are older than 35 who did not go to a city school. These selection categories yield either one or two mask vectors. In the former case, we compute the second mask vector by flipping all the bits in the existing mask vector. Hence, we can always consider the version where case and control groups are determined by two mask vectors.

In the following, let $[\![a]\!]$ be the value vector we are testing and let $[\![m_1]\!]$ and $[\![m_2]\!]$ be mask vectors for case and control groups, respectively. Then $[\![n_i]\!] = \mathbf{sum}([\![m_i]\!])$ is the count of subjects in the corresponding population.

The tests need to compute the mean, standard deviation or variance of a population. We do this by evaluating the standard formulae using SMC. For improved precision, these metrics should be computed using real numbers.

Student's t-tests. The two-sample Student's t-test is the simplest statistical tests that allows us to determine whether the difference of group means is significant or not compared to variability in groups. There are two common flavours of this test [32] depending on whether the variability of the populations is equal.

In some cases, there is a direct one-to-one dependence between case and control group elements. For example, the data consists of measurements from the same subject (e.g. income before and after graduation), or from two different subjects that have been heuristically paired together (e.g. a parent and a child). In that case, a paired t-test [32] is more appropriate to detect whether a significant change has taken place.

The algorithm for computing both t-tests is a straightforward evaluation of the respective formulae using SMC with privacy-preserving real number operations. Both algorithms publish the statistic value and the population sizes.

Wilcoxon Rank Sum Test and Signed Rank Test. T-tests are formally applicable only if the distribution of attribute values in case and control groups follows the normal distribution. If this assumption does not hold, it is appropriate to use non-parametric Wilcoxon tests. The Wilcoxon rank sum test [24] works on the assumption that the distribution of data in one group significantly differs from that in the other.

A privacy-preserving version of the rank sum test follows the standard algorithm, but we need to use several tricks to achieve output privacy. First, we need a more complex version of the cutting procedure to filter the database, the cases and controls using the same filter. Second, to rank the values, we sort the filtered values together with their associated masks by the value column.

Similarly to Student's paired t-test, the Wilcoxon signed-rank test [49] is a paired difference test. Often, Pratt's correction [24] is used for when the values are equal and their difference is 0. In a privacy-preserving version of this algorithm, we again need to cut several columns at once. We also need to obliviously separate absolute values and signs from the signed inputs values and later sort these two vectors by the sign vector.

The computation of both tests is simplified by the fact that most operations are done on signed integers and secure real number operations are not required before computing the final z-score statistic. Both algorithms only publish the statistic value and the population sizes.

The χ^2-tests for Consistency. If the attribute values are discrete such as income categories then it is impossible to apply t-tests or their non-parametric counterparts and we have to analyse frequencies of certain values in the dataset. The corresponding statistical test is known as χ^2-test.

The privacy-preserving version of the χ^2-test is implemented simply by evaluating the algorithm using SMC operations. The algorithm can be optimised, if the number of classes is small, e.g. two. The algorithm publishes only the statistic value and the population sizes.

8 Practical Implementation and Benchmarks

We have implemented the described privacy-preserving statistics algorithms on the SHAREMIND SMC system. For an overview of the implementation, see Appendix A. Figure 2 shows our benchmarking scenario. Artificial data was used in the benchmarks, as the PRIST study is still in progress. We conducted the experiments on a SHAREMIND installation running on three computers with 3 GHz 6-core Intel CPUs with 8 GB RAM per core. While monitoring the experiments, we did not see memory usage above 500 MB per machine. The computers were connected using gigabit ethernet network interfaces.

Table 2 contains the operations, input sizes and running times for our experimental scenario. The output of the operations was checked against reference results from the R statistical toolkit and was found to be correct. We see that most operations in our experimental study take under a minute to complete.

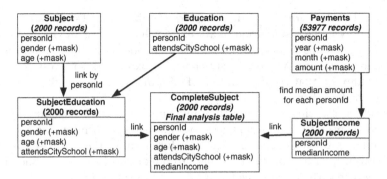

Fig. 2. The data model and table transformations in our experiment

Table 2. Running times of privacy-preserving statistics (in seconds)

Step 1: Data import

Operation	Record count	Time
Data import from offsite computer	2 000	3 s
	53 977	24 s

Step 2: Descriptive statistics

Operation	Record count	Time
5-number summary (publish filter size)	2000	21 s
	20000	97 s
5-number summary (hide filter size)	2000	27 s
	20000	107 s
Frequency table	2000	16 s
	20000	222 s

Step 3: Grouping and linking

Operation	Record count	Time
Median of incomes by subject	53 977	3 h 46 min
Linking two tables by a key column	2000×5 and 2000×3	28 s
Linking two tables by a key column	2000×7 and 2000×2	29 s

Step 4: Statistical tests

Operation	Record count	Time
Student's t-test, equal variance	2000	167 s
	20000	765 s
Student's t-test, different variance	2000	157 s
paired t-test, known mean	2000 and 2000	98 s
paired t-test, unknown mean	2000 and 2000	102 s
χ^2-test, 2 classes	2000	9 s
	20000	10 s
χ^2-test, n-class version, 2 classes	2000	20 s
χ^2-test, n-class version, 5 classes	2000	23 s
Wilcoxon rank sum	2000	34 s
Wilcoxon signed-rank	2000 and 2000	38 s

The most notable exceptions is the group median computation, as median computation has to be applied to the payments of 2000 subjects. This time can be reduced by vectorising the median invocations or conduct this aggregation before the data are converted into secret-shared form.

To check scalability, we performed some tests on ten times larger data vectors. We found that increasing input data size 10 times increases running time about 5 times. Only histogram computation is actually slower, because it uses a more detailed frequency table for larger databases, actually increasing the work done.

The improved efficiency per input data element is explained by the use of vectorised operations of the SHAREMIND framework. The operations in the SHAREMIND framework are more efficient when many are performed in parallel using the SIMD (single instruction, multiple data) model.

9   Conclusions

In this paper, we study the problem of performing privacy-preserving statistical studies on data collected from sources connected to a single federated database infrastructure. Our proposed solution is to use secure multi-party computation as a privacy-enhancing technology. The paper provides a description of the solution with an explanation of the privacy-guarantees and implementation guidelines. We have also validated the need for this technology with the end users.

We present practical designs for statistical analysis algorithms and their implementations on the SHAREMIND secure multi-party computation system. Experimental results show that our approach is sufficiently fast for practical use in non-real-time applications such as a statistical study. The technical strengths of our solution are generality, precision and practicality. First, we show that secure multi-party computation is flexible enough for implementing complex applications. Second, our use of secure floating point operations makes our implementation more precise. Third, we use the same algorithms as popular statistical toolkits like GNU R without simplifying the underlying mathematics.

We introduce a project that will validate the solution in practice—the linking of tax and education records in Estonia to study what kinds of specialists are needed in the ICT sector. A statement from the Estonian Data Protection Inspectorate indicates that our solution does not process personally identifiable information. This suggests that secure multi-party computation can provide a completely new level of privacy protection in the analysis of federated databases.

Acknowledgements. This research was supported by the European Regional Development Fund through Centre of Excellence in Computer Science (EXCS) and Competence Centre in Electronics-, Info- and Communication Technologies (ELIKO); the European Social Fund Doctoral Studies and Internationalisation programme DoRa; and by the Estonian Research Council under Institutional Research Grant IUT27-1. The end user validation and the development of privacy-preserving statistical tools is funded by the European Union Seventh Framework Programme (FP7/2007-2013) under grant agreement no. 284731.

The authors wish to thank the interviewees for their time and cooperation and the Estonian Center for Applied Research for their help in generating the artificial data used in the experiments of this paper.

References

1. Aggarwal, G., Mishra, N., Pinkas, B.: Secure computation of the median (and other elements of specified ranks). Journal of Cryptology 23(3), 373–401 (2010)
2. Ansper, A., Buldas, A., Freudenthal, M., Willemson, J.: Scalable and Efficient PKI for Inter-Organizational Communication. In: Proceedings of ACSAC 2003, pp. 308–318 (2003)
3. Ansper, A., Buldas, A., Freudenthal, M., Willemson, J.: High-Performance Qualified Digital Signatures for X-Road. In: Riis Nielson, H., Gollmann, D. (eds.) NordSec 2013. LNCS, vol. 8208, pp. 123–138. Springer, Heidelberg (2013)
4. Ansper, A., Buldas, A., Freudenthal, M., Willemson, J.: Protecting a Federated Database Infrastructure Against Denial-of-Service Attacks. In: Luiijf, E., Hartel, P. (eds.) CRITIS 2013. LNCS, vol. 8328, pp. 26–37. Springer, Heidelberg (2013)
5. Asharov, G., Lindell, Y., Zarosim, H.: Fair and Efficient Secure Multiparty Computation with Reputation Systems. In: Sako, K., Sarkar, P. (eds.) ASIACRYPT 2013, Part II. LNCS, vol. 8270, pp. 201–220. Springer, Heidelberg (2013)
6. Ben-David, A., Nisan, N., Pinkas, B.: FairplayMP: A system for secure multi-party computation. In: Proceedings of ACM CCS 2008, pp. 257–266 (2008)
7. Bogdanov, D.: Sharemind: programmable secure computations with practical applications. PhD thesis. University of Tartu (2013)
8. Bogdanov, D., Laud, P., Randmets, J.: Domain-Polymorphic Programming of Privacy-Preserving Applications. Cryptology ePrint Archive, Report 2013/371 (2013), http://eprint.iacr.org/
9. Bogdanov, D., Niitsoo, M., Toft, T., Willemson, J.: High-performance secure multiparty computation for data mining applications. International Journal of Information Security 11(6), 403–418 (2012)
10. Bogdanov, D., Talviste, R., Willemson, J.: Deploying secure multi-party computation for financial data analysis. In: Keromytis, A.D. (ed.) FC 2012. LNCS, vol. 7397, pp. 57–64. Springer, Heidelberg (2012)
11. Bogetoft, P., et al.: Secure Multiparty Computation Goes Live. In: Dingledine, R., Golle, P. (eds.) FC 2009. LNCS, vol. 5628, pp. 325–343. Springer, Heidelberg (2009)
12. Breunig, M.M., Kriegel, H.-P., Ng, R.T., Lof, J.S.: Identifying density-based local outliers. In: Proceedings of CM SIGMOD 2000, pp. 93–104 (2000)
13. Burkhart, M., Strasser, M., Many, D., Dimitropoulos, X.A.: SEPIA: Privacy-Preserving Aggregation of Multi-Domain Network Events and Statistics. In: Proceedings of USENIX 2010, pp. 223–240 (2010)
14. Canetti, R., Ishai, Y., Kumar, R., Reiter, M.K., Rubinfeld, R., Wright, R.N.: Selective private function evaluation with applications to private statistics. In: Proceedings of PODC 2001, pp. 293–304. ACM (2001)
15. Cybernetica. Income analysis of the Estonian Public Sector. Online service, https://sharemind.cyber.ee/clouddemo/ (last accessed December 13, 2013)
16. Damgård, I., Geisler, M., Krøigaard, M., Nielsen, J.B.: Asynchronous multiparty computation: Theory and implementation. In: Jarecki, S., Tsudik, G. (eds.) PKC 2009. LNCS, vol. 5443, pp. 160–179. Springer, Heidelberg (2009)

17. Damgård, I., Pastro, V., Smart, N., Zakarias, S.: Multiparty computation from somewhat homomorphic encryption. In: Safavi-Naini, R., Canetti, R. (eds.) CRYPTO 2012. LNCS, vol. 7417, pp. 643–662. Springer, Heidelberg (2012)
18. Du, W., Atallah, M.J.: Privacy-preserving cooperative statistical analysis. In: Proceedings of ACSAC 2001, pp. 102–110 (2001)
19. Du, W., Chen, S., Han, Y.S.: Privacy-preserving multivariate statistical analysis: Linear regression and classification. In: SDM 2004, pp. 222–233 (2004)
20. Dwork, C.: Differential privacy. In: Bugliesi, M., Preneel, B., Sassone, V., Wegener, I. (eds.) ICALP 2006. Part II. LNCS, vol. 4052, pp. 1–12. Springer, Heidelberg (2006)
21. Feigenbaum, J., Pinkas, B., Ryger, R., Saint-Jean, F.: Secure computation of surveys. In: EU Workshop on Secure Multiparty Protocols (2004)
22. Gentry, C.: Fully homomorphic encryption using ideal lattices. In: Proceedings of STOC 2009, pp. 169–178. ACM (2009)
23. Goldreich, O., Ostrovsky, R.: Software Protection and Simulation on Oblivious RAMs. Journal of the ACM 43(3), 431–473 (1996)
24. Hollander, M., Wolfe, D.A.: Nonparametric statistical methods, 2nd edn. John Wiley, New York (1999)
25. Hoonhout, H.C.M.: Setting the stage for developing innovative product concepts: people and climate. CoDesign, 3(S1),19–34 (2007)
26. Hyndman, R.J., Fan, Y.: Sample quantiles in statistical packages. The American Statistician 50(4), 361–365 (1996)
27. Jawurek, M., Kerschbaum, F.: Fault-tolerant privacy-preserving statistics. In: Fischer-Hübner, S., Wright, M. (eds.) PETS 2012. LNCS, vol. 7384, pp. 221–238. Springer, Heidelberg (2012)
28. Kalja, A.: The X-Road Project. A Project to Modernize Estonia's National Databases. Baltic IT&T review 24, 47–48 (2002)
29. Kalja, A.: The first ten years of X-road. In: Estonian Information Society Yearbook 2011/2012, pp. 78–80. Department of State Information System, Estonia (2012)
30. Kalja, A., Vallner, U.: Public e-Service Projects in Estonia. In: Proceedings of Baltic DB&IS 2002, vol. 2, pp. 143–153 (June 2002)
31. Kamm, L., Bogdanov, D., Laur, S., Vilo, J.: A new way to protect privacy in large-scale genome-wide association studies. Bioinformatics 29(7), 886–893 (2013)
32. Kanji, G.K.: 100 statistical tests. Sage (2006)
33. Kerschbaum, F.: Practical privacy-preserving benchmarking. In: Jajodia, S., Samarati, P., Cimato, S. (eds.) Proceedings of IFIP TC-11 SEC 2008, vol. 278, pp. 17–31. Springer, Boston (2008)
34. Kiltz, E., Leander, G., Malone-Lee, J.: Secure computation of the mean and related statistics. In: Kilian, J. (ed.) TCC 2005. LNCS, vol. 3378, pp. 283–302. Springer, Heidelberg (2005)
35. Lane, J., Heus, P., Mulcahy, T.: Data Access in a Cyber World: Making Use of Cyberinfrastructure. Transactions on Data Privacy 1(1), 2–16 (2008)
36. Laur, S., Talviste, R., Willemson, J.: From Oblivious AES to Efficient and Secure Database Join in the Multiparty Setting. In: Jacobson, M., Locasto, M., Mohassel, P., Safavi-Naini, R. (eds.) ACNS 2013. LNCS, vol. 7954, pp. 84–101. Springer, Heidelberg (2013)
37. S. Laur, R. Talviste, J. Willemson.: From Oblivious AES to Efficient and Secure Database Join in the Multiparty Setting (extended version). Cryptology ePrint Archive, Report 2013/203 (2013), http://eprint.iacr.org/

38. Laur, S., Willemson, J., Zhang, B.: Round-Efficient Oblivious Database Manipulation. In: Lai, X., Zhou, J., Li, H. (eds.) ISC 2011. LNCS, vol. 7001, pp. 262–277. Springer, Heidelberg (2011)
39. Lettl, C.: User involvement competence for radical innovation. Journal of engineering and technology management 24(1), 53–75 (2007)
40. Li, N., Li, T., Venkatasubramanian, S.: t-closeness: Privacy beyond k-anonymity and ℓ-diversity. In: Proceedings of ICDE 2007 (2007)
41. Y. Lindell, K. Nissim, C. Orlandi.: Hiding the input-size in secure two-party computation. Cryptology ePrint Archive, Report 2012/679 (2012), http://eprint.iacr.org/
42. Machanavajjhala, A., Kifer, D., Gehrke, J., Venkitasubramaniam, M.: L-diversity: Privacy beyond k-anonymity. ACM Transactions on Knowledge Discovery from Data (TKDD) 1(1) (March 2007)
43. P. Pruulmann-Vengerfeldt, L. Kamm, R. Talviste, P. Laud, D. Bogdanov.: Deliverable D1.1—Capability model (2012), http://usable-security.eu/files/D1.1.pdf.pdf
44. Samarati, P.: Protecting respondents identities in microdata release. IEEE Transactions on Knowledge and Data Engineering 13, 1010–1027 (2001)
45. Shamir, A.: How to share a secret. Communications of the ACM 22, 612–613 (1979)
46. Suber, P.: Open Access. MIT Press (2012)
47. Subramaniam, H., Wright, R.N., Yang, Z.: Experimental analysis of privacy-preserving statistics computation. In: Jonker, W., Petković, M. (eds.) SDM 2004. LNCS, vol. 3178, pp. 55–66. Springer, Heidelberg (2004)
48. Sweeney, L.: K-anonymity: A model for protecting privacy. Int. J. Uncertain. Fuzziness Knowl.-Based Syst. 10(5), 557–570 (2002)
49. Wilcoxon, F.: Individual Comparisons by Ranking Methods. Biometrics Bulletin 1(6), 80–83 (1945)
50. Willemson, J.: Pseudonymization Service for X-Road eGovernment Data Exchange Layer. In: Andersen, K.N., Francesconi, E., Grönlund, Å., van Engers, T.M. (eds.) EGOVIS 2011. LNCS, vol. 6866, pp. 135–145. Springer, Heidelberg (2011)
51. Willemson, J., Ansper, A.: A Secure and Scalable Infrastructure for Inter-Organizational Data Exchange and eGovernment Applications. In: Proceedings of ARES 2008, pp. 572–577. IEEE Computer Society (2008)
52. Yang, Z., Wright, R.N., Subramaniam, H.: Experimental analysis of a privacy-preserving scalar product protocol. Computer Systems Science & Engineering 21(1) (2006)
53. Yao, A.C.-C.: Protocols for Secure Computations (Extended Abstract). In: Proceedings of FOCS 1982, pp. 160–164. IEEE (1982)

A   Overview of Implemented Operations

Figure 3 showcases our privacy-preserving statistical functionality and its dependencies. The implementation is built on the arithmetical, comparison and oblivious vector operations provided by SHAREMIND. However, our algorithms can be ported to any SMC framework that provides the same set of features.

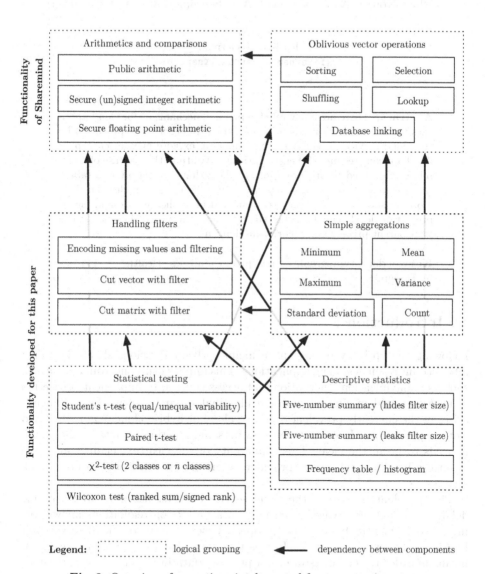

Fig. 3. Overview of operations implemented for our experiments

Privacy by Encrypted Databases

Patrick Grofig, Isabelle Hang, Martin Härterich, Florian Kerschbaum,
Mathias Kohler, Andreas Schaad, Axel Schröpfer, and Walter Tighzert

SAP
Karlsruhe, Germany
{firstname.lastname}@sap.com

Abstract. There are a few reliable privacy mechanisms for cloud applications. Data usually needs to be decrypted in order to be processed by the cloud service provider. In this paper we explore how an encrypted database can (technically) ensure privacy. We study the use case of a mobile personalized healthcare app. We show that an encrypted database can ensure data protection against a cloud service provider. Furthermore we show that if privacy is considered in application design, higher protection levels can be achieved, although encrypted database are a transparent privacy and security mechanism.

Keywords: Cryptography, Encrypted Databases, Healthcare, Privacy by Design.

1 Introduction

Following the "privacy by design" principle privacy decisions should be taken into account when designing applications. This implies using the available means, such as anonymization, encryption and access control, to implement protection of necessary and minimized personal identifiable data. An unsolved challenge arises in the currently prevalent design of cloud or hybrid cloud, e.g. mobile and cloud, applications. In order to process personal identifiable data in the cloud, it needs to be in the clear. This availability of the cleartext enables all kinds of misuse by the cloud service provider, originally intended only to provide IT services.

This problem of trust in the cloud service provider has generated a public debate. It is not clear whether current data protection regulations allow storing personal identifiable data of European Union citizens on cloud servers not hosted in the European Union. In this paper we explore the use of a technical means in order to securely store (and process) data in the cloud. In particular, we investigate the use of an encrypted database. In our database, all data is encrypted at the client which also retains the key. Therefore the cloud service provider has only access to ciphertexts.

For all fairness, the legal debate whether encrypted personal identifiable data (without the key) is still personal identifiable data has also not been settled. In this paper we will nevertheless not explore the legal dimension. For a technically

B. Preneel and D. Ikonomou (Eds.): APF 2014, LNCS 8450, pp. 56–69, 2014.

educated person, it seems convincing that encryption solves the problem. In this paper we will show that when using a transparent encryption mechanism such as an encrypted database precautions also in the design of the application should be taken.

We use the example of a mobile personalized health care app that stores data in the cloud. Clearly, personal health records are sensitive personal identifiable data and subject to the strongest data protection regulations. We will show how to design such an app, so that it ensures confidentiality of this data against a cloud service provider using an encrypted database.

The remainder of the paper is structured as follows. In the next Section we describe related work and how we implement our encrypted database using it. In Section 3 we describe how this encrypted data works and is used. Then, in Section 4 we describe our use case of a mobile personalized healthcare app. And, finally, in Section 5 we present our conclusions for ensuring privacy by an encrypted database.

2   Processing Queries on Encrypted Data

We briefly describe how we implement our encrypted database using adjustable encryption. Security is a major concern for outsourced databases [1,8,13]. In the database-as-a-service model [13] an independent service provider offers its database to clients. The clients need to entrust their data to the cloud service provider without having control over unwanted disclosures, e.g., to insiders or hackers.

The solution to this outsourced security problem is to encrypt data before sending it to the cloud. Of course, the decryption key needs to remain only at the client. This is easy to implement for simple storage, but the clients must remain able to query the database. Therefore the service provider has to solve the complicated task of querying on the encrypted data. There are several proposals for processing many SQL queries on this encrypted data [2,11,12,29,31]. We implement a slightly modified version of Popa et al.'s adjustable encryption [29].

Order-preserving encryption (OPE) [2,4,5,28], deterministic encryption (DET) [3,27] and (additively) homomorphic encryption (HOM) [25] offer a (partial) solution to the encrypted data querying problem. These different encryption schemes have different algebraic properties. Let $c = E_T(x)$ denote the encryption of plaintext x in encryption type $T \in \{OPE, DET, HOM\}$. We denote $D_T(c)$ the corresponding decryption. Order-preserving encryption has the property that it preserves the order of plaintexts, i.e.

$$x \leq y \Longleftrightarrow E_{OPE}(x) \leq E_{OPE}(y)$$

Deterministic encryption preserves the equality of plaintexts, i.e.

$$x = y \Longleftrightarrow E_{DET}(x) = E_{DET}(y)$$

In (additively) homomorphic encryption multiplication of ciphertexts (modulo a key-dependent constant) maps to addition of the plaintexts, i.e.

$$D_{HOM}(E_{HOM}(x) \cdot E_{HOM}(y)) = x + y$$

Using these algebraic properties we can implement the relational operators for most SQL queries on the ciphertext, i.e. without decrypting the data. Consider a table scan with equality or range selection conditions. One can implement these on order-preservingly or even deterministically encrypted data. Similarly, one can implement join operators using these conditions – assuming the columns use the same key. Also, grouping (group by clause) can operate on deterministically encrypted data. Even, some data functions, such as minimum, maximum or counting, work on ciphertexts only. Note that for these operations it is not necessary to modify the relational operator implementation compared to a regular, non-encrypted database implementation. The operators perform the same computation on the ciphertexts as they would on the plaintexts[1].

For aggregation – sum or average functions – we can use homomorphic encryption. If the database multiplies the (selected) ciphertexts, it obtains a ciphertext of the aggregate. This requires only a small change to the operator implementation which one can implement by user-defined functions.

This leads to a convincing result: Using the appropriate encryption type a large subset of SQL queries can be implemented on encrypted data. Still, one has to choose the appropriate encryption type for one's data. This choice is important, because the encryption types have different security levels and may be incompatible.

Incompatible encryption makes executing a query impossible. For example, consider data encrypted using homomorphic encryption and performing a range query on it. This is impossible. Such combinations of encryption schemes may be even required by specific queries. Consider the query

SELECT x FROM T GROUP BY y HAVING SUM(z) > 100.

The sum function requires homomorphic encryption and the greater-than comparison requires order-preserving encryption. Such queries simply cannot be executed on encrypted data in the server's database, since no appropriate encryption scheme exists.

The different encryption types also have different security levels. Homomorphic encryption, such as Paillier's encryption scheme [25], is semantically secure. Semantic security means that it is computationally impossible to distinguish two ciphertexts, even if the adversary may choose their plaintexts. Semantic security implies that ciphertexts are randomized, i.e., equality is not preserved under encryption.

Deterministic encryption leaks this equality and is therefore considered less secure. Security guarantees have been established under the assumption that the plaintexts have high entropy [3]. Order-preserving encryption is not only deterministic, but also leaks the order of the plaintexts (and is therefore less secure). The security of order-preserving encryption is still under debate. Boldyreva et al. proposed an order-preserving encryption that has the best security possible assuming it is non-modifiable and stateless [4]. They later showed that it leaks

---

[1] Although the data type of the ciphertexts may be different.

the upper half of the bits of the plaintext [5]. Popa et al. proposed a modifiable, stateful scheme that has ideal-security, i.e., it leaks only the order [28].

In summary we have: homomorphic (or standard) encryption is more secure than deterministic encryption which is more secure than order-preserving encryption. This observation implies that the client should carefully choose its encryption types for data outsourcing. It should only use order-preserving or deterministic encryption if necessary to enable its queries in order to achieve the highest security level. Yet, the set of executed queries may be unknown at design time making this choice undecidable.

Popa et al. offer an intriguing solution to the encryption type selection problem [29]. First, they introduce a further encryption type RND for standard, randomized encryption. This encryption type only allows retrieval, but no queries. Note that order-preserving encryption enables a proper superset of queries to deterministic encryption. They therefore compose a layered ciphertext called onion. For each data item x they compute the following sequence of encryptions

$$E_{RND}(E_{DET}(E_{OPE}(x)))$$

This onion at first only allows retrieval – due to the randomized encryption. When the client encounters a query that requires deterministic encryption, e.g., a selection using equality, then it updates the database. It sends the key $D_{RND}()$ for decrypting the randomized encryption to the database. The database uses a user-defined function to perform the update, such that now the database stores $E_{DET}(E_{OPE}(x))$. This enables the new query to be executed. The same procedure occurs in case of a query that requires order-preserving encryption to execute.

Homomorphic encryption is handled slightly differently and stored in a separate column. The separate column also enables aggregation operations, but does not harm security, since homomorphic encryption is semantically secure. A layering is not possible, since homomorphic encryption needs to encrypt the plaintext x for the correct result in aggregations.

This algorithm represents an adjustment mechanism of the database to the series of executed queries. It enables to dynamically adjust the encryption types, i.e., without knowing all queries in advance. We call such a database *adjustably encrypted*. Furthermore, the adjustment is unidirectional. Once decrypted to deterministic or order-preserving encryption, it is never necessary to return to a higher encryption level to enable a subsequent query. Yet, security against the cloud service provider has already been weakened, because the less secure ciphertext has been revealed at least once and can therefore be used in cryptanalysis.

3   Database Adjustment

As described before the database encryption level is adjusted to the queries performed. In this section we further deepen into the SQL features and their corresponding adjustment. We then also present how an application can use our encrypted database. It is particularly important that its use is transparent to the application, i.e. an application developer usually does not have to worry about the encryption. In this paper we argue, however, that better privacy results can be obtained, if the developer carefully designs his application and queries.

We consider the database operations of selection, grouping, joins, sorting, aggregation and further functions. For each operation we identify the corresponding encryption level. The adjustment algorithm decrypts the database to this level (or below). We do not explain the semantics of the operations, but refer the reader to an SQL introduction.

Selection: There are two types of selection criteria: equality and range query. An example of an equality selection is

SELECT x FROM T WHERE y = 100

After this query the column x is either encrypted using deterministic or order-preserving encryption. An example of a range selection is

SELECT x FROM T WHERE y > 100

In this case the column x is afterwards encrypted using order-preserving encryption.

Grouping: Grouping is a common operation particularly in analytical queries. It combines groups of row with a common, equal attribute(s) value(s). An (relatively stupid) example of grouping is

SELECT x FROM T GROUP BY x

Afterwards, the column x is encrypted using deterministic encryption. Note that grouping can be combined with selection using the HAVING clause. An example leading to order-preserving encryption would be

SELECT x FROM T GROUP BY x HAVING x > 100

Joins: Joins can be algebraically represented by cross-products, i.e. the all-pairs combination of the relations. This implies that joins per se are neutral for the encryption. A cross-product can always be built, even on randomized encryption. An example is

SELECT x, y FROM T1, T2

Still, cross-products significantly extend the size of the results table and joins are usually combined with a selection. Using the selection criterion, joins can be implemented using significantly faster algorithms, e.g. hash joins or sort-and-merge joins. The selection criterion can be again equality or range as before and has the same impact on the encryption level. In the following example column z is encrypted using deterministic encryption.

SELECT x, y FROM T1, T2 WHERE T1.z = T2.z

Note that for cross-column selection conditions both columns need to be encrypted using the same key. We adjust the encryption key before the query as well. Proxy re-encryption offers to change the encryption key without intermediate decryption. We follow the strategy outlined by Kerschbaum et al. [20].

Sorting: Values can be returned sorted from a query. An example is

```
SELECT x FROM T ORDER BY x
```

Afterwards, the column x is encrypted using order-preserving encryption. Also rank-based statistical function such as maximum (MAX) and minimum (MIN) are based on order-preserving encryption.

```
SELECT MIN(x), MAX(x) FROM T
```

Aggregation: We consider three aggregation functions: SUM, AVG, and COUNT.

```
SELECT SUM(x), AVG(x), COUNT(x) FROM T
```

Summation is performed using homomorphic encryption. This requires the operator to be modified. This can be implemented using a user-defined function or by modifying the database. A decryption to an onion level is not necessary, since homomorphic encryption is stored in parallel to the leveled onion. The mean is computed as SUM(x)/COUNT(x) where the division is performed on the client. Summation is implemented as before and counting can be implemented using any encryption. The count operator can perform on any encryption level, again even randomized encryption. Note that the count operator requires to implement NULL (in addition to 0) values. While this has been criticized to lead to incomplete logic, it is commonly supported in off-the-shelf databases.

Functions: SQL offers a wide variety of further functions, e.g. for string manipulation. We do not provide specific support for these, but implement them on the client on the decrypted cleartexts.

We have shown that there is a wide spectrum of SQL functions and corresponding encryption levels. Some operations, such as equality selection, even operate on multiple encryption levels. We therefore have carefully select the encryption level (and onion) to operate on when there are multiple options and intertwined conditions from the query. The problem is complicated, if the user can configure the available encryption options. We follow again the algorithm by Kerschbaum et al. [21].

An obvious question to ask is whether adjustable encryption actually provides more security. Given an infinitely long sequence of random queries, one would expect all columns to be decrypted to order-preserving encryption. Fortunately, real sequences are not infinite. We have performed a number of experiments in order to study the security provided by adjustable encryption. We executed the sequences of TPC-H, TPC-C and of a live SAP system on our adjustable encryption scheme. The TPC-H benchmark simulates analytical queries whereas the TPC-C benchmark and the SAP system perform transactional workloads. We have summarized our findings in Table 1.

Table 1. Encryption State of Exemplary System

	TPC-H	TPC-C	Live SAP System
Total Queries	22	20	406
Total Tables	8	9	2
Total Columns	61	71	248
RND (columns / %)	17 / 27.9%	49 / 69,0%	157 / 63.3%
DET (columns / %)	24 / 39.3%	17 / 23,9%	74 / 29.8%
OPE (columns / %)	20 / 32.8%	5 / 7,0%	17 / 7.9%

In order to judge the benefit of encrypted databases for privacy it is important to understand their use. An application developer implementing its application on top of an adjustably encrypted database needs to make few modifications. All he needs is the driver for the encrypted database. In our case this is a standard JDBC driver for JAVA applications. He can then use the encrypted database similarly to any other, non-encrypted database, i.e. he executes SQL queries and retrieves the results. The driver interface is unchanged and all encryption and decryption operation occur inside the driver. The driver only needs to be given a reference to the database instance (and key store if it is not the default). Figure 1 shows some example Java code for using our database.

```
Class.forName("com.sap.research.seeed.jdbc.SEEEDDriver");

Properties props = new Properties();
props.put(SEEEDDriver.extDriverURLPropKey, ServerInformation.HANA_Uri);

Connection conn = DriverManager.getConnection(
                  "jdbc:sap-research:seeed", props);

Statement stmt = conn.createStatement();
ResultSet rs = stmt.executeQuery("SELECT * FROM \"MyTable\"");
```

Fig. 1. Java code for using encrypted database

The encryption of the database is *transparent* to the application developer. He does not need to make any major modifications when operating on an encrypted database. On the hand, this is a significant advantage, since integration is easy and privacy and security benefit. On the other hand, this may lead the application developer to unsafe choices and in this paper we highlight that the application developer can further enhance privacy when paying attention to his design.

Secure outsourcing could also be solved by other techniques, such as secure multi-party computation [10,15,18,19,30] which has been used for supply chain management [7,17,22,23,26] and statistical benchmarking [6,16,24], but this requires a more significant redesign of the application and the user and developer experience.

4   Personalized Healthcare App

4.1   Basic Functions

Next, we briefly describe the design of our healthcare app. Personalized health-care is a current trend enabled by ubiquitous availability of computing devices, such as smartphones. These can monitor health indicators, such as blood pressure, blood sugar, heart rate, temperature, etc., or simply record mood and feelings. The collected set of measurements can be used in treatment of illnesses. It can even be used in order to identify preventive treatment when early symptoms arise.

Each measurement is a tuple. Let id be the identifier of the person. Let $time$ be the time of measurement. Let loc be the location of the measurement. Let val be the data value of the location (with an implicit type). The tuple then consists of

$$\langle id, time, loc, val \rangle$$

This tuple also represent the start of a schema for our personalized healthcare app. All basic data, i.e. measurements, are collected in this form and stored in relations. We can simplify the tuple by removing the identifier and using specialized forms of multi-tenancy. Each person using its app has its own user identifier in the database and can share the same schema. Since user need not and should not share data, this form of multi-tenancy simplifies the tuple to the relation

$$\langle time, loc, val \rangle$$

Our healthcare app has a very simple user interface for entering such tuple, if they are not collected automatically. A person incrementally builds a record of measurements. Let $PlainData$ be the name of the table. Each time the app performs the exemplary following query

```
(I) INSERT time = '16.12.2013 23:59', loc = 'Karlsruhe',
         val = '120' INTO PlainData
```

This collection of data would be mostly used, if it were not used for some analysis. A typical form of analysis are histograms, i.e. we group the data by categories, e.g. time slots or locations, and count the number of occurrence, e.g. of unhealthy events. From such a histogram one can, for example, see the time of the day with the highest blood pressure. Our app offers a simple user interface for retrieving the most common and useful such histograms. Each time it performs the following exemplary query

```
(II) SELECT loc, COUNT(loc)
      FROM PlainData GROUP BY loc
    WHERE val > 100 ORDER BY COUNT(loc)
```

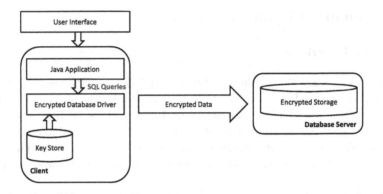

Fig. 2. Basic app architecture

4.2 Integration with Encrypted Database

We propose to use an adjustably encrypted database as described in Section 2 in order to protect the data against the service provider. Figure 2 shows the basic architecture of our app with our encrypted database. We highlight in red the interface between application code and database driver, namely SQL queries. As we have already described in detail in Section 3 the encryption state of the database adjusts to the queries performs. So, we need to investigate how this adjustment is done for our personalized healthcare app.

Initially the database starts with all onions encrypted using randomized encryption, i.e. each column is encrypted using a semantically secure encryption scheme, such as AES128-CBC. When performing query I (insert of plain values), each value will be encrypted to this onion level. As a result all personal identifiable data is encrypted using a standard, commonly recommended encryption scheme.

When performing query II (computation of histograms), several selection criteria are given. First all data is grouped by its location (or time slot). Hence, the location column is decrypted to deterministic encryption. Furthermore, all values greater than 100 are selected (because they likely indicate an unhealthy measurement). Hence, the value column is decrypted to order-preserving encryption.

If we assume that also histograms for time slots are computed, all columns will be decrypted: time and value to order-preserving encryption and location to deterministic. As Islam et al. point out, already searchable encryption which is still stronger than deterministic encryption allows frequency analysis when side information is available [14]. In our example it would probably be easy to determine the plaintexts of most ciphertexts if someone trailed a person for some time. The observer obtains a sample of locations which is likely similarly distributed to the ones stored in the database. The security of order-preserving encryption is less investigated, but even more debated. As a result our healthcare while using an encrypted database would offer little protection of personal identifiable data.

4.3   Better Solution

Fortunately, there is a much better solution if the app designer pays a little attention. Instead of computing the histograms on the fly, the designer can pre-select the most important ones. He does that anyway, since few app users are skilled enough to select a sensible analysis by themselves. The designer thereby provides an additional service of offering the most useful analyses to his customers.

As an example, we consider the histogram query from above. Instead of executing query II the app can incrementally compute the statistics. The can simply store the aggregations in the following relation

$$\langle time, loc, count \rangle$$

Let $AggregateData$ be the name of the corresponding database table It then inserts new values as follows

```
(III) UPDATE count = (SELECT count
WHERE time = '16.12.2013 23:59' AND loc = 'Karlsruhe') + 1
                     INTO AggregateData
   WHERE time = '16.12.2013 23:59' AND loc = 'Karlsruhe'
```

In order to retrieve a histogram it simply executes

```
(IV) SELECT * from FROM AggregateData
```

Note that sorting of query IV can be performed locally without any additional cost, since all data values need to be transferred anyway. Yet, if we consider the encryption state in our encrypted database, we see a significant improvement. Query (III) performs selection with equality conditions for the time and location column. Therefore these columns also need to be encrypted using deterministic encryption. Nevertheless, there is a significant improvement in security. Each ciphertext is unique. Hence, frequency analysis attacks as by Islam et al. are thwarted.

This is similarly to the index built for searchable encryption by Curtmola et al. [9]. They first encrypt each keyword using deterministic encryption and then build an encrypted list of documents. This significantly speeds up search time which is also useful in our application, but they also show that it maintains security. We omit a formal analysis here, but it is easy to see that all ciphertexts can be simulated by random numbers if the key is unknown.

The count column is encrypted using homomorphic encryption. Homomorphic encryption, such as Paillier's [25] is also semantically secure. Using homomorphic encryption query III can be performed entirely on the database, i.e. without performing the sub-select and addition locally first.

Clearly, this design improves the privacy of the app user and may even allow storing this personal identifiable data in the cloud. All, data is encrypted using provably secure encryption schemes and known attacks are avoided. Still, the mobile healthcare app is still able to function as before. We have achieve a major step forward in securing privacy in a hybrid cloud application as it is prevalent in current software development.

4.4   Sharing the Data

Sometimes it is desirable to share one's data. Such sharing should, of course, only be initiated on the user's request and with his informed consent. Unintentional sharing is likely a privacy violation.

We consider two types of sharing for our mobile healthcare app: among different systems or application and with third parties. A user may operate different system, e.g. a smartphone, a tablet and a PC. He may want to use or analyze his data on all three systems potentially using different applications. Note that in this case the person accessing the data remains the data owner, but he is accessing it using different systems.

In the other case the data owner may want to share his data with third parties, e.g. his physician or a medical expert. In this case the data is accessible by this third party and a potential privacy violation may occur. We again do not investigate the legal obligations for such sharing – for the data owner or the recipient. Instead, we focus on the implementation of appropriate cryptographic security mechanisms.

4.5   Sharing across Systems

In this case the access rights remain the same, i.e. the data owner is allowed to access its data, but nobody else. Therefore no additional cryptographic keys are necessary, as long as the data owner remains in sole possession of the key. Note that this also ensures technical protection against the cloud service provider.

Often it is not possible or too cumbersome to directly link two systems, such as smartphone and tablet. Instead each device is connected to the Internet sharing common access to servers, such as the cloud server of the health care application. Fortunately, there is a standardized way of securely transferring data between the systems using this server.

Note that the only information (state) that needs to be shared are the cryptographic keys. All other information is stored encrypted in the cloud server's database. Cryptographic keys can be securely stored in a password protected file. The password is used to generate a cryptographic key which encrypts the other cryptographic keys. This is a common mechanism for implementing secure key stores.

The design idea for a shared tablet, mobile app application is now to store this key store also in the cloud. At the start of the application, it loads the key store from the cloud. Then, the user enters a password which is used to decrypt the keys for the encrypted database. All systems can securely use the keys in this manner. There is no additional effort for the user, since he needs to authenticate using a password in any case.

4.6   Sharing with Third Parties

In this case an additional party gets access and there is need for an additional key. Not all data may be shared eternally and hence the user should not share his key. Instead, he should make a copy and make this copy available to the third party.

A simple solution for this data sharing problem is using public keys. The user downloads the data he wants to share to his system and encrypts it with the public key of the recipient. For example, for e-mail messages there is the quasi-standard of PGP.

A public-key encrypted message can only be read by the recipient. Of course, the key exchange needs to be secured, but the availability of a public key infrastructure can be assumed. It is likely that a cloud service provider for health data offers its customers a connection secured by the transport layer security (TLS – formerly SSL) protocol. This protocol already requires the server to obtain a certificate from an authority part of a public key infrastructure.

5   Conclusions

We have shown how an adjustably encrypted database operates and how to use it. Based on this we have done a case study for a mobile personalized healthcare app. This app uses our encrypted database and we have shown its basic functions. We have first applied a straight-forward approach to the SQL queries and showed its impact on the encryption state of the database. Then, we have further improved the protection by modifying the queries. Ultimately, we reached a state where only provably encrypted data is revealed. We therefore conclude that with proper use an encrypted database may protect personal identifiable information in the cloud against the service provider. It is therefore a technical alternative to organizational measures, such as storing personal identifiable information of European Union citizens only on servers hosted in the European Union. Hence, we further conclude that all cloud or hybrid applications designed with privacy in mind should consider the use of an encrypted database. It provides technical data protection even when combined with organizational measures. We envision such transparent database protection to become a standard measure for technical privacy protection in the cloud economy.

References

1. Agrawal, D., Abbadi, A.E., Emekçi, F., Metwally, A.: Database management as a service: challenges and opportunities. In: Proceedings of the 25th International Conference on Data Engineering, ICDE (2009)
2. Agrawal, R., Kiernan, J., Srikant, R., Xu, Y.: Order preserving encryption for numeric data. In: Proceedings of the 2004 ACM International Conference on Management of Data, SIGMOD (2004)
3. Bellare, M., Boldyreva, A., O'Neill, A.: Deterministic and efficiently searchable encryption. In: Menezes, A. (ed.) CRYPTO 2007. LNCS, vol. 4622, pp. 535–552. Springer, Heidelberg (2007)
4. Boldyreva, A., Chenette, N., Lee, Y., O'Neill, A.: Order-preserving symmetric encryption. In: Joux, A. (ed.) EUROCRYPT 2009. LNCS, vol. 5479, pp. 224–241. Springer, Heidelberg (2009)

5. Boldyreva, A., Chenette, N., O'Neill, A.: Order-preserving encryption revisited: improved security analysis and alternative solutions. In: Rogaway, P. (ed.) CRYPTO 2011. LNCS, vol. 6841, pp. 578–595. Springer, Heidelberg (2011)

6. Catrina, O., Kerschbaum, F.: Fostering the uptake of secure multiparty computation in e-commerce. In: Proceedings of the 3rd International Conference on Availability, Reliability and Security, ARES (2008)

7. Chaves, L.W.F., Kerschbaum, F.: Industrial privacy in rfid-based batch recalls. In: Proceedings of the International Workshop on Security and Privacy in Enterprise Computing, INSPEC (2008)

8. Curino, C., Jones, E.P.C., Popa, R.A., Malviya, N., Wu, E., Madden, S., Balakrishnan, H., Zeldovich, N.: Relational cloud: A database-as-a-service for the cloud. In: Proceedings of the 5th Conference on Innovative Data Systems Research, CIDR (2011)

9. Re. Curtmola, J., Garay, S., Kamara, R.: Ostrovsky.: Searchable symmetric encryption: improved definitions and efficient constructions. Journal of Computer Security 19(5) (2011)

10. Dreier, J., Kerschbaum, F.: Practical privacy-preserving multiparty linear programming based on problem transformation. In: Proceedings of the 3rd IEEE International Conference on Privacy, Security, Risk and Trust, PASSA (2011)

11. Hacigümüs, H., Iyer, B., Mehrotra, S.: Efficient execution of aggregation queries over encrypted relational databases. In: Lee, Y., Li, J., Whang, K.-Y., Lee, D. (eds.) DASFAA 2004. LNCS, vol. 2973, pp. 125–136. Springer, Heidelberg (2004)

12. Hacigümüs, H., Iyer, B.R., Li, C., Mehrotra, S.: Executing sql over encrypted data in the database-service-provider model. In: Proceedings of the 2002 ACM International Conference on Management of Data, SIGMOD (2002)

13. Hacigümüs, H., Mehrotra, S., Iyer, B.R.: Providing database as a service. In: Proceedings of the 18th International Conference on Data Engineering, ICDE (2002)

14. Islam, M., Kuzu, M., Kantarcioglu, M.: Access pattern disclosure on searchable encryption: ramification, attack and mitigation. In: Proceedings of the 19th Network and Distributed System Security Symposium, NDSS (2012)

15. Kerschbaum, F.: Simple cross-site attack prevention. In: Proceedings of the 3rd International Conference on Security and Privacy in Communications Networks, SECURECOMM (2007)

16. Kerschbaum, F.: Building a privacy-preserving benchmarking enterprise system. Enterprise Information Systems 2(4) (2008)

17. Kerschbaum, F.: An access control model for mobile physical objects. In: Proceedings of the 15th ACM Symposium on Access Control Models and Technologies, SACMAT (2010)

18. Kerschbaum, F.: Automatically optimizing secure computation. In: Proceedings of the 18th ACM Conference on Computer and Communications Security, CCS (2011)

19. Kerschbaum, F., Biswas, D., de Hoogh, S.: Performance comparison of secure comparison protocols. In: Proceedings of the International Workshop on Business Processes Security, WSBPS (2009)

20. Kerschbaum, F., Härterich, M., Grofig, P., Kohler, M., Schaad, A., Schröpfer, A., Tighzert, W.: Optimal re-encryption strategy for joins in encrypted databases. In: Wang, L., Shafiq, B. (eds.) DBSec 2013. LNCS, vol. 7964, pp. 195–210. Springer, Heidelberg (2013)

21. Kerschbaum, F., Härterich, M., Kohler, M., Hang, I., Schaad, A., Schröpfer, A., Tighzert, W.: An encrypted in-memory column-store: the onion selection problem. In: Bagchi, A., Ray, I. (eds.) ICISS 2013. LNCS, vol. 8303, pp. 14–26. Springer, Heidelberg (2013)
22. Kerschbaum, F., Oertel, N.: Privacy-preserving pattern matching for anomaly detection in rfid anti-counterfeiting. In: Ors Yalcin, S.B. (ed.) RFIDSec 2010. LNCS, vol. 6370, pp. 124–137. Springer, Heidelberg (2010)
23. Kerschbaum, F., Sorniotti, A.: Rfid-based supply chain partner authentication and key agreement. In: Proceedings of the 2nd ACM Conference on Wireless Network Security, WISEC (2009)
24. Kerschbaum, F., Terzidis, O.: Filtering for private collaborative benchmarking. In: Müller, G. (ed.) ETRICS 2006. LNCS, vol. 3995, pp. 409–422. Springer, Heidelberg (2006)
25. Paillier, P.: Public-key cryptosystems based on composite degree residuosity classes. In: Stern, J. (ed.) EUROCRYPT 1999. LNCS, vol. 1592, pp. 223–228. Springer, Heidelberg (1999)
26. Pibernik, R., Zhang, Y., Kerschbaum, F., Schröpfer, A.: Secure collaborative supply chain planning and inverse optimization–the jels model. European Journal of Operational Research 208(1) (2011)
27. Pohlig, S.C., Hellman, M.E.: An improved algorithm for computing logarithms over gf(p) and its cryptographic significance. IEEE Transactions on Information Theory 24(1), 106–110 (1978)
28. Popa, R.A., Li, F.H., Zeldovich, N.: An ideal-security protocol for order-preserving encoding. In: Proceedings of the 34th IEEE Symposium on Security and Privacy (2013)
29. Popa, R.A., Redfield, C.M.S., Zeldovich, N., Balakrishnan, H.: Cryptdb: protecting confidentiality with encrypted query processing. In: Proceedings of the 23rd ACM Symposium on Operating Systems Principles, SOSP (2011)
30. Schröpfer, A., Kerschbaum, F., Müller, G.: L1 – an intermediate language for mixed-protocol secure computation. In: Proceedings of the 35th IEEE Computer Software and Applications Conference, COMPSAC (2011)
31. Tu, S., Kaashoek, M.F., Madden, S., Zeldovich, N.: Processing analytical queries over encrypted data. In: Proceedings of the 39th International Conference on Very Large Data Bases, PVLDB (2013)

Accountable Surveillance Practices: Is the EU Moving in the Right Direction?

Fanny Coudert

KU Leuven – Interdisciplinary Centre for Law & ICT (ICRI) –
iMinds – B-CCENTRE, Leuven, Belgium
fanny.coudert@law.kuleuven.be

Abstract. The European Union is introducing into the Data Protection Package a new data protection principle, the principle of accountability. Data controllers will be compelled to adopt policies, organizational and technical measures to ensure and be able to demonstrate compliance with the legal framework. The expected benefits are threefold: to foster trust in personal data management practices of data controllers, to increase visibility of personal data processing activities and to raise data controllers' privacy awareness. Surveillance practices, because of their inherent opacity, could greatly benefit from reinforced accountability obligations to gain public's trust. This paper critically analyses whether the policy options taken by the European Union to operationalise the principle of accountability are likely to meet this goal.

Keywords: Privacy, Data Protection, Accountability, Surveillance.

1 Introduction

While surveillance systems are being deployed on a larger scale, citizens start developing tactics to resist. One strategy consists in holding surveillance systems owners into account by raising the level of transparency of the surveillance activities. Smart mobile devices make the task easier and more effective. They facilitate the documentation of events, the monitoring of behavior or the reporting on the video surveillance infrastructure [1]. As a way of example, the Institute for Applied Autonomy's has developed a web-based application which allows users to chart the locations of closed-circuit television (CCTV) surveillance cameras in urban environments. As advertised on their website, with this app, *"users can find routes that avoid these cameras ("paths of least surveillance") allowing them to walk around their cities without fear of being "caught on tape" by unregulated security monitors"*[2].

Another example is the SurveillanceWatch app developed by a Canadian research project of the same name [1]. The goal of this project is to make video surveillance in the private sector and the related privacy issues more transparent, understandable and accountable to Canadians citizens. This project has developed a smartphone app that will enable individuals to take photos of cameras and signs of video surveillance installations, uploading these to a shared database with tags to indicate key privacy features of the installation. Users will in return be able to view the location and

B. Preneel and D. Ikonomou (Eds.): APF 2014, LNCS 8450, pp. 70–85, 2014.

privacy compliance of installations in their immediate vicinity or anywhere in the world. The level of compliance is indicated through a color code which shows to the user whether the observed surveillance system meets the requirements of minimal compliance, is lacking information for minimal compliance or do not comply with Canadian privacy regulation. Requirements include high visibility of the cameras, a clear indication of the installation's owner and operator, a description of why the area is being surveilled and a description of the installation's properties (whether the images are monitored or recorded, contact information for the individual responsible for protecting personal information captured by the cameras as well as a reference to the legislation that governs the handling of this information).

Both initiatives show how the opaqueness of surveillance systems generate feeling of powerlessness and mistrust, which the legal obligations to inform users or the legal enforcement mechanisms, based on complaints and redress procedures, seem not being able to overcome. Indeed, information notices have usually little visibility, are insufficient or are written in terms difficult to understand for citizens. Legal oversight mainly occurs when something goes wrong, thus the protection often comes too late and it is uncertain in its outcome. These initiatives thus intend to restore the balance in power by holding surveillance system owners to account before any harm occur. The need for accountability mechanisms rely on the observation that knowing that surveillance system owners should act within strict legal boundaries is not sufficient to trust they will do as expected. They lie with the hope of turning "blind trust" into "proven trust" [3]. In front of such initiatives, revisiting the way data holders are accountable to the people they monitor therefore appears as an unavoidable step when defining adequate legal safeguards to frame surveillance practices.

While it has been stressed elsewhere that accountability can come in various meaning and shapes [4], this paper will focus on accountability from a legal viewpoint, i.e. as a means to foster legal compliance. After reviewing the expected benefits of the introduction of the principle of accountability in the European Data Protection Package, the provisions of both the General Data Protection Regulation (the "lex generalis", applicable by default whenever a personal data processing is taking place) and the Law Enforcement Data Protection Directive (the "lex especialis", only applicable to law enforcement authorities) will be reviewed and assessed in order to define whether they are likely to meet their goals.

2 Accountability: Trust, Transparency and Privacy-Awareness

While the principle of accountability has always been underlying the data protection framework, when not referred to explicitly (see e.g. OECD Guidelines, PIPEDDA (Canadian privacy framework) or the APEC privacy framework), the data protection community has only regain interest in this principle for the last years. The accountability discourse, mainly generated in the US, has developed as a way to deal with the advent of big data related-technologies and the increasing pervasiveness of computing in everyday life [5] and with cross-border data flows [6]. As it appears each time more difficult to restrict data collection, some authors advocate to focus on the regulation of data uses [see as latest example: 7]. In this context, it becomes paramount to increase the transparency of data processing activities and to require data controllers to act proactively in demonstrating the compliance of their data management practices with the legal framework. The Accountability Projects, led by the Centre for Information Policy Leadership, intended to operationalize the principle for its introduction into the data protection framework [8]. One of the main drivers of this initiative was to facilitate international data flows. They however managed to reactivate the interest of Academia in the principle and discussions flourished around the very concept of accountability and its relation with other concepts such as answerability or liability [4, 3], and its policy goals, meaning and operationalization within the privacy framework [9, 6].

The debates around the principle of accountability found their way through the discussions taking place for the revision of the European Data Protection Framework. Article 29 Data Protection Working Party [10] was the first to suggest the introduction of an explicit principle of accountability. It would serve to "move data protection from theory to practice" [10] as data protection principles and obligations were regarded as often insufficiently reflected in concrete internal measures and practices. Following Article 29 Data Protection Working Party, the European Commission approached the introduction of an explicit principle of accountability as a tool for a more effective application of the data protection framework [11]. The principle of accountability is here expected to enhance data controllers' responsibility by compelling them to put in place effective policies and mechanisms to ensure compliance with the rules.

This paper will focus on how the principle of accountability is being shaped within the new Data Protection Package. From this perspective, the principle of accountability and the provisions that operationalize it are expected to bring three main benefits, namely: (1) to create trust in the way how personal data are handled by data controllers (2) to increase the transparency of data processing practices (3) and ultimately to promote privacy-minded behaviors within organizations, thus fostering the emergence of a data protection culture.

2.1   Trust

Trust is "*a response to risk in which the individual accepts to take a risk and assume others' ability to behave or perform as expected*"[12]. Trust is thus "*the willingness to enter into interaction under the face of uncertainty*" [12]. It follows that trust is a highly dynamic process "*where the premises of trust are constantly monitored and reassessed*" [12]. Trust is fragile, easy to damage, difficult to rebuild.

In addition, imbalance of power and information asymmetries have a significant impact on the building of trust [12] in the sense that the more unbalanced the relationship, the more assurance the party in power will have to give to the "weak party". This is the case of surveillance activities. They operate covertly, creating uncertainty about the real content of the surveillance activity. The intrusive nature of the surveillance into individuals' life and the increased power given to the surveillance entity by the technology could generate a sense of weakness and exposure amongst individuals. Even when the person monitored knows about the surveillance, although she might understand the goal or the means, she rarely is provided assurance about the fact that the surveillance system is operated respectful of her fundamental rights, more specifically respectful of her privacy. In addition, the increase complexity of surveillance systems (and information systems in general) and the multiplicity of actors involved makes it more difficult for citizens to clearly identify who is the owner of the surveillance system and for supervision authorities to enforce the law, failing to provide the required assurance.

The data protection framework participates to building trust by regulating data processing activities created by the surveillance. As shown by Gutwirth and De Hert [13], whereas the right to privacy mainly functions negatively in that it ensures the non-interference in private matters of the individual, acting in that sense as an 'opacity tool', data protection laws act instead as a set of 'transparency tools', i.e. they regulate rather than prohibit personal data processing. It follows that when faced with an intrusive technology, the right to privacy (and other relevant fundamental rights) will serve as reference to define whether the technology should be allowed and when, whereas the right to data protection will come into the play only in a second phase, in order to regulate these deemed acceptable uses in the democratic society. This does not mean that data protection laws do not contain some "opacity tools" which limit data collection practices (e.g. through the principle of data minimization). But their rationale is mainly directed towards the regulation of data processing activities. In the same line of arguments, Diaz et al. show that data protection laws contain an inherent tension between "principles that assume that data controllers are trusted entities, cognizant and respectful of individual rights (e.g. principle of choice, purpose limitation, security and accountability), and principles that, (...) treat data controllers with distrust (data minimization and collection limitation)" [14].

This means that the data protection framework entrusts data controllers with a duty of care, they act as "custodians of personal information" [14], as "fiduciaries for individual rights" [14]. In this context, the principle of accountability will merely aim at compelling data controllers to show they are trustworthy custodians. They will be expected to be able to demonstrate they have implemented all required and expected measures to ensure they are compliant with the obligations set up under the data protection framework. The introduction of a principle of accountability into the European Data Protection Package should thus look at defining a liability and responsibility structure that can back-up "proven trust" and convince citizens that their personal data are processed according to their legitimate expectations. It should introduce sufficient assurance mechanisms to be able demonstrate compliance with the legal framework to Data Protection Authorities and transparency tools towards citizens, so that they can easily identify whether a data controller has proven to be trustworthy.

2.2   Transparency

Accountability is the fact of being account-*able*, i.e. the ability to give an account. According to the Oxford Dictionary, being accountable is to be required or expected to justify actions or decisions. Accountability is thus a process which involves an accountor who is called by an accountee to make visible to others the motives and content of its decisions and actions. Accountability mechanisms are processes tending to increase visibility, thus the transparency of data processing activities.

Accountability mechanisms will act by *"making bad –* and good- *acts visible"* [5]. Accountability schemes allow organizations to show all the active and assignable steps taken to achieve the objective pursued [5]. In that sense, the Article 29 Data Protection Working Party stressed that accountability is about showing *"how responsibility is exercised and making it verifiable"* [10], i.e. about making data processing practices transparent to data protection authorities and data subjects.

The concept of accountability differs from the one of legal compliance in that accountability mechanisms are only expected to demonstrate compliance. Accountability does not guarantee compliance but it does contribute to make compliance easier than violation [5]. In words of Weitzner et al. *"for those rare cases where rules are broken, we are well aware that we may be held accountable through a process that looks back through the records of our actions and assess them against the rules"* [5]. These authors show the importance of visibility in ensuring compliance as *"the vast majority of legal and social rules that form the fabric of our societies are not enforced perfectly or automatically, yet somehow most of us still manage to follow most of them all the time"* [5]. This is because we *"follow rules because we are aware of what they are and because we know there will be consequences, after the fact, if we violate them"* [5].

The concept of accountability also differs from the one of liability, i.e. the state of being legally responsible for something. Both concepts can however interact in that *"a system of legal responsibility or liability can be based either on a logic of compliance or on a logic of account giving"* [3]. While the previous data protection framework, under the 95/46/EC Directive, focused on a logic of compliance and to that effect it created specific supervisory authorities with enforcement powers, the new framework includes a logic of account giving by incorporating a series of obligations that will tend to make data processing activities transparent and verifiable, facilitating both compliance and enforcement.

It follows that the introduction of a principle of accountability within the data protection framework is often accompanied with, on the one hand, the warning that the implementation of accountability mechanisms will not waive data controllers' legal liability from lack of compliance, and on the other hand, with the expressed need to articulate both concepts, i.e. to what extent accountability mechanisms can contribute to demonstrate compliance and thus to modulate data controllers' liability [9].

Transparency requirements under the principle of accountability will be operationalized through provisions tending to ensuring the verifiability of data controllers' policies, procedures and practices by both Data Protection Authorities and data subjects.

2.3   Fostering the Emergence of a Data Protection Culture

The Art 29 Working Party feared that *"unless data protection becomes part of the shared values and practices of an organization, and responsibilities for it are expressly assigned, effective compliance will be at considerable risk, and data protection mishaps are likely to continue"* [10]. Accountability is expected, in that sense, to foster the emergence of a data protection culture.

Indeed, because accountability is concerned with the demonstration that the entity complies with the legal framework, it gives the incentives to adapt internal structures and processes as to ensure that compliance can be accounted for. This comes down to designing adequate internal procedures to raise privacy awareness within the organization and to integrate privacy safeguards into internal business processes. This is often realized through the design of a privacy management program which will involve all units and levels of an organization and which will ultimately ensure that sufficient and convincing evidence is produced whenever required by the authorized third party. In that sense, the revised OECD Guidelines points to Privacy Management Programs as the way to implement the principle of accountability. By turning privacy concerns into a primary goal to be achieved because of the possibility to be asked to account for internal privacy practices, it ultimately becomes part of day-to-day business processes, improving the understanding of privacy issues and the compliance with the legal framework.

The introduction of a principle of accountability into the European framework should thus lead to the implementation by data controllers of "data governance schemes", i.e. programs which cover " *all legal, technical and organisational means by which organisations ensure full responsibility over the way in which data are handled, such as planning and control, use of sound technology, adequate training of staff, compliance audits, etc"* [15].

3   Accountability into the European Data Protection Package

On 25 January 2011, the European Commission published a Data Protection Package which contains two instruments. First, a proposal for a Regulation on the protection of individuals with regards to the processing of personal data and on the free movement of such data (the "General Data Protection Regulation"), which will repeal the current Data Protection Directive (95/46/EC Directive) and act as "lex generalis". Second, a proposal for a Directive on the protection of individuals with regard to the processing of personal data by competent authorities for the purposes of prevention, investigation, detection or prosecution of criminal offences or the execution of criminal penalties, and the free movement of such data (the "Law Enforcement Data Protection Directive"), which will repeal Council Framework Decision 2008/977/JI and act as "lex especialis". Both proposals being part of a single package, the amendments and opinions tabled to the text often stress the need to ensure consistency between both instruments. The European Parliament has approved within LIBE Committee a long list of amendments and has started the negotiations with the Council with the aim of coming to a consensual text by Spring 2014. This section discusses the latest versions of the texts, after the vote in the European Parliament LIBE Committee in October 2013. Reference is made to previous versions whenever relevant.

3.1   The Principle of Accountability

The principle of accountability is now explicitly referred to as one of the main data protection principle in article 5 of the General Data Protection Regulation. The principle means that personal data should be processed under the responsibility and liability of the controller, who shall ensure and be able to demonstrate compliance with the provisions of the Regulation.

In the Law Enforcement Data Protection Directive, the principle of accountability is not mentioned expressly but Article 4 f) reproduces the same wording as Article 5 of the General Data Protection Regulation. The European Parliament has restored the wording contained in the leaked text of the Directive in November 2011. Indeed, all references to accountability and to the obligation to be able to demonstrate compliance with the Directive had been removed from the proposal published in January 2012. This was heavily criticised by both the European Data Protection Supervisor [16] and the Article 29 Data Protection Working Party [17].

Accountability thus entails no more than an assumption and acknowledgment of responsibility and an obligation to demonstrate compliance upon request. Accountability obligations are thus procedural by nature. They get their full meaning when understood in the accountability relationship at stake. Under the new Data Protection framework, data controllers are expected to account for the compliance of their personal data processing operations with the provisions of General Data Protection Regulation (or the Law Enforcement Data Protection Directive) to the competent supervisory authorities.

It is worth noting that the accountability relationship considered by the Regulation and the Directive is between data controllers and DPAs. Data subjects do not hold any right of authority against data controllers over the suitability of their policies, procedures and practices to comply with the data protection framework. Data subjects are given other means to call data controllers into account over the way they handle their personal data such as through the exercise of their right of access, complaint and re-dress procedures, etc. Indeed, the principle of accountability is introduced as a way to improve legal compliance whose control is entrusted to DPAs, not to data subjects. However, data subjects are the recipients and the main reason why accountability mechanisms are installed. They are the ones who, in the first place, entrust data controllers with their personal data for specific purposes. Accountable personal data management practices are only meant to ensure their personal data are processed with due care.

3.2   Oversight and Assurance Practices

In the General Data Protection Regulation

Oversight will be provided by DPAs. However, data controllers can also rely on internal and external assurance mechanisms to monitor and evaluate their level of compliance. In addition, the Regulation provides for a certification mechanism as well as obligation to publish accountability mechanisms implemented into annual corporate reporting, allowing to make good data management practices visible to data subjects.

Internal assurance mechanisms are promoted through the prominent role given to the Data Protection Officer ("DPO"). This new figure appears as key in any accountability scheme in that she will be responsible for ensuring that policies, procedures and practices are adequate, effective and regularly updated through the regular monitoring of their implementation. She will also be responsible for conducting internal audits. Compliance can however also be verified by an independent internal or external auditor (Recital 60).

Furthermore, article 39 provides for the possibility for data controllers to request the certification of the compliance of their personal data processing with the Regulation. The Regulation follows Article 29 Data Protection Working Party's initial recommendation to introduce certification schemes as a tool of legal certainty by giving data controllers assurance with regard to the adequacy of the accountability mechanisms put in place [10]. Under the Regulation, certification is voluntary and should bear in particular on compliance with the data protection principles (as set under article 5), such as the principle of purpose specification, data minimisation, accountability with the principles of data protection by design and by default, with security obligations, with the obligations of data controllers and processors as well as with data subjects rights. Certification is granted by DPAs or by any external auditor accredited by DPAs. This allows data controllers to use a mark, the "European Data Protection Seal". Data controllers are thus given a double incentive to apply for certification: they can show to data subjects they are trustworthy and, as the seal is granted by data protection authorities, this should give them a presumption of compliance in the context of enforcement actions.

Certification of products is also contemplated under article 39. The European Data Protection Board is given the competence to certify that a data protection-enhancing technical standard is compliant with the Regulation.

Finally, article 22 contains an obligation to include in any regular general report of the activities of the controller, such as the obligatory reports by publicly traded companies, a summary description of the aforementioned policies and measures. This provision contributes to give visibility to the actions taken by data controllers to ensure good data governance and to reach to data subjects.

In the Law Enforcement Data Protection Directive

The Directive adopts a slightly different approach with regard to assurance mechanisms. Article 18.3 only imposes a general obligation for data controllers to ensure the verification of the adequacy and effectiveness of the measures implemented under the accountability principle (as defined under article 18.1). The requirement to have the measures implemented verified by independent internal and external auditors is only applicable "if proportionate".

However, contrary to the Regulation, the designation of a DPO is mandatory. Recital 44 refers to the DPO as a person who would assist the controller or processor to monitor and demonstrate compliance with the provisions adopted pursuant to this Directive. Article 32 entrusts the DPO with the task of monitoring the implementation and application of policies, including the assignment of responsibilities, as well as the compliance with the obligations set forth by the Directive.

In addition, the Directive implements data tracking obligations. Recital 40a (art. 24) now mandates that every processing operation is recorded in order to enable the verification of the lawfulness of the data processing as well as self-monitoring. Assurance is provided in this context through technology.

3.3   Verifiability

In the General Data Protection Regulation
Article 22 ("Responsibility and accountability of the controller") sets an obligation for data controllers to adopt appropriate policies and implement appropriate and demonstrable technical and organizational measures to ensure and be able to demonstrate in a transparent manner compliance with the Regulation. The requirement to demonstrate compliance "in a transparent manner" is not further explained nor in the text of the article or in the recitals. However, it could be assumed that such wording refers to the general requirement of verifiability (by the competent DPA) of the actions taken by data controllers to ensure and be able to demonstrate compliance. Article 22 specifies that such actions should refer to policies, technical and organizational measures which are adequate and effective to ensure compliance with the legal framework.

The verifiability of data controllers' data management practices will go through a thorough review of the documentation. Recital 60 and 65 both state that liability of data controllers will be established, amongst other, on the basis of the documentation produced. Indeed, the Regulation contains several obligations to document compliance with its provisions. This concerns first and foremost the content of internal policies, organizational and technical measures implemented, but also risks assessments, data protection assessments, data protection compliance reviews, data breaches and the tasks performed by the Data Protection Officer to raise awareness about data protection obligations both under the Regulation and internal procedures.

In the Law Enforcement Data Protection Directive
Article 18 of the Directive also integrates the obligation to be able to demonstrate, in a transparent manner, for each processing operation, that the processing of personal data is performed in compliance with the provisions of the Directive. Likewise, the meaning of the terms "in a transparent manner" not being further explained nor in the text of the article or in the recitals, it should be assumed that such wording refers to the general requirement of verifiability (by the competent supervisory authority) of the actions taken by data controllers to ensure and be able to demonstrate compliance. Article 18 contains an indicative list of the measures this obligation entails, namely: (1) keeping documentation referred to in article 23 ("Documentation"), (2) performing data protection impact assessments, (3) complying with the requirements of prior consultation, (4) implementing data security requirement, (5) designating a data protection officer, (6) implementing specific safeguards when processing personal data about children.

The difference with the Regulation is that the Directive is much more detailed about the information that data controllers should maintain about all processing systems and procedures under their responsibilities, including the result of the verification of the measures. In addition, it contains an obligation to keep records of any data collection, alteration, consultation, disclosure, combination or erasure indicating the purpose, date and time of such operations, the identification of the person who accessed the data (as far as possible) and the identity of the recipient of the data. These records are kept for the purposes of verification of the lawfulness of the data processing, self-monitoring, ensuring data integrity and security and for purposes of auditing. These records should be made available upon request to the supervisory authority.

3.4 Data Governance

Accountability mechanisms compel data controllers to adjust their business processes to deal with data protection concerns in an adequate and effective way. It follows that accountability, as a data protection principle, will foster the design and implementation of an internal structure for data governance.

In the General Data Protection Regulation

Good data governance will allow organizations to demonstrate good practice and compliance. Indeed, ensuring that the policies, organizational and technical measures are duly documented is not sufficient to demonstrate compliance. Recital 65 states that "equal emphasis and significance should be placed on good practice and compliance". This is thus the adequacy and efficiency of the whole data governance structure put in place by the data controller that will be assessed by the Data Protection Authorities. Article 22.3 clearly specifies that the controller should be able to demonstrate the adequacy and effectiveness of policies and organizational and technical measures implemented. This obligation extends to compliance policies and procedures.

Indeed, in order to leave sufficient flexibility and to allow the scalability of accountability mechanisms, the Regulation does not specify which policies, organizational and technical measures should be implemented (article 22.1). It rather sets a list of criteria that should govern their design: state of the art, nature of personal data processing, context, scope and purposes of the processing, risks for the rights and freedom of the data subjects and the type of organization. Such assessment should be carried out both at the time of the determination of the means for processing (before the personal data are collected) and at the time of the processing itself (covering the whole life cycle of the processing). Similarly, compliance policies and procedures should be designed taking into account the state of the art and the cost of implementation.

Data governance is also fostered through the key role given to DPOs. They are not only entrusted with the task of raising awareness, informing and advising about the content of the Regulation but they are given a significant role in monitoring the effective implementation of policies, organizational and technical measures. The creation of a specific position, to be filled by someone with sufficient privacy expertise and entrusted with the management of internal policies, procedures and practices related to privacy within the organization should drive data governance to happen in practice.

Additional provisions of the Regulation foster the implementation of a data governance scheme, by promoting the integration of privacy concerns into specific business processes and the design of systems, products and services.

Article 23 introduces a new obligation to take into account data protection concerns during the entire lifecycle management of personal data through the principles of data protection by design and data protection by default. Both principles aim at the introduction of technical measures into system design that will ensure compliance. By integrating privacy safeguards into technology, both principles could be used as to provide evidence of compliance under the principle of accountability.

The principle of data protection by design requires data protection to be embedded within the entire life cycle of the technology, from the very early design stage, right through its ultimate deployment, use and final disposal. Privacy by design covers the entire lifecycle management of personal data systematically focusing on comprehensive procedural safeguards regarding the accuracy, confidentiality, integrity, physical security and deletion of personal data.

The principle of data protection by default, on the other hand, requires privacy settings on services and products which should by default comply with the general principles of data protection (recital 61). Data protection by default means that only those personal data which are necessary for each specific purpose of the processing and are especially not collected, retained or disseminated beyond the minimum necessary for those purposes, both in terms of the amount of the data and the time of their storage. In particular, those mechanisms shall ensure that by default personal data are not made accessible to an indefinite number of individuals and that data subjects are able to control the distribution of their personal data.

Similarly, Section 3 of Chapter 4 "Lifecycle data protection management" introduces an obligation for data controllers to carry out a risk analyses of the potential impact of the processing on the fundamental rights and freedom of data subjects. It further defines additional obligations in case specific risks are identified. This goes from the designation of a representative when the controller is not established in the Union, to the performance of Data Protection Impact Assessments, the appointment of a DPO or an obligation to consult the DPO or the DPA.

In the Law Enforcement Data Protection Directive
The provisions fostering data governance schemes are similar in the Directive. The Directive not only imposes an obligation to document all measures taken to ensure compliance with the Directive, it also compels data controllers to implement appropriate and proportionate technical and organizational measures and procedures to ensure the processing will meet the requirements of the provisions of the Directive. The role of the Data Protection Officer is substantially the same, her role being reinforced in the Directive in that her appointment is mandatory and she should be appointed for four years. Finally, the Directive also introduces the principles of privacy by design and privacy by default in the same way as the Regulation does.

4   Limits and Opportunities of the New Framework

As elaborated in section 2, the definition of any accountability scheme within the data protection framework involves three main aspects: (1) to ensure that the outcome of the process increase the level of trust in data controllers' practices; (2) to provide for efficient oversight mechanisms by giving sufficient visibility to data management practices; and (3) to foster the deployment of an internal governance structure that will ensure that privacy is integrated in the internal policies, procedures and practices of the accountable organization in conformity with the applicable legal framework. This section assesses to what extent the General Data Protection Regulation and the Law Enforcement Data Protection Directive meet these objectives.

4.1   Trust Mechanisms

The introduction of a principle of accountability into the data protection framework involves defining the right frame to ensure that accountability relationships will increase the level of trust into the data controllers' personal data management.[1]

In that sense, the Regulation provides for the possibility to advertise compliance to data subjects through the "European Data Protection Seal". The role of Data Protection Authorities would thus be substantially modified, moving from a purely enforcement approach to a more preventive approach. Data Protection Authorities would play a key role in the development of referential, models, etc. and would be able to enforce their implementation. They will also certify the certifiers. It however raises the question of how DPAs will be able to combine both roles of certifier and enforcer. One can wonder to what extent an organization which has been certified is protected from further enforcement actions from DPAs. Compliance could also be advertised through the publication of a summary of the data governance scheme adopted in public reports of the data controllers.

It is however not clear how the Directive articulate the change-over from blind trust to proven trust. While increased technical auditing mechanisms are provided for, as well as the role of DPOs in providing assurance is reinforced, it is not clear how this will transpire to citizens. The equation between the need to maintain certain opacity for law enforcement activities and the need to provide for transparency mechanisms to increase citizens' trust is not solved. While the Directive introduces an accountability scheme, this seems to remain a relationship between supervisory authorities (which are not necessarily DPAs) and law enforcement agencies. It is not defined how the outcome of the accountability process will reach to citizens. It is thus doubtful that such measures would have a real impact on citizens' trust.

4.2   Oversight

Accountability schemes involves the granting of rights of authority to competent authorities, in this case DPAs (or supervisory authorities under the Law Enforcement Data Protection Directive), public agencies especially entrusted with the task of enforcing the data protection framework. Such rights should enable supervisory authorities to verify the accuracy of the account given, as well as the adequacy and effectiveness of the procedures put in place. In other words, to verify the truth of the story told by data controllers.

---

[1] Enhanced information obligations through icons as provided under article 13a of the Regulation fall out of the scope of this section in so far as they only rely on an unilateral statement made by data controllers. As such, they cannot qualify as accountability mechanism.

In that sense, and following Raab [4], the process of account giving pursues two main objectives, namely (1) to enable the third party with rights of authority to better understand the organizations' intentions and its understanding, or theory, of its own situation or how it might act in it, and (2) to give visibility to the organization's actions that are by nature invisible and must be represented.

The Regulation introduces in several provisions the obligation to make available, upon request, the required documentation to the DPA. Similarly, it creates a proactive obligation for data controllers to demonstrate they are legally compliant. In addition, DPOs, actors with sufficient knowledge in privacy, are designated as point of contact of the organization with the DPA. This should ease the dialogue of account giving between data controllers and the DPA. All these features intend to increase the visibility and the verifiability of the measures implemented by data controllers by DPAs.

However, it is not clear how the dialogue between the DPA and data controllers will be articulated. Both the Regulation and the Directive merely refer to the traditional enforcement powers of DPAs in terms of access to data controllers' information, systems and premises and of sanctions in case of lack of compliance. Yet, a series of questions remain unaddressed, such as, for example: how often can DPAs request access to this information under the principle of accountability; to which extent DPAs will have access to the controller's data or system in order to test and challenge the story told by data controller (most particularly when the controller rely on internal/external audit); which are the consequences of finding of lack of compliance, i.e. will this automatically trigger the start of an enforcement procedure or will the DPA only suggest modifications/corrections.

4.3   Governance

Accountability from the perspective of the data protection framework also means that data holders have to implement a data governance structure that will aim at ensuring and demonstrating compliance with the legal framework. Bennett [9] made clear that, in the context of data protection, the account should not only bear on the content of policies, but also on internal procedures implemented to comply with the legal framework and on the organization's practices, i.e. the day-to-day of the organization, its products and services.

Both the General Data Protection Regulation and the Law Enforcement Data Protection Directive include provisions that compel data controllers not only to adopt adequate policies and to document them but also to design adequate and effective organizational and technical measures that will ensure compliance with the legal framework and enable them to demonstrate their compliance. Insistence on the implementation of good practices and on the adoption of a risk management approach to data processing operations are expected to force data controllers to identify the risks posed to citizens' fundamental rights and to incorporate countermeasures to mitigate such risks. The Law Enforcement Data Protection Directive is even stricter in this regard as it compels data controllers to implement precise technical safeguards such as record keeping in order to facilitate technological audit of the processing of personal data.

5   Accountable Surveillance Practices: Raising the Level of Trust

Trust and Surveillance appear at first sight as antithetical terms. One can only trust that surveillance will occur under a pre-defined and legitimate set of conditions, clearly established within the law. To that end, surveillance has to be not only legitimate but also predictable.

Accountability participates to making surveillance predictable, in that it ensures the transparency of the surveillance practices, it provides assurance through external oversight, it raises privacy awareness and it encourages data controllers to implement data governance schemes to ensure they take due care of the personal data they are entrusted with. Accountability is however only part of the solution and only contributes to generate trust in institutions and market players engaged in surveillance to the extent that these are compelled to give an account of their practices. They do not legitimate surveillance practices, they only increase the visibility of the way how data controllers minimise the impact of their practices on citizens' fundamental rights.

This paper has shown that the introduction of an accountability principle into the European Data Protection Package will encourage data controllers to define internal policies, procedures and practices for data management and it will lead them to take into account privacy at all levels of the organization and all stages of product and system development. The European Data Protection Package also contains measures to increase the visibility of privacy-enhancing measures.

For these measures to manage to increase trust in surveillance systems, citizens should be convinced that their owners are operating them with their fundamental rights in mind. To that end, they should be provided with sufficient assurance. The Regulation makes a move in that direction, opening a path towards proven trust, by introducing an obligation to publish the measures taken to comply with the principle of accountability in corporate public reports and through the establishment of a certification mechanism and the granting, by DPAs, of a "European Data Protection Seal". It however remains to be seen to what extent these measures will have an impact on the transparency of data processing activities towards data subjects and to what extent they will be effectively implemented by data controllers. The new Data Protection Package do not provide specific incentives, e.g. through sanctions, to compel data controllers to do so.

The Law Enforcement Data Protection Directive does not contain any tool on which law enforcement authorities can rely to demonstrate citizens they make a good and reasonable use of surveillance technologies. While a seal does not appear to be an appropriate answer in the specific context of law enforcement, alternative mechanisms are necessary to demonstrate to citizens they can trust a given surveillance system to be designed as to minimize the impact on their fundamental rights but also to be used in full compliance with the legal framework. It is indeed difficult to anticipate that accountability mechanisms by themselves, without any way for citizens to identify compliant surveillance systems, i.e by only trusting the fact that supervisory authorities are holding data controllers accountable for their personal data management practices, will manage to raise the level of citizens' trust.

Acknowledgements. This paper was made possible thanks to the funding and work performed for the PARIS project (PrivAcy pReserving Infrastructure for Surveillance), EU FP7, under Grant Agreement n° No: 312504 and the B-CCENTRE project, Prevention of and Fight against Crime Programme of the EU, European Commission, DG Home Affairs.

References

1. McPhail, B., Clement, A., Ferenbok, J., Johnson, A.: I'll be watching you, Awareness, Consent and Accountability in Video Surveillance. In: 2013 IEEE International Symposium on Technology and Society (ISTAS), June 27-29, pp. 276–284 (2013), doi:10.1109/ISTAS.2013.6613130
2. Institute for Applied Autonomy (IAA), n.d., iSeeproject, available at: https://www.appliedautonomy.com/isee.html
3. De Hert, P.: Accountability and system responsibility: New Concepts in Data Protection Law and Human Rights Law. In: Guagnin, D., Hempel, L., Ilten, C., Kroener, I., Neyland, D., Postigo, H. (eds.) Managing Privacy Through Accountability, p. 199. Palgrave Macmillan (2012)
4. Raabs, C.: The Meaning of 'Accountability' in the Information Privacy Context. In: Guagnin, D., Hempel, L., Ilten, C., Kroener, I., Neyland, D., Postigo, H. (eds.) Managing Privacy Through Accountability, Palgrave Macmillan (2012)
5. Daniel, J., Weitzner, et al.: Information accountability. Communications of the ACM 51(6), 84–87 (2008)
6. Alhadeff, J., Van Alsenoy, B., Dumortier, J.: The Accountability Principle in Data Protection Regulation: Origin, Development and Future Directions. In: Guagnin, D., Hempel, L., Ilten, C., Kroener, I., Neyland, D., Postigo, H. (eds.) Managing Privacy Through Accountability, pp. 49–82. Palgrave Macmillan (2012)
7. Cate, F.H., Cullen, P., Mayer-Schönberger, V.: Data Protection Principles for the 21st Century, Revising the 1980 OECD Guidelines (December 2013)
8. Centre for Information Policy Leadership, Accountability projects, details over the initiatives and published papers, http://www.informationpolicycentre.com/accountability-based_privacy_governance/
9. Bennett, C.J.: The Accountability Approach to Privacy and Data Protection: Assumptions and Caveat. In: Guagnin, D., Hempel, L., Ilten, C., Kroener, I., Neyland, D., Postigo, H. (eds.) Managing Privacy Through Accountability, pp. 33–48. Palgrave Macmillan (2012)
10. Article 29 Data Protection Working Party, Opinion 03/2010 on the Principle of Accountability (adopted on July 13, 2010)
11. European Commission, Communication on "A comprehensive approach on personal data protection in the European Union", COM(2010) 609 final, Brussels (November 4, 2010)
12. Friedewald, M., Leimbach, T., Wright, D., Gutwirth, S., De Hert, P., González Fuster, G., Langheinrich, M., Ion, I.: Privacy and Trust in the Ubiquitous Information Society. Final Study Report (D4), Prepared for the European Commission, DG INFSO (March 27, 2009)
13. Gutwirth, S., De Hert, P.: Privacy, data protection and law enforcement. Opacity of the individual and transparency of power. In: Claes, E., Duff, A., Gutwirth, S. (eds.) Privacy and the Criminal Law, pp. 61–104. Intersentia, Antwerp (2006)
14. Díaz, C., Tene, O., Gürses, S.: Hero or Villain: The Data Controller in Privacy Law and Technologies. Ohio State Law Journal 74 (2013)

15. European Data Protection Supervisor, Opinion of the European Data Protection Supervisor on the Communication from the Commission and to the European Parliament and the Council on an area of freedom, security and justice serving the citizen, OJ C276/8, 42 (2009)
16. European Data Protection Supervisor, Opinion on the Data Protection Reform Package, §310 (March 7, 2012)
17. Article 29 Data protection Working Party, Opinion 01/2012 on the data protection reform proposals, WP 191, p. 27 (March 23, 2012)

TAM-VS: A Technology Acceptance Model for Video Surveillance

Erik Krempel[1] and Jürgen Beyerer[1,2]

[1] Fraunhofer Institute of Optronics, System Technologies and Image Exploitation
IOSB, Karlsruhe, Germany
[2] Vision and Fusion Laboratory, Karlsruhe Institute of Technology, Karlsruhe,
Germany
{erik.krempel,juergen.beyerer}@iosb.fraunhofer.de

Abstract. Video surveillance became omnipresent in our everyday live
and is a lively field of research. While early research was focused on
functionality, e.g., face recognition or violence detection, nowadays also
privacy and transparency related work is done. While this research helps
us to design systems that combine functionality and privacy, only little understanding is present how the people under video surveillance
will react to the new systems. The average citizen does not understand
technological details and is unable to distinguish between systems with
varying privacy protection. Overall, surveillance has a bad reputation in
most countries. To understand the acceptance of surveillance within a
society, many questionnaires were made to ask people, if they support
it in special places, e.g., airports, public transport and shopping malls,
which led to many statistics about surveillance. Their outcome depends
on recently happened events, e.g., a terrorists attack or a reported misuse of a video sequence. The underlying factors are not considered and
no generic model for the acceptance exists. This work presents a model,
based on the well known Technology Acceptance Model (TAM). It is
shown, which factors lead to a personal level of acceptance. The results
presented in this paper can be used to design accepted and efficient
surveillance systems.

1 Introduction

The discussion about video surveillance in public places is still ongoing and it is
influenced by different factors. E.g., authorities try to solve problems by closed-
circuit television (CCTV) cameras which are abused as a cheap replacement for
security personal. Due to a missing understanding of the technical limitations,
the discussion is mostly not objective. The emotional debate about safety and
privacy resulted to many false conclusions. In 2002 Michael McCahill and Clive
Norris [1] published their estimated number of 4.2 million surveillance cameras
in the United Kingdom. This number, although well-known and often cited,
is likely far of the real amount. In 2011 the CCTV user group of the ACPO
estimated that there are only about 1.85 million CCTV cameras in the UK [2].

B. Preneel and D. Ikonomou (Eds.): APF 2014, LNCS 8450, pp. 86–100, 2014.
© Springer International Publishing Switzerland 2014

Even if the real number is uncertain, there is an ongoing trend towards video surveillance systems all over the world. More and more systems are deployed and at the same time more powerful technology hits the market. Ten years ago CCTV-systems basically consisted of analog cameras streaming pictures to an operator. The development is impressive, modern "smart video surveillance systems" provide a broad variety of features to support the operator. They can, e.g., detect abnormal behavior [3], track individuals over multiple cameras [4] or even fulfill entire surveillance tasks on their own [5].

With increasing performance, new privacy risks occurred. In [6] Hempel et al. point out that 40% of the European society thinks that CCTV invades privacy. The acceptance differs in between the member countries, but it is obvious that developers must consider acceptance, when designing systems.

Early work on privacy, enforces protection by blurring or scrambling faces of observed people, who are wearing special markers for identification [7]. Other approaches modify the entire picture and only present necessary elements of the scene to the operator [8]. The newest development only shows video to the operator, when some kind of algorithm detects a situation that is specified as critical [9]. To increase the transparency of the data processing, a new approach allows the observed persons to directly interact with the system [10]. This aims to restore trust in the systems and thereby increase acceptance. Another upcoming development are smart video surveillance systems that offer additional services to the observed subjects, so they become a user of the system. People might want to book a surveillance service when walking home in the dark or demand special observation for their car in public parking. Also non-security related services as in-house navigation are possible[9].

With the development of video surveillance at an enormous pace, one topic stayed unobserved. With all the improvements on video surveillance nobody can predict how the acceptance of the systems will be or what factors will affect it. While some might argue that new systems will be accepted solely because they improve security other search for a balance between security and privacy, or even systems that offer benefits not related to security. With that many different approaches a methodical analysis of video surveillance systems is required. With TAM-VS a model for understanding acceptance is proposed. In a first survey with non-random participants the model fulfilled all common quality criteria and allows stating some hypothesis about the acceptance of video surveillance.

This work is structured as follows. Section 2 gives an overview about important and recent work on technology acceptance models. Section 3 introduces to structural equation modeling. Sections 4 then points out why none of the existing models is sufficient for video surveillance, before Sect. 5 explains the new technology acceptance model for video surveillance (TAM-VS). Section 6 describes the assessment of data used in Sect. 7. Following Sect. 8 summarizes the implications of the TAM-VS for developers of video surveillance systems. Finally Sect. 9 concludes the presented work.

2   Related Work

The Technology Acceptance Model (TAM) by Davis et al. [11] is still the most widely used theoretical model in the area of information systems. It extends the Theory of Reasoned Action (TRA) [12] and sees two factors for the acceptance of technology: *Perceived Ease of Use* and *Perceived Usefulness*. The two factors try to measure the degree of how a person believes that using a particular system would be free from effort and how much they believe a certain technology will improve their job performance. TAM is a robust model [13] and was successfully applied to many different technologies, e. g., e-mail, WWW and e-Health. An article by Lee et al. [13] counted in total 698 journal citations until the year 2003 for the original TAM publication by Davis.

Several research groups extended TAM to improve the overall quality of predictions how much a technology will be used after it was introduced in a certain work group. Venkatesh and Davis [14] propose the TAM2 model that examines how the Perceived Usefulness is influenced by other factors, e. g., *Output Quality* and *Image*. Venkatesh et al. [15] suggest with the Unified Theory of Acceptance and Use of Technology (UTAUT) an even more complex model. It adds extra factors affecting parts of the decision, e.g., *Performance Expectancy*, *Effort Expectancy*, *Social Influence*, *Gender*. The new factors allow a better prediction, but the simplicity of the original model is lost. When applying a model to a new field as video surveillance, the dependencies between the big number of factors make it difficult to identity the key factors for acceptance. Hence, the original TAM is the best starting point to analyze the acceptance of video surveillance.

Spiekermann et al. [16] developed an acceptance model, especially designed to understand and predict the acceptance of ubiquitous computing (UC) systems. It considers *Usefulness*, *Risk,Privacy* and *Control*. They argue that these factors influence the *Cognitive Attitude*, the *Affective Attitude* and the *Behavioral Intention to Use*. Although the model is sufficient for UC systems, it seems to be to complex for a first approach towards a better understanding of the acceptance of video surveillance. Especially Control cannot be mapped to surveillance directly, which contradicts as well.

3   Short Introduction to Structural Equation Modeling

TAM and descending approaches are based on structural equation modeling (SEM). To understand the TAM-VS model basic knowledge about SEM is required and imparted in this section.

SEM is a statistical technique for testing and estimating relations between multiple factors. It can be used for exploratory and confirmatory modeling, i. e., it can be used for development or testing of a theory. In this work it is used as the latter. When used as a confirmatory tool, usually a number of *hypotheses* is represented in a causal model. The model and the underlying hypothesis are tested against the obtained measurement data to determine how well the model fits. The greatest strength of SEM compared to factor analysis or path analysis

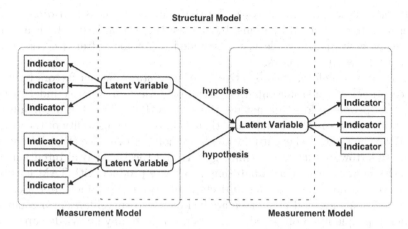

Fig. 1. Structural Equation Modeling

is that *latent variables*, also called *factors* or *constructs* can be used. Latent variables are effects that cannot be measured directly but are estimated by a number of *indicators*. E. g. to estimate how useful a new technology is to a user, he needs to be asked about the change in productivity, effectiveness and performance.

To cope with latent variables SEM is separated into *measurements models* that measure the value of the latent variables and a *structural model* representing the hypotheses, which describes the influence of the of latent variables on each other. Figure 1 provides an overview over used semantics and important components of SEMs.

4   Shortcomings of TAM for Video Surveillance

Understanding the acceptance of video surveillance systems differs highly from understanding systems TAM was originally designed for. As shown in Fig. 2a, TAM assumes two factors, Perceived Usefulness (PU) and Perceived Ease Of Use (PEOU), influencing the Attitude towards using a technology (A). This Attitude influences the Behavioral Intention (BI), which at last influences the Actual Use (AU).

- **Perceived Usefulness (PU)**
  The degree to which a subject believes that the system would enhance his performance.
- **Perceived Ease of Use (PEOU)**
  The degree to which a subjects thinks a system can be used easily.
- **Attitude towards using a technology (A)**
  The attitude the subject has towards a certain technology.
- **Behavioral Intention (BI)**
  The degree to which a subjects states to use the technology in the future.

All these factors are latent variables that cannot be measured directly, but rather need to be covered by items. In contrast the Actual Use (AU) is a simple assessment how many people use a provided technology after a certain time, e. g., actual use after 6 weeks.

As mentioned before, the objective is to understand, which factors influence the acceptance of video surveillance systems of subjects in an area under surveillance. The people in focus do not use the system themselves, but are monitored by it. So it is not suitable to measure their believe in the usability of the system (PEOU) or how they believe it may alter their job performance (PU). Measuring the attitude towards using a technology (A) and the Behavioral Intention (BI) raises the same issues. When analyzing a software product with TAM it is possible to record how many of the subjects really use the product after a certain time (AU). This method cannot be applied on video surveillance. To count the number of people in an observed area does not lead to any knowledge about the acceptance of the surveillance task. People might be dead set against a video surveillance system, but have no other choice than to walk through the observed area.

5   TAM-VS

Neither TAM nor any existing approach based on the model is suitable to analyze the acceptance of surveillance technology. A new model needs to be created that is especially designed to understand acceptance factors common in security related technology, especially video surveillance.

The factors examined in this study were identified by multiple expert interviews and two group discussions. Following a first draft of TAM-VS was created and the indicators, used to measure the latent variables, were tested with a convenient sample of 18 people. The results improved the wordings of indicators and the model. Figure 2b shows the final model. The identified factors are:

PUS: The Perceived Usefulness of the system.
RI: The Perceived Personal Risk due to malfunction or abuse of the system.
TR: The Transparency achieved by the system. Do people understand how the system works and the data handling done by it.
EE: The overall Emotional Attitude towards the surveillance system.
AC: The overall Acceptance of the surveillance system.

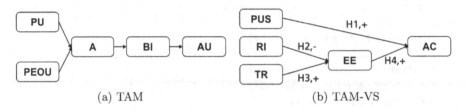

(a) TAM   (b) TAM-VS

Fig. 2. TAM by Davis et al. [11] and the developed TAM-VS

Following, the different factors and their indicators in the measurement model are described in detail. The original questionnaire was used in Germany was therefore written in German, please see the Appendix for a translated version.

Perceived Usefulness: Perceived Usefulness of the surveillance system to ensure safety in the observed area. In contrast to classical TAM, TAM-VS addresses the subjects' opinion about the functionality, i. e., can the system ensure safety in the area. As the system is used by an operator and not by the observed subjects, four items are relevant for measuring: simplifies the job of security personal, increases overall security, simplifies the detection of crime, is a appropriate tool to increase the safety.

Perceived Personal Risk: The Perceived Risk of the subjects when walking through the observed area. Two items were identified: fear of disadvantages through the processing and collection of data and fear of disadvantages through malfunctions in the processing or collection of data.

Transparency: The overall perceived Transparency of the system. Expressed by three items: understanding of the collection of data, understanding of the processing of data, knowing the responsible person for the system.

Emotional Attitude: The Emotional Attitude of subjects towards surveillance systems. This factor is included because discussion showed that people might find surveillance systems quite useful to ensure safety, but still dislike them for personal reasons. As they address emotions, these questions are difficult to translate and they might need some extra care before using them in an English questionnaire. Three different items are used: use of such systems is sensible, I do not worry because of the system and I feel comfortable in the monitored area.

Acceptance: The last factor measures the overall Acceptance of the surveillance system. Three items are used: "I like such systems", "Such systems should be forbidden by law" and "More systems like this should be used". The second item was negative and the scores were inverted before further analyzing the results.

All items are scaled (-2) – (+2), where (-2) is strong disagreement and (+2) is strong agreement. A reflexive model is chosen, because the factors have multiple dimensions and are hard to capture by formative models. Please see external literature when you are interested in the differences between reflexive and formative models or measurement model design for example [17].

Together with the model four different hypotheses are formulated about how the factors influence each other:

H1: There will be a positive relationship between the perceived usefulness and the acceptance.

H2: There will be a negative relationship between the perceived risk and the emotional attitude.

H3: There will be a positive relationship between the transparency of the system and the emotional attitude.

H4: There will be a positive relationship between the emotional attitude and the acceptance.

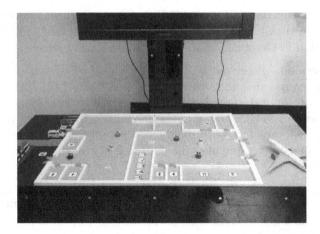

Fig. 3. Airport demonstrator used in the field study

6 Method of Assessment

After the new model was created and the measurement model had passed initial quality checks, the whole model was tested in a broader field study. A first pen and paper questionnaire with short presentations of the technologies in scope was done. The pen and paper version with initial presentations was chosen against online questionnaire, because we felt that the technology under review might demands some individual explanations. The participants were recruited via multiple mailing lists as well as social networks. We actively decided to not perform the questionnaire in the Karlsruhe Institute of Technology because the highly technology affine students might have biased the results. It was held in the Berlin University of the Arts where a much higher variety in the field of study exists.

In total five different appointments were held with about 15 persons each. Appointments were distributed over three days to enable every interested person to participate. Every participant was offered an incentive of about $20 for their time to ensure high levels of motivation and concentration through the whole interview. It took one hour to present different technologies and to answer the complete form.

In total 82 valid questionnaires were filled out. The participant poll does not reflect the entire German population, 62.2 % of the study was answered by woman and 34.1% by man, some unknown. Further the sample was a bit younger and had a higher education than the average population. Most likely this is because the questionnaire was held at a university which had impact on the people attending. However the difference is uncritical for the testing of the TAM-VS model and it is likely that the results in the sample can be translated to the entire German population.

The developed model was tested in two different scenarios, a classical and smart video surveillance. Both take place in an airport, because it offers a surrounding which is typically protected by video surveillance and most people are familiar with airports. As seen in Fig. 3 a model of an airport was built to make the scenarios as vivid as possible. Before the questionnaire was distributed the sample was invited to have a closer look at the model. It consists of all areas typical found on an airport, namely areas for public and private transport on the left, a security checkpoint and airline check-in counters in the center, two gates on the right and baggage claims and customs at the top. Additional areas such as restrooms and restaurants were added to get an typical airport layout. In this airport model colored blocks were used to visualize individuals. The two blue blocks represent security personal while all the other blocks represent individual passengers. A monitor positioned in top of the model allows the visualization needed to explain conventional and smart video surveillance.

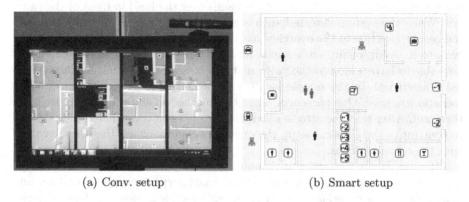

(a) Conv. setup   (b) Smart setup

Fig. 4. Visualization used for surveillance scenarios

After demonstrating the layout of the airport and answering occasional questions to it, the group was invited to sit down. First the classical setup was introduced. Here the monitor was used to display video streams of different cameras observing the airport as seen in Fig. 4a. This represents a state of the art video surveillance system. Multiple video sources are displayed at the same time and one or more operators are present to observe the area. To represent real conditions there is some overlap in the video streams as well as some blind spots. To further demonstrate the operation a sample incident was shown. Therefore one of the colored markers performed an assault on another one. It was assumed that the operator would detect the assault in the video stream and could react accordingly. After some time the attacker fled the crime scene and was pursued by security officers coordinated by the operators viewing the video stream. Here especially the complexity of detecting crimes and tracking of fleeing subjects over multiple video stream was shown.

After the conventional scenario was demonstrated the form was distributed and the participants had sufficient time to completely answer it. The form was composed of a single page of paper, printed on front and back. After every participant had finished compete the form the second part of the form was distributed.

The second half of the study started with the demonstration of a smart surveillance system. Here special care was take to explain that such systems are not yet in operation but are in development and will be ready in the near future. The demonstrated system helps the operators by performing some advanced tasks. Instead multiple video streams the operators see a overview map of the airport as shown in Fig. 4b. In this overview the system marks the current position of all passengers with black icons and the two security officers with special security-officer icons. The system is capable to track persons over multiple cameras. Intelligent situation assessment algorithms process the video data and try to detect trained patterns. In the demonstration system it was possible to raise the systems awareness by holding both hands over the head in front of the camera. When the system detected such a gesture it uses red markers to visualize the gesture position in the overview map as well as purple markers for all people next to it. Additionally an acoustic alarm is send to the operators which are now able to have a look at the video material to assess the situation the system rated as critical. In the sample incident the same procedure as in the classical scenario was used. One passenger assaulted another on and the system detected the event. After that the attacker fled and the operator coordinated the pursuit. In contrast to the classical setup the operators could now use the overview map with the colorized icons.

After the smart scenario was demonstrated all participants had time to ask questions concerning the basic concepts of smart surveillance to prevent misunderstandings. All questions concerning moral or ethical issues or detailed technical questions were shifted to after the questionnaire was completed, to not influence individual opinions. After all the participants had finished answering the questionnaire additional technical ideas were presented. Here a idea was presented and directly afterward the subjects were asked to answer some questions concerning the just presented technology. These questions are not part of the publication and came after the presentations and questionnaires of the acceptance model were finished.

7   Analyzing Results

The model and hypothesis is tested with Partial Least Squares SEM (PLS-SEM). PLS-SEM is well suited for predictive analysis [18] and is broadly used to understand technology acceptance. In addition it offers a variety of benefits [19] compared to the also widely used covariance-based SEM. It generates stable results with smaller sample sizes and formative measurement models with fewer items. Hence, PLS-SEM is a well suited tool for the first analyzes of the model. The PLS analysis is realized with the software SmartPLS [20] by Ringle et al. which is available for everybody interested.

7.1 Test of the Measurement Model

Following the PLS-SEM approach, the quality of the outer measurement model was tested at first. Table 1 shows the composite reliability of all factors. Every single value is above the suggested threshold of 0.7 stating a good internal consistency. The average variance extracted (AVE), also displayed in Table 1 of every factor is higher than the common accepted threshold of 0.5 indicating good convergent validity. Table 2 shows the outer loadings of all indicators. In the conventional setup only two of the 15 items are below the quality criteria threshold of 0.7 suggested by Chen[18]. In the smart video surveillance scenario all indicators are above 0.7. This implies that the indicators have a sufficient validity in both scenarios. Furthermore, Cronbachs-α values summarized in Table 1 show a high internal consistency. Only in the conventional scenario the value of perceived risk is below the threshold of 0.7. The last commonly accepted quality criteria for reflexive measurement models is the Fornell-Larckers criteria [21]. It states that the square root of AVE should be higher than the construct correlation in the off-diagonal columns and rows to imply that every construct shares more variance with its indicators than it shares with the other model constructs. As seen in Table 3The Fornell-Larckers criteria is fulfilled for every factor in both scenarios.

Table 1. Measurement model quality criteria

	AVE	Composite Reliability	Cronbachs-α
Conv. Surveillance			
AC	0.707840	0.878452	0.794066
EE	0.670080	0.858944	0.753734
PUS	0.644682	0.877343	0.819268
RI	0.630850	0.773585	0.415230
TR	0.680621	0.860885	0.760067
Smart Surveillance			
AC	0.749515	0.899311	0.832256
EE	0.657845	0.852009	0.740204
PUS	0.678104	0.893421	0.843380
RI	0.768672	0.869119	0.701441
TR	0.669105	0.858297	0.754194

7.2 Test of the Structural Model

After successfully checking the measurement model, the next part of the analyzes checks, if the hypotheses made earlier are true. The first important criteria is R^2 of all factors which are influenced by other factors, i. e., EE and AC, as it indicates the predictive power of the model. With higher value of R^2 the model is able to predict more the change observed in the depending factors. Which values

Table 2. Indicator Loadings

Indicator	Conv. Surveillance	Smart Surveillance
AKZ1	0.918905	0.933550
AKZ2	0.764134	0.783964
AKZ4	0.833806	0.783964
EE1	0.831000	0.851816
EE4	0.789727	0.766001
EE5	0.834273	0.813134
PUS1	0.806567	0.738721
PUS2	0.852455	0.842124
PUS3	0.638302	0.802907
PUS5	0.891106	0.901595
RI1	0.779312	0.900915
RI3	0.808933	0.851878
TR2	0.907956	0.807389
TR3	0.924056	0.860591
TR4	0.602991	0.784105

of R^2 are satisfying is still a source of discussions. Chen[18] defines values of $R^2 > 0.67$ as substantial, $R^2 > 0.33$ as moderate and $R^2 > 0.19$ as weak. Others, e.g., Schloderer et al. [22] argue that smaller values of R^2 can occur, when some influence factors are (deliberately) ignored without rendering the latent variable unimportant. I. e., the value for the explained Acceptance (AC), 0.6413 in the conventional setup and 0.7359 in the smart setup, is highly satisfying. The values for the Emotional Attitude (EE), 0.3016 in the conventional setup and 0.3423 in the smart setup, are sufficient at least. The study focuses on explaining the acceptance of video surveillance rather than it was focused on understanding all influences on the emotional factor. Therefore smaller values of R^2 in EE are acceptable in the first test. Nonetheless more research is planed to get a better understanding of the factors influencing EE. To finally asses the hypotheses the path coefficients and the corresponding significance are shown in Fig. 5. The significance was computed by bootstrapping as proposed when using PLS-SEM [19]. The first path value is the conventional scenario, the second the smart video surveillance scenario. Sellin and Keeves [23] state that that absolute value of the path coefficient should be at least 0.1 to have an important effect. Other sources state that all coefficients show an effect as long as they are significant and the effect direction is the same as predicted by the hypothesis. In both scenarios the effect of the coefficients is as predicted and above the threshold of 0.1. Therefore all four hypotheses are validated by the given data. As expected, perceived risk has a negative effect on emotional attitude towards video surveillance, while transparency has a positive effect. What is more surprising is how much stronger the influence of emotional attitude on the acceptance is compared to perceived usefulness. In the next chapter a deeper look at the implications for practice is given.

Table 3. Discriminant validity of measures: Square root of AVE diagonal and cross construct correlation off-diagonal

	Cronbachs-α	AC	EE	PUS	RI	TR
Conv. Surveillance						
AC	0.794066	0.841332277				
EE	0.753734	0.796781	0.818584144			
PUS	0.819268	0.544515	0.6031	0.802920918		
RI	0.41523	−0.344786	−0.357956	−0.25834	0.794260663	
TR	0.760067	0.466133	0.453001	0.331051	−0.108993	0.824997576
Smart Surveillance						
AC	0.832256	0.865745344				
EE	0.740204	0.84534	0.811076445			
PUS	0.84338	0.690587	0.692482	0.823470704		
RI	0.701441	−0.432879	−0.473521	−0.285993	0.876739414	
TR	0.754194	0.536	0.511639	0.452006	−0.423025	0.817988386

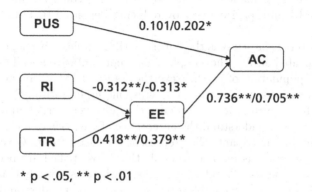

* p < .05, ** p < .01

Fig. 5. Path coefficients and significance (conv./smart)

8   Implications of the TAM-VS for Practice

After finishing the first study and validating the acceptance model some conclusions for the development of new surveillance systems and redesign of existing systems can be made. On the first glance the results of the study are not surprising. Both Perceived Usefulness and Emotional Attitude have a significant impact on the Acceptance of video surveillance systems. These potential relationships are long presumed and the first important finding of the study is to confirm these influences with a methodical study.

A deeper look at the results shows a somewhat surprising result. In the conventional scenario the weight of the Perceived Usefulness is only slightly higher than the threshold proposed by Sellin and Keeves. In The smart scenario the effect of Perceived Usefulness is stronger but in both cases the Emotional Attitude is much more important. This confirms the thesis that Acceptance of video surveillance is a mostly emotional topic and guaranteed safety has only a small impact. While the safety is a absolutely necessary part of acceptance it seems that improving safety alone will not result in highly accepted and wanted systems.

With the Emotional Attitude such an strong factor for acceptance developers should aim to improve it. The results imply that Perceived Risk has a negative impact on the Emotional Attitude. Because the factor is highly individual it seems hard to influence. For a practical approach the Transparency of a given systems seem to be the more promising factor. When developers succeed to improve this, i.e., by explaining better how their systems operate and integration more transparency enhancing tools, smart surveillance systems have great opportunity to gain higher acceptance. More research would be valuable to find what other factors further influence the Emotional Attitude. The mediocre value of R^2 in Emotional Attitude suggests, that a least one more strong factors is hidden. This factor might be another promising approach to increase the acceptance of video surveillance. It is reasonable to assume that privacy protection and integration of Privacy Enhancing Technologies (PETs) could be this factor or at least influence EE in a positive way by reducing Perceived Risk and improving transparency.

One limitation of the study is the nature of the sample. With slightly younger and better educated adults, the sample is not representative for all Germans far less the whole population of earth. Nevertheless the TAM-VS model passed all quality checks commonly found in the corresponding literature. Even when the results might not be valid for all Germans, they give very strong indication that TAM-VS is usable to understand the acceptance of video surveillance by polling higher numbers of participants that represent the focus group. Given the open method of recruiting it is further arguable that those polled are people with a high interest in the topic. Therefore it is reasonable to assume that their opinion will have a big influence in the public opinion. Thus a good understanding of their motivation is important to design systems which can reach better acceptance in the whole population.

9   Conclusion

TAM is a great way to predict how systems under development will be accepted. To solve the limitations of TAM not being usable for all variation of technologies, system depending models got introduced. With TAM-VS a new TAM model was developed to measure and understand which factors influence the acceptance of surveillance systems. The designed model was tested by a user study in two scenarios, one presenting the current state of the art video surveillance systems and the second one predicting how video surveillance will develop in the near future. The newly developed TAM-VS model was shown adequate in both scenarios. Thus confirming existing theories what influences acceptance of video surveillance today and helping engineers to develop new systems fulfilling the need of people. This will result in new surveillance systems which are accepted by the majority of people and still are able to perform their surveillance tasks.

References

1. McCahill, M., Norris, C.: Cctv in london. Report deliverable of UrbanEye project (2002)
2. Gerrard, G., Thompson, R.: Two million cameras in the uk. CCTV Image 42, 10–12 (2011)
3. Zelniker, E., Gong, S., Xiang, T., et al.: Global abnormal behaviour detection using a network of cctv cameras. In: The Eighth International Workshop on Visual Surveillance-VS(2008)
4. Monari, E., Maerker, J., Kroschel, K.: A robust and efficient approach for human tracking in multi-camera systems. In: Sixth IEEE International Conference on Advanced Video and Signal Based Surveillance, AVSS 2009, pp. 134–139. IEEE (2009)
5. Moßgraber, J., Reinert, F., Vagts, H.: An architecture for a task-oriented surveillance system: A service-and event-based approach. In: 2010 Fifth International Conference on Systems (ICONS), pp. 146–151. IEEE (2010)
6. Hempel, L., Töpfer, E.: Cctv in europe. final report. Urbaneye WorNing Paper (15) (2004)
7. Senior, A., Pankanti, S., Hampapur, A., Brown, L., Tian, Y.L., Ekin, A.: Blinkering surveillance: Enabling video privacy through computer vision. Technical report, IBM (August 2003)
8. Senior, A., et al.: Enabling video privacy through computer vision. In: Security & Privacy, 3rd edn. pp. 50–57. IEEE (June 2005)
9. Vagts, H., Krempel, E., Beyerer, J.: User-centric protection and privacy in smart surveillance systems. In: Future Security - Security Research Conference 2012 (Future Security 2012), Bonn, Germany (September 2012)
10. Vagts, H., Beyerer, J.: Enhancing the acceptance of technology for civil security and surveillance by using privacy enhancing technology. In: Future Security: 6th Security Research Conference. Fraunhofer Verlag (2011)
11. Davis, F.D.: Perceived usefulness, perceived ease of use, and user acceptance of information technology. MIS quarterly 13, 319–340 (1989)
12. Fishbein, M.: A theory of reasoned action: Some applications and implications. Nebraska Symposium on Motivation (1979)
13. Lee, Y., Kozar, K., Larsen, K.: The technology acceptance model: Past, present, and future. The Communications of the Association for Information Systems 12(1), 53 (2003)
14. Venkatesh, V., Davis, F.D.: A theoretical extension of the technology acceptance model: Four longitudinal field studies. Management science 46(2), 186–204 (2000)
15. Venkatesh, V., Morris, M., Davis, G., Davis, F.: User acceptance of information technology: Toward a unified view. MIS quarterly 27, 425–478 (2003)
16. Spiekermann, S.: User control in ubiquitous computing: Design alternatives and user acceptance. Shaker Verlag (2008)
17. St, E.L.L., Ronald, D.: An Assessment of Formative and Reflective Constructs in IS Research. In: 15th European Conference on Information Systems, University of St. Gallen (2007)
18. Chin, W.: The partial least squares approach for structural equation modeling. Modern Methods for Business Research, 295–336 (1998)
19. Hair, J., Ringle, C., Sarstedt, M.: PLS-SEM: Indeed a silver bullet. The Journal of Marketing Theory and Practice 19(2), 139–152 (2011)
20. Ringle, C.M., Wende, S., Will, A.: SmartPLS 2.0 (M3) Beta (2005)

21. Fornell, C., Larcker, D.: Evaluating structural equation models with unobservable variables and measurement error. Journal of marketing research, 39–50 (1981)
22. Schwaiger, M., Meyer, A.: Theorien und Methoden der Betriebswirtschaft: Handbuch für Wissenschaftler und Studierende. Vahlen (2011)
23. Sellin, N., Keeves, J.: Path analysis with latent variables. International encyclopedia of education, 4352–4359 (1994)

A   Appendix

Here the translated version of the full wording of the questionnaire is presented for possible reuse in other studies. All items were scaled (-2) – (+2), where (-2) was strong disagreement and (+2) was strong agreement. The items missing, e. g., PUS4, were eliminated after a first test in item development. Please keep in mind that especially the items concerning emotional attitudes are difficult to translate and show be reevaluated by a native speaker.

PUS1: The system facilitates the work of the security officers.
PUS2: The system increases the safety in the observed area.
PUS3: The system enables the security officers to secure large areas.
PUS5: I think the system is useful to increase safety.
 TR2: I am well informed what data is collected by the system.
 TR3: I am well informed how the system is processing data.
 TR4: I know who is responsible for the system.
 R11: The processing of data has a negative impact on me.
 RI3: I could be disadvantaged through errors in collection or processing of data by the system.
 EE1: I Think the use of such systems is sensible.
 EE4: I do not worry because of such systems.
 EE5: I feel more safe when such a system is in use.
AKZ1: I like such systems.
AKZ2: Such systems should be illegal.
AKZ4: More systems like this should be used.

Towards a Multidisciplinary Framework to Include Privacy in the Design of Video Surveillance Systems

Zhendong Ma[1], Denis Butin[2], Francisco Jaime[3], Fanny Coudert[4],
Antonio Kung[5], Claire Gayrel[6], Antonio Maña[3], Christophe Jouvray[5],
Nathalie Trussart[6], Nathalie Grandjean[6], Víctor Manuel Hidalgo[7],
Mathias Bossuet[8], Fernando Casado[3], and M. Carmen Hidalgo[3]

[1] Austrian Institute of Technology
[2] Inria, Université de Lyon
[3] Universidad de Málaga
[4] KU Leuven - Interdisciplinary Centre for Law & ICT - iMinds
[5] TRIALOG
[6] Université de Namur
[7] Visual Tools
[8] THALES

Abstract. Privacy impacts of video surveillance systems are a major concern. This paper presents our ongoing multidisciplinary approach to integrate privacy concerns in the design of video surveillance systems. The project aims at establishing a reference framework for the collection of privacy concepts and principles, the description of surveillance contexts, surveillance technologies, and accountability capabilities.

Keywords: Video surveillance, privacy, accountability, multidisciplinarity, SALT, PARIS.

1 Introduction

Despite contested views on its usefulness [15], video surveillance has been widely deployed to protect individuals and assets in public and private spaces. Over the past decades, video surveillance technologies have made tremendous advances, from analogue closed-circuit television (CCTV) to digital and network-based systems. State of the art video surveillance systems are labelled as "smart" and "intelligent", in which different types of information systems are integrated for correlating information from multiple sources. For example, biometric systems can be integrated into video surveillance for individual identification. In addition, advanced video analytic capabilities enable the system to monitor, detect, and search objects and events, e.g., for motion, behaviour, and abandoned object detection. As the systems are often network-based, real-time video streams and recorded video data can be distributed or remotely accessed using existing network infrastructure across geographic and organizational boundaries.

B. Preneel and D. Ikonomou (Eds.): APF 2014, LNCS 8450, pp. 101–116, 2014.

Privacy has always been a concern in surveillance systems. A large amount of work has been carried out in the past, e.g., from political science [21] to technological solutions [17]. However, the rapid development of technologies and the increasing market demand for surveillance capabilities outpace the development of regulations, social norm, and protection mechanisms. As a result, many areas remain partially or entirely undefined, which poses serious privacy risks if they are not handled correctly during the system planning, design, and development phases.

Video surveillance systems can be deployed in disparate contexts and often integrate subcomponents such as access control, communications, and mission management systems. Usually the system design process is driven by operational missions and generic specifications, in which system designers fulfill the technical and operational specifications. During the design process, many options exist and numerous decisions must be taken. This makes it demanding to include and address privacy concerns in the design. For example, perceptions of privacy vary according to context. Notably, expectations in public spaces are usually different from expectations in private ones; yet the demarcation between public and private spaces is sometimes blurry. Accordingly, social, political, and ethical approaches are required to deal with the complexities of those varying perceptions. Furthermore, just within Europe, regulations differ considerably even across member states. Even when only a given country is under consideration, it often remains difficult to find synthetic information about statutory law or case law related to specific surveillance scenarios. A parallel challenge is how to make all the privacy solutions practical, i.e., we must find optimal solutions for individuals' right to privacy on one side and the public need for safety and (homeland) security on the other side.

This paper presents our ongoing work on the establishment of a multidisciplinary framework that includes privacy concerns in the design of video surveillance systems. Specifically, the framework serves as a foundation for the collection of concepts and principles and for the description of surveillance context as well as surveillance technologies and accountability capabilities. It takes into account views from different stakeholders such as policy makers, regulators, national Data Protection Authorities, law enforcement, public authorities, and video surveillance system providers and operators. The framework is envisioned to help designers and other stakeholders facing these complexities to create video surveillance systems taking into account privacy requirements in a methodological, principled, systematic, and accountable way. To this aim, the framework provides reusable, generic and synthetic guidelines, reference information and criteria to be used or modified by experts and other stakeholders.

The remainder of the paper is structured as follows. We describe the privacy challenges and motivate the need for a multidisciplinary framework in § 2. We then give an overview of our approach and the rationales in § 3. The framework and its associated processes are presented in § 4 and § 5, respectively, followed by a summary in § 6.

2 Privacy Challenges and Motivations for Developing a Framework

Privacy is multifaceted, subjective, and evolving. The definition and perception of public and private spaces are constantly shaped under social, political, legal, and cultural influences. Therefore, a consistent basis is needed for describing the context concerning the balance between privacy and surveillance. Otherwise, it is difficult to determine the nature of personal and sensitive information in the surveillance context. Even though privacy can be seen from many angles, we base our analysis on the *Seven Types of Privacy* taxonomy [13], a recent framework (published in 2013) broadening the definition of privacy to account for novel threats introduced by technologies such as surveillance systems. This taxonomy enumerates the following categories: the privacy of the person, privacy of behaviour and action, privacy of communication, privacy of data and image, privacy of thoughts and feelings, privacy of location and space and privacy of association. While we also included more technical perspectives on privacy in our literature review, the above taxonomy provides a comprehensive categorization independently of specific practical measures to counteract privacy threats.

A chief challenge to video surveillance is the tension between surveillance functionality and privacy. Modern computer vision algorithms are capable of transforming and masking regions of video images that are considered private [10]. However, the willingness of surveillance operators to embrace these solutions in their systems and their effectiveness to protect privacy in systems with multiple information sources are still questionable. Besides, the reliability of these privacy protection components in large scale surveillance systems are yet to be proved. Surveillance systems are not much different from other IT systems that have various potential risks. Any data breach resulting from accidental disclosure or from a malicious attack will have an impact on privacy as well. To make the matter more complex, the trend in surveillance systems is towards multi-model and multi-operator system with increasing system interoperability, which leads to higher co-operation and exchange of information at the organizational level as well as at the system level.

Another challenge to privacy is the imbalance of power between citizens and surveillance system owners, introduced by the massive collection of personal data by surveillance system owners in an opaque way. The lack of knowledge about what is recorded and the absence of an individualised relation with controllers put data subjects in an overly weak position. Because of their inherent opacity, surveillance systems cannot rely on informed consent to legitimate personal data processing. Therefore, data subjects can only rely on *ex post* protection, i.e., complaints and redress procedures. Such protection often come too late and is uncertain in its outcome.

Costs can also be a challenge if alterations or extensions required to support privacy in a system are significant and expensive. Adopting a privacy-by-design approach and taking into account such requirements early on in system design can mitigate this issue.

The number of entities generally involved in surveillance systems yield additional difficulties. Numerous interacting entities generate a multitude of communication channels, often carrying sensitive data. This imbalance and complexity motivate the need to increase the accountability obligations of data controllers for their data processing. By accountability [9], we do not merely mean legal compliance but (1) the demonstration and verifiability of compliance at all levels through transparency about policies, actual processing and the explicit definition of technical compliance and (2) the possibility for an independent third party to actually check the evidence of both legal and technical compliance (e.g., procedure documentation and audit logs). A good definition of the spirit of accountability can be found in an Article 29 Working Group's Opinion [6], which affirms in particular accountability's role of "showing how responsibility is exercised and making this verifiable". Rather than a part of privacy, we consider accountability as a principle and a set of tools that can be used to support it.

While it could be argued that the inherent imbalance of power in any surveillance system brings an ethical obligation upon data controllers to act in a transparent way towards data subjects, the upcoming European General Data Protection Regulation [12] introduces a legal obligation to be able to demonstrate compliance with the data protection framework. This obligation goes through the implementation of adequate policies, procedures and technical measures tending to evidence compliance. Therefore, data subjects or their representatives are owed "accounts", but this is not sufficient; this evidence of the actions of controllers must be analysed and the conclusions of legal and technical compliance checking made available. The regulation foresees that assurance is provided through internal or external audit and legal compliance checked by Data Protection Authorities. However, in terms of technical compliance, both the accounts and the obligations against which they are to be verified often remain vague, impeding meaningful analysis and the reaching of clear conclusions. Furthermore, technical compliance checking on the system level, if it is not completed by links to higher-level principles, may seem excessively technical or disconnected from the big picture to stakeholders. A framework with sufficient generality is therefore needed to integrate the technical and high-level aspects of accountability into a unified approach.

2.1 Existing Work on Privacy and Video Surveillance

Existing research work addresses privacy from either social or computer science perspective, or the combination of both. In recent years, the European Commission funded a number of research projects that touch upon privacy and ethics of surveillance systems. The IRISS project [1] looks at the impact of surveillance technologies on basic rights and their social and economic influences. The SAPIENT project [3] aims at developing a Privacy Impact Assessment (PIA) methodology for surveillance technology. The SurPRISE project [4] assesses criteria and factors influencing European citizens' acceptance of surveillance technology. VideoSense [5] works on privacy preserving video analytics.

Existing solutions fostering accountability include PIA [22]. PIA forces data controllers not only to identify the impact the system developed will have on privacy and implement the necessary safeguards, but also to ensure that compliance with the legal framework is ensured throughout the whole lifecycle of the system which means allocating responsibilities for compliance between the different actors and implementing the required procedures to provide regular reviews and assurance.

PIA should integrate accountability as a system design prerequisite to ensure obligations are fulfilled. In particular, accountability over actual data handling practices is important to increase transparency regarding real system activity. This aspect is often neglected in PIA, yet seems essential to take into account accountability requirements. Even though checks related to accountability are not always part of PIA, adequate technical tools already exist. Available means to achieve this accountability of practice include privacy policy languages such as EPAL [7] or PPL [20], which allow the precise specification of (technical) data handling policies. These standardised policies can then be used to analyze system operation traces (audit logs) through a posteriori technical compliance control [8, 11].

Many technical solutions have surfaced addressing the privacy issue along the line of software, hardware, and system architecture. For example, digital signal processors can be embedded in the so-called "smart cameras", which are then programmed to selectively de-identify, mask, or scramble a certain region in the video [10]. The access to the raw video data is limited. Instead, metadata is used to fulfill the requirement of the surveillance operators. Therefore, video data from the smart cameras is split into two streams: a metadata stream for describing objects, events, behaviour, and other situations in the video; and an image stream which is the original video data.

Senior et al. [18] proposed to foster privacy through a layered access model enforced by a multilevel access control system architecture. The access model derives access rights from the following questions: (1) what data is present, (2) has the subject given consent, (3) what form does the data take, (4) who sees the data, (5) how long is data kept, and (6) how raw is the data. The answers to these questions lead to a layered access model. The raw video stream is further processed, and information is extracted to generate versions of different image details. For example, the access model can include three layers for three types of users: ordinary users can only access statistical information, privileged users can access limited individual information, and law enforcement agencies can access raw video information. For privacy protection, video data are rendered to transform a person's image into a bar, a box, or only its silhouette. Commercial systems such as IBM Smart Surveillance Solutions [16] claim to feature video analytics-based privacy protection mechanisms, including the limitation of access to camera and functions, information extraction from videos, and fuzzy metadata representation.

3   The SALT Approach

The previous section shows that systematically addressing privacy in video surveillance systems requires careful considerations from multiple perspectives. To include privacy from the very beginning of a video surveillance project is crucial for ensuring privacy after the system is deployed and operated, until it is decommissioned. Designers are challenged by choices reflecting concerns from various aspects. Therefore, in order to include privacy in the design of video surveillance systems, a methodological approach is required to systematically address multidisciplinary concerns.

We aim at ensuring that the designed system supports both public security interests and minimal impact on individuals' privacy. Accountability mechanisms are further given specific attention to increase transparency and help reinforcing citizen rights in a surveillance society (or faced with surveillance systems). To achieve these goals, a methodology is defined based on a two-step process:

1. System owners[1] are first guided through a reflexive process to assess the legal/socio-contextual[2] and ethical opportunity of the system envisioned, i.e. to assess the necessity and proportionality of the technology in relation to the stated purposes. Assessment of the impact on individuals' privacy as framed under the *Seven Types of Privacy* terminology [13] is a key at that stage. This phase could lead to discard, validate or mitigate the options initially taken.
2. During the design process, designers[3] are referred to socio-contextual, ethical and legal considerations that should be taken into account in order to reduce the impact of the system on individuals' privacy. They are presented with state-of-the-art privacy preserving technologies to mitigate such impact and with accountability features to increase the level of transparency of the system and the traceability of the actions performed by such system.

The outcome of these two stages (opportunity assessment and system requirements) are documented in order to enable legal validation but also to enhance the transparency of the decision-making process.

Two pillars are defined to support the methodology:

– A decision support in the form of a knowledge base to assist the understanding of common concerns in complex and evolving environments and to facilitate the decision-making process. We identify the social-contextual, ethical, legal, and technological aspects as the most influential factors in the

---

[1] In this paper, system owners are defined as a legal entity (for basic systems, this can be a person or a group of persons) that has the ownership of the system (meaning its hardware and software components).

[2] We use the word "contextual" to emphasize the need to take into account local (at the country or regional level) perceptions of privacy and surveillance.

[3] We define system designers as the entities producing sufficient, coherent and testable specifications for a given system.

decision support, which is referred to as the SALT framework. The SALT framework is envisioned to provide a guidance for system designers to design and integrate privacy and accountability into the system and to enforce high level requirements in technical terms during the product lifecycle. § 4 describes the SALT framework.

– Processes associated with the SALT framework, which specify what knowledge should be included in the SALT framework, and how to use the knowledge to support the design of video surveillance systems that integrate privacy and accountability from the start, i.e., privacy-by-design and accountability-by-design. §. 5 describes the processes in details.

4   SALT Framework

The SALT framework is a collection of concepts and overarching principles concerning privacy including social-contextual, ethical, legal, and technical viewpoints. It is envisioned to be a reference for decision support during the design of video surveillance systems. The present section describes how to collect and synthesize knowledge from various views into the framework, and how to process and manage the knowledge in the framework.

4.1   Overview

The SALT framework relies on the SALT management tool, a set of computer programs that enable a user (a person acting for a surveillance system operator or a domain expert), to interact with concepts and information stored in the computer. The work on knowledge capture and management in the SALT framework is inspired from the principles and methods of knowledge engineering, in which building a knowledge-based system is regarded as a modelling process, i.e., constructing computer models for realizing problem-solving capabilities comparable to the ones of a domain expert [19].

Fig. 1 provides an overview of the SALT framework. It relies on literature and domain experts as knowledge sources. The literature includes academic research articles, legal texts, institutional and policy documents, and studies funded by the European Commission. In addition, a possible extension to the knowledge source can be the opinions of other stakeholders such as citizens and relevant associations and organisations. Initially, the domain experts are mainly the individuals creating the SALT framework. SALT knowledge is selectively captured in a number of ways that are deemed relevant. In this stage, experts' effort will be needed to evaluate the relevance of captured knowledge. Since SALT knowledge comes from different disciplines and individuals, work is also needed to identify links and synthesize knowledge coherently.

The analysed knowledge is transferred from textual description to defined models which facilitate the management of captured knowledge. In other words, models are structured, machine-readable presentations of information related to privacy and video surveillance. The SALT knowledge repository stores these models from various sources. The purpose of knowledge application is to assist system designers to apply the knowledge to solve similar problems in an efficient and correct way. In other words, given the information on a specific context such as legal system and surveillance project requirements, one can retrieve tailored references for decision support in system design phase. This specific information helps designers to take proper design decisions to develop surveillance systems and to enforce social, ethical, and legal requirements in technical terms such as appropriate access control models and the implementation of audit trails.

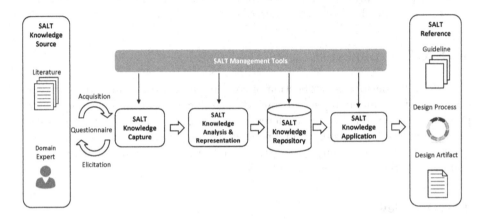

Fig. 1. Knowledge engineering in SALT framework

As a collection of knowledge from various sources, the SALT framework will be accessed and edited by different users in a cooperative way. Thus the role of the SALT management tools is to provide tool support for the creation, edition, search, and extraction of the knowledge in the SALT framework.

The SALT compliant design process is envisioned to ensure the proportionality of the surveillance purpose and of the system designed, by integrating privacy requirements into the design process according to the instantiated SALT framework.

For instance, the aspect of the design process focusing on accountability takes into account a number of aspects at different levels, involving corresponding disciplines. Its overarching goal is to encourage controllers into increased transparency. At the most general level, enabling accountability requires identifying all entities involved in the surveillance infrastructure, which data they have access to and under which conditions. The responsibilities of all actors in terms of protecting privacy and processing personal data in compliance with the data protection framework must also be clarified.

For the controller to be able to account for its policy, policies regulating data users should be transparent to Data Protection Authorities. This involves not only compliance with the legal framework but also the active demonstration of links between the privacy policy and the legal obligations to which they correspond to. This simplifies subsequent verification of legal policy compliance.

In addition, subjects must know what is recorded and which entities can access which recordings under which conditions. For instance, in some surveillance systems, massive amounts of recording channels exist with thousands of cameras deployed in urban areas. Thus multiple control centers are required to handle this kind of data production, making it extremely complex to identify all data flows, access authorizations, purposes of the data processing and ultimately to enforce the internal privacy policy of the organization. In such cases, the importance of accountability, i.e., of the transparency of the data processing operations as well as a proper allocation of responsibilities, is vital to mitigate privacy risks.

At a different but equally important level, appropriate procedures must be implemented. They involve integrating privacy concerns into business processes, carrying out PIA, appointing a Data Protection Officer who is responsible for ensuring internal compliance, training staff and carrying out periodic audits.

Finally, policies and procedures should translate into practice. Technical measures can help data controllers to demonstrate that their practices actually meet the requirements of the legal framework. In SALT compliant design process, this involves taking a closer look at the details of the entire data lifecycle, including the exact nature of recorded data, temporal parameters such as the maximal duration of storage and storage security (which may use cryptography). Because data is recorded in public spaces, there can be no one-on-one data handling policy negotiation between a subject and the controller. Instead, a representative of the public may defend the interests of individual subjects by globally negotiating privacy policies during the SALT complaint design process. Some traditional data protection principles, such as data minimization, may be difficult to apply in some cases, for instance when images are recorded. However, specific techniques, for instance the automatic blurring of faces, may be available to promote this principle. These techniques are a part of the possible design artifacts presented to system designs.

4.2 SALT Knowledge Management

In the initial phase, the knowledge input of the SALT framework mainly relies on systematic literature review and guided interview of domain experts. In the systematic literature review, a team of researchers and engineers from various disciplines has conducted a breadth-first survey of existing body of knowledge on privacy and surveillance. The scope of the survey covers psychosocial, social, political, ethical, legal, and computer engineering topics related to privacy in surveillance systems. Our literature review also includes topics on accountability-by-design, privacy-by-design, and PIA [14].

Another source of knowledge input comes from domain experts or other stakeholders through proactive elicitation. The elicitation process is conducted and guided by questionnaires. The questionnaires are carefully designed to capture knowledge related to specific aspects of the SALT framework. For example, our preliminary questionnaire for eliciting legal knowledge for surveillance systems include questions in three stages: (1) a preliminary assessment of legitimacy and overall proportionality of surveillance systems in relation to the stated purpose;

(2) the assessment of surveillance system following Article 29 Working Party guidance and Directive 95/46 principles; and (3) the assessment of balancing *stricto sensu*. The knowledge is captured in an iterative process, i.e., the analysis of the knowledge acquired will provide additional guidance on how knowledge is elicited by modifying the structure and content of the questionnaire.

The knowledge in the SALT framework must also be accessed and extended to account for the evolving nature of privacy concerns. In order to do so in an efficient and user-friendly way, the knowledge in SALT framework should be machine-readable, i.e. we need to transfer the knowledge into an appropriate computer representation such that a computer is able to work on it. The computer-readable representation of the SALT knowledge can be realised in various ways, depending on the type of technology and platform chosen. Typical examples include XML, JSON, or a Wiki-based structure. However, independently of the representation language and platform, it is important to have a high level definition of the structure and format of the SALT knowledge. From a computer engineering point of view, it is analogous to the definition of models for representing and processing information. In the case of the SALT framework, this model is what we call a *SALT template*. Whenever a piece of knowledge is added to the SALT framework, it follows the structure given by the SALT template, that is, we instantiate the SALT template according to the knowledge and then we store it. We name the result a *SALT instance* or a *SALT reference*[4].

The proposed SALT template must fulfil the following properties: (1) it must allow to differentiate each particular instance, (2) each instance must be uniquely identified, (3) it must prove the reliability of the information that it stores, (4) it must include the key information regarding the privacy or accountability concerns that it handles, and (5) it must provide a mechanism that allows for storing information coming from the four different categories, which may need different ways of handling the information.

In order to achieve these requirements, we have devised the structure depicted in Fig. 2. A SALT template contains several types of components. At the first level, it includes the instance information and the content. *Instance information* is unique to each SALT instance and is used to differentiate instances. An instance includes *Identification*, which identifies the SALT instance, typically an instance identifier or a version number; and *Trust information*, which is used to guarantee SALT information trustfulness. To ensure the integrity and authenticity of the reference information, trust mechanisms such as digital signatures, authority identifiers, certifications or trusted-party endorsements can be included. Another part of a SALT instance is the *Content* component, which stores the information related to the actual concerns. The content includes *Core information*, which identifies what type of concern is stored within the SALT instance, e.g. concern identifiers and concern categories, and *Extensions*, which provides the rationale and information related to a specific concern. For example, *Ethical extension* includes information on topics such as types of privacy likely to be

---

[4] In this paper, "SALT reference" and "SALT instance" will be used interchangeably since they refer to the same concept but reflect different disciplinary perspectives.

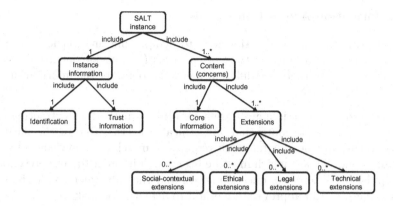

Fig. 2. Structure and components of SALT instance

impacted by the surveillance system, stakeholders who need the system, affected individuals' basic rights and so on.

Each new instance will include the information on the origin of the knowledge and the author(s) of the instance such that the content of the instance can be checked if necessary. Since decisions on privacy-related issues are results of specific contexts, such as the case of different interpretations of the same law, it is possible that there might be overlapping instances. A probable solution is to provide all related instances to system designers to help them to make a decision. Since concerns have different levels of specificity, for example, legal concerns usually depend on specific cases while social concerns can be linked to more general context, the SALT template is designed to be flexible enough to be useful for both specific and general cases.

5 SALT Process

Three independent processes are closely associated with the SALT framework and define how privacy concerns are captured, managed, and applied. The processes can be divided into two groups according to their purposes: SALT knowledge building processes and SALT knowledge use process. With SALT knowledge building processes, we decide what relevant information to take into account and how to integrate it into the SALT framework. For this purpose, two different processes are defined: *Information acquisition process* and *Information representation process*. SALT knowledge use process describes how information gathered by previous processes can be used to guide system designer during the system design phase. In the context of SALT framework, this process is called *SALTed design process*.

5.1 Information Acquisition Process

We define this process to describe how to acquire information for the SALT framework. Depending on the type of concerns (i.e., socio-contextual, ethical, legal and technical), there are different methods to gather the information.

Questionnaires. Questionnaires are a convenient method for extracting information regarding socio-contextual and ethical concerns. Due to the nature of these concerns, any meaningful result requires to match the knowledge of a sample group of individuals, which must be big enough in order to be representative of a population. Therefore, questionnaires, and the subsequent analysis of the obtained data, are an appropriate method to achieve this task.

Primary Sources. This method involves the systematic review of documents and reports for objective information, i.e. information that is less likely to be influenced by personal and subjective feelings and interpretations. Legal and technical concerns in the SALT framework are the ones that clearly benefit from this type of documentation. Numerous legal documents (constitutions, licenses, proclamations, statements, sureties, tax forms, treaties, etc.) and technical reports are widely accepted and trusted. They provide objective information and views to the SALT framework.

Secondary Sources. Apart from the two previous methods for information acquisition, domain experts can provide valuable input as a direct result of their own expertise in the form of personal opinions and decisions that may apply to ambiguous issues. For example, a lawyer could provide a possible interpretation of a given law applied to a determined context.

5.2 Information Representation Process

As its name states, this process handles the task of representing the information acquired from the information acquisition process. The information is modeled and stored in the knowledge repository. Therefore, the structure and format of a SALT instance is crucial, since they directly affect to the performance of the knowledge management. The modeling of a SALT instance is covered in §. 4.2.

5.3 SALTed Design Process

The SALTed design process designates the SALT reference usage process that will guide system designers in the design of a SALT compliant surveillance system. SALT compliance signifies that the system design process includes relevant privacy concerns and follows the guidelines specified by the SALT framework. It starts from the SALT instances selection and ends with the creation of a system design specification. The SALTed design process is designed in a way that makes it likely to be adopted by system designers (usually engineers or other technical staff) while minimizing interference with existing system design processes and workflows. Besides, in order to assess the reliability of the content provided by these experts, an evaluation mechanism might be created in the future to decide their level of expertise.

Tab. 1 presents use cases related to the SALTed design process. Use cases are commonly employed by software engineers to visualise a system architecture and to understand a system's main functionalities. A use case typically describes the interactions between an actor and a system. An actor in the use case represents the role of a user. We use the same approach to describe the various activities involved in the SALTed design process and the interactions of the users with the SALT framework. For each use cases, we identify the primary actor and describe its actions performed in the use case description. Note that the naming of the actor only reflects a user's role with respect to the SALT framework from a software engineering point of view.

Table 1. Use cases related to a SALTed design process

Use case	Description	Primary actor
SALT template modification	Modification of the formatting structure used to store SALT references (privacy and accountability related information) into a given repository	SALT authority
Creation of a SALT framework reference	Creation and storage (within a repository) of a standard SALT framework reference	Standards body
Extension of a SALT framework reference	Extension and storage (within a repository) of a standard SALT framework reference	Standards body
Creation of a SALT framework project reference (SFPR)	Creation and storage (within a repository) of a SALT framework project reference (references specific to a given project)	Project stakeholder
Surveillance system design	Design of an entire surveillance system	System designer
Providing technological components capabilities	Delivery of technical components capabilities	Technology provider

Note that we envision that at the beginning, the experts who initialise the SALT framework will assume the role of SALT authority. The Standards body could also be called "standards committee", which refers to persons with sufficient knowledge to create a SALT framework reference. They can be considered as experts in social-contextual, ethical, legal and technical concerns.

Based on the use cases specification, we use an activity diagram to show the interactions between the actors and their actions within the SALTed design process. The activity diagram in Fig. 3 depicts all actors and how their roles are

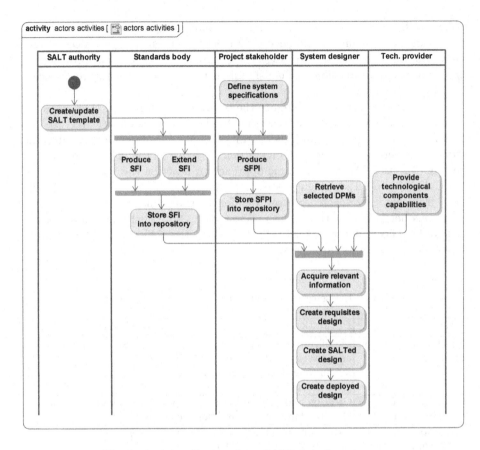

Fig. 3. Activity diagram for a SALTed design process

related. In general, the following activities can be involved in a SALTed design
process:

– First, a SALT template is created if it does not yet exist. If the SALT template is already available, it is necessary to check whether the template needs
  to be updated according to the new information that is going to be included
  in the repository. Therefore, the template will be updated when needed.
– Second, information is collected according to the fields specified in the template. As the template is a part of the SALT knowledge repository, the repository is populated with related knowledge by various actors. For example, the
  standard body can either create or extend existing knowledge, update and
  store this information, i.e. SALTed Framework Instances (SFIs), into the
  repository. The project stakeholder can specify system requirements (considered as high level system specifications), create and store this information,
  i.e. SALT framework project instances (SFPIs), into the repository. In addition, the technology provider can provide information on their component
  capabilities.

– Third, the system designer acquires the relevant information produced in the second step. Besides, the system designer can also include domain specific privacy knowledge represented as Domain Privacy Models (DPMs) in the SALT framework. A system design is created by the system designer. At first, a required system design without the SALT information is generated. Taking into account SALT information, then the system designer converts the design to a SALT compliant design. A final deployed system design is produced according to component capabilities and deployment scenarios. Note that the system design can be an iterative process.

6 Conclusion

We have presented a multidisciplinary approach to take into account privacy in the design of video surveillance systems. The SALT framework is a set of concepts, overarching principles, and knowledge relative to the social-contextual, ethical, legal, and technical aspects of surveillance, as well as concepts related to privacy-by-design and accountability-by-design. With the associated processes, the SALT framework serves as a decision support to assist system designer and other stakeholders in coping with complex privacy requirements in a systematic and methodological way.

The work performed so far has concentrated on the design of an architecture for the SALT Framework and reining the vision of the project. The forthcoming challenges include giving an adequate representation of social knowledge in a computer-readable format, as well as the development of tools to access, update and use the stored knowledge. The project aims at testing the methodology in two different settings: the design of a video surveillance system and a biometric system.

The approach presented here stems from the ongoing PrivAcy pReserving Infrastructure for Surveillance (PARIS) project [2]. The project gives us a unique opportunity to work together with researchers and engineers from different disciplines and backgrounds to address privacy in surveillance in a coherent way. Our interaction underlines contrasting approaches to privacy, even among consortium partners. This convinces us that a multidisciplinary approach, although sometimes difficult, is fruitful to systematically address privacy and cross-boundary issues.

Acknowledgement. This work was partially funded by the European Commission though the project PrivAcy pReserving Infrastructure for Surveillance (PARIS) with contract FP7-SEC-2012-1-312504. We thank all reviewers for their invaluable and detailed comments.

References

1. Increasing Resilience in Surveillance Societies (IRISS), http://irissproject.eu
2. PrivAcy pReserving Infrastructure for Surveillance (PARIS),
   http://www.paris-project.org
3. Surveillance, Privacy and Ethics (SAPIENT), http://www.sapientproject.eu

4. Surveillance, Privacy and Security (SurPRISE), http://surprise-project.eu
5. The VideoSense Network of Excellence, http://www.videosense.eu
6. Article 29 Data Protection Working Party: Opinion 3/2010 on the principle of accountability (2010)
7. Ashley, P., Hada, S., Karjoth, G., Powers, C., Schunter, M.: Enterprise Privacy Authorization Language (EPAL). Tech. rep. IBM Research (2003)
8. Butin, D., Chicote, M., Le Métayer, D.: Log Design for Accountability. In: 2013 IEEE Security & Privacy Workshop on Data Usage Management, pp. 1–7. IEEE Computer Society (2013)
9. Butin, D., Chicote, M., Le Métayer, D.: Strong Accountability: Beyond Vague Promises. In: Gutwirth, S., Leenes, R., De Hert, P. (eds.) Reloading Data Protection, pp. 343–369. Springer (2014)
10. Cavallaro, A.: Privacy in Video Surveillance. IEEE Signal Processing Magazine 24(2), 166–168 (2007)
11. Cederquist, J., Corin, R., Dekker, M., Etalle, S., den Hartog, J.: An Audit Logic for Accountability. In: Sahai, A., Winsborough, W. (eds.) Proceedings of the Sixth IEEE International Workshop on Policies for Distributed Systems and Networks, pp. 34–43. IEEE Computer Society Press (2005)
12. European Commission: Proposal for a Regulation of the European Parliament and of the Council on the Protection of Individuals with Regard to the Processing of Personal Data and on the Free Movement of such Data (2012)
13. Finn, R.L., Wright, D., Friedewald, M.: Seven Types of Privacy. In: Gutwirth, S., Leenes, R., Hert, P.D., Poullet, Y. (eds.) European Data Protection: Coming of Age, pp. 3–32. Springer (2013)
14. Gayrel, C., Trussart, N., Coudert, F., Maña, A., Jaime, F., Hidalgo, C., Casado, F., Ma, Z., Strobl, B., Hidalgo, V.M., Bossuet, M., Le Métayer, D., Kung, A., Jouvray, C.: PARIS Deliverable 2.1: Contexts and Concepts for SALT Frameworks, http://www.paris-project.org/images/Paris/pdfFiles/PARIS_D2.1_v1.0.pdf
15. Gill, M., Spriggs, A.: Home Office Research Study 292: Assessing the impact of CCTV (2005), https://www.cctvusergroup.com/downloads/file/Martin%20gill.pdf
16. Russo, S.: Digital Video Surveillance: enhancing physical security with analytic capabilities (2008), http://www-935.ibm.com/services/us/gts/pdf/sp_wp_digital-video-surveillance.pdf
17. Senior, A.W. (ed.): Protecting Privacy in Video Surveillance. Springer (2009)
18. Senior, A.W., Pankanti, S., Hampapur, A., Brown, L.M.G., ITian, Y., Ekin, A., Connell, J.H., Shu, C.F., Lu, M.: Enabling Video Privacy through Computer Vision. IEEE Security & Privacy 3(3), 50–57 (2005)
19. Studer, R., Benjamins, V.R., Fensel, D.: Knowledge Engineering: Principles and methods. Data Knowl. Eng. 25(1-2), 161–197 (1998)
20. Trabelsi, S., Njeh, A., Bussard, L., Neven, G.: PPL Engine: A Symmetric Architecture for Privacy Policy Handling. W3C Workshop on Privacy and data usage control (2010)
21. Webster, C.W.R., Töpfer, E., Klauser, F.R., Raab, C.D. (eds.): Video Surveillance: Practices and Policies in Europe. IOS Press (2012)
22. Wright, D., Gellert, R., Gutwirth, S., Friedewald, M.: Minimizing Technology Risks with PIAs, Precaution, and Participation. Technology and Society Magazine, IEEE 30(4), 47–54 (2011)

A Framework for Privacy Analysis of ICN Architectures

Nikos Fotiou[1], Somaya Arianfar[2], Mikko Särelä[2], and George C. Polyzos[1]

[1] Mobile Multimedia Laboratory, Athens University of Economics and Business,
Athens, Greece
{fotiou,polyzos}@aueb.gr
[2] Department of Communication and Networking, Aalto University,
Helsinki, Finland
{somaya.arianfar,mikko.sarela}@aalto.fi

Abstract. Information-Centric Networking (ICN) has recently received increasing attention from the research community. Its intriguing properties, including identity/location split, in-network caching and multicast, have turned it into the primary paradigm for many recent inter-networking proposals. Most of these are mainly concerned with core architectural issues of ICN including naming, routing, and scalability, giving little or no attention to *privacy*. Privacy issues however, are together with security, an integral part of any contemporary communication technology and play a crucial role for its adoption. Since the core functions of an ICN architecture are content name based, many opportunities for privacy related attacks–such as user profiling–are created; being aware of these privacy threats, users might completely dismiss the idea of using an ICN-based network infrastructure. Therefore, it is important to investigate privacy as an integral part of any ICN proposal. To this end, in this paper, we develop a privacy framework for analyzing privacy issues in different ICN architectures. Our framework defines a generic ICN model as well as various design choices that can be used in order to implement the functions of this model. Moreover it considers a comprehensive list of privacy attack categories, as well as various types of adversaries.

1   Introduction

Information-Centric Networking (ICN) is an emerging paradigm that has received increasing attention in recent years. ICN is believed to overcome various limitations of the current networking architectures, including inefficient mobility handling, lack of effective multicast, insecurity and distorted business environment. A key property of ICN architectures[1] is the use of content names as a new abstraction layer between applications and the network. In contrast to the IP model that relies on endpoints location and IP addresses, ICN relies on content names to provide the expected networking functionality. Communicating entities in ICN architectures reveal the name of the content to the network, either

---

[1] See [15] for a survey on ICN research efforts.

B. Preneel and D. Ikonomou (Eds.): APF 2014, LNCS 8450, pp. 117–132, 2014.

to make it available to others or to ask for the network to retrieve it. Using this information, it is believed, that the network can provide better services to networked applications and to interconnect different application domains [14].

This change in the communication model also changes the privacy model of the network [8]. Today, the network only sees the IP-address of entities that communicate with each other. A secure encrypted channel can be established in order to prevent the network from seeing what is actually being transmitted between endpoints. However, in an ICN based architecture, where users access the network using content names, the network should be able to recognize this information and use it in various networking functions. In addition to exposing the content name to the network, various forms of privacy threats can be created depending on the specific design and implementation choices.

Discussing these new forms of privacy threats, before anything else, requires the understanding of an ICN architecture and this includes the breaking down of the architecture into core components and the identification of the ways these components interact with each other. Since the ecosystem of ICN is composed by a significant number of heterogeneous architectures, defining a common model that captures all of them is not a trivial task. A significant part of this work is devoted to creating such a common and proposal-independent model of ICN design. This model identifies roles and functions that are common in many ICN proposals and presents various design choices for implementing these functions.

Understanding and modeling an ICN architecture is the first step towards its privacy analysis. However in order to reach this target another step is required: the identification and documentation of the privacy threats. To this end, we present a thorough list of privacy attacks categories, we define various adversary types and we use an existing methodology for documenting threats.

The reminder of the paper is organized as follows. We discuss related work in Section 2. We define a generic model of ICN and we present available design choices in Section 3. In Section 4, we discuss types of privacy attacks and adversaries and we use the DREAD [9] methodology to analyze privacy threats. In Section 5 we present various research efforts in the area of ICN privacy. Finally conclude our paper in Section 6

2   Related Work

To our knowledge privacy in ICN has only been discussed in a few other works, mainly by Lauinger et al. [11] and by Chaabane et al. [3]. Lauinger et al. [11] identify three privacy threats: *information leakage through caches, censorship* and *surveillance*. In the first type of attacks a malicious entity tries to learn which users are interested in a content item by requesting this item and by measuring the response time: small response times are an indication that the requested item has been cached close to the malicious entity. If caches are used at lower aggregation levels then the number of users that share a cache will be limited, therefore it might be possible to associate cached content items with the users that originally requested it. Moreover, censorship and surveillance attacks are possible since content items in ICN are uniquely identified, therefore it is easier for a privileged malicious entity to either block specific items or monitor the users that access specific items.

Chaabane et al. [3] identify four categories of privacy attacks related to: *caching, content, naming* and *signatures*. Similar to [11], cache privacy attacks exploit response times and–potentially–reveal the preferences of a group of users. Chaabane et al. distinguish the adversaries with respect to this kind of attack, into *immediate* neighbors and *distant* neighbors, with immediate and distant referring to the network distance between the adversary and the target. Content privacy attacks aim at monitoring and censoring users and they are facilitated by the fact that content is cached, therefore an attacker has more time to inspect the data. Name based privacy attacks are enabled due to the semantic correlation between the content and its name. These attacks are amplified by the fact that content name cannot be easily encrypted, because it is needed by the networking functions. Finally signature privacy attacks refer to attacks that target a content owner that has digitally signed content data in order to protect its *provenance*.

Both works by Lauinger et al. [11] and by Chaabane et al. [3] assume certain design choices, inspired by the NDN ICN architecture [10]. Although the same privacy threats may exist under different setups, their impact and their method of exploitation varies. Our work is not limited to particular design choices. On the contrary, we propose a generic model for ICN, we discuss various design choices and we argue how these design choices affect the feasibility and the impact of privacy attacks. The attacks described in these works are captured by our model and they are discussed in more detail. Moreover our model defines additional privacy threats and proposes a richer adversary model. Finally these works propose solutions for these attacks, based on the NDN ICN architecture. The goal of our paper is not to propose a specific security solution: its goal is to set the foundations of a privacy framework that will allow the assessment of a privacy risk and the measurement of the effectiveness of a privacy solution.

Any generic privacy analysis framework (e.g., [4]) can be used (with small or big modifications) for the privacy analysis of an ICN architecture. However, we believe that a framework tailored for this paradigm can accelerate this process and facilitate the detection of new privacy threats and of critical design choices.

3   An ICN Model

In this section we identify the main roles and functions that may exist in an ICN network. We then dicuss different design choices available to support the expected functionalities.

3.1   Roles and Functions in ICN

Generally an ICN architecture is composed of the following entities[2]

- (Content or information) Owner: The entity that creates and owns a content item. The owner is responsible for assigning names to content items and for creating (if necessary) access control rules that govern who can access each item. The role of owner captures real world entities (e.g., an author, a university, a company, a government)
- Consumer: The entity that is interested in receiving (access) a content item. A consumer is a real world entity that interacts with the network through a device (e.g., a computer, a mobile phone). In the rest of the paper when stated that a consumer interacts with the network, it is always meant through his access device.
- Storage node: A network entity that actually hosts a content item. A storage node may be under the full control of an owner (e.g., the web server of a university), but it may also be (semi-)independent (e.g., proxy caches and CDN servers). Storage nodes may either have been appointed by the owners themselves (e.g., a university may host a content item in its web server, or pay a CDN to host it), or may act opportunistically (e.g., an in-network cache).
- Resolver: A network entity that acts as an indirection point between consumers' devices and storage nodes. A resolver's main functionality is to accommodate consumers' interests for particular content items. All the resolvers of an architecture form the *resolution network*.

These entities interact with each other in the following manner: An owner creates a content item, assigns a *name* to it and stores a copy of this item in at least one storage node. The storage nodes *advertise* the content items they host. The advertisement of an item is received and kept by some resolvers in the network. A consumer sends a content *lookup* request that is routed through the resolution network and eventually reaches a resolver that has a matching entry for that item of interest. A successful match will ultimately result in the content being *forwarded* from a storage node to the interested consumer(s). Intermediate nodes may opportunistically *cache* a forwarded item, and act as additional storage nodes for that item in the future.

3.2   Design Choices for Content Naming

The choice of a naming structure for an ICN, depends on various properties expected from each naming scheme. Some basic properties include:

Security bindings. In ICN, the network has to ensure the *authenticity* of the content items. Therefore, the network–or some specific entity in the network– has to make sure that a name is associated with the correct content item. This requires either a direct or an in-direct binding between the content and its name. With a direct binding, the name or a part of the name is

---

[2] The terminology is not entirely standard because various architectures, designs and research efforts more generally, have different priorities.

cryptographically derived from the content. With an in-direct binding, the name is securely bound to an entity which can vouch for the rightfulness of the link between a content item and a name.

Human readability. Human readable names can be easily memorized by users. Usually they are of varying length, and because they are meaningful and distinguishable to the users some names become more popular than others. Thus, in some cases using human readable names require the existence of a naming assignment authority that handles various issues, such as, copyrights. Names that are not human readable, are usually of constant size and indistinguishable by users. Non-human readable names can be derived by using mechanisms such as (secure) hash functions. With these names usually a search engine-like mechanism is required, in order to map a human readable description to a content name.

Mutability. A content name can be mutable or immutable. Mutable names are short lived. When mutable names are used, mechanisms for finding the current name of a content item and for examining if this name is still valid, should be considered. Immutable names are long lived. When immutable names are used, entities that assign names may be required, otherwise the architecture may suffer from conflicts among owners who wish to use the same name for their different content.

Content to name mapping. The final property of a naming scheme concerns how many names can a content item have simultaneously. A content item may have multiple names or a single one. When an item has multiple names it may (or may not) be possible to tell if two names identify the same object or not.

3.3   Design Choices for Advertisement and Lookup

Content advertisement creates state in the resolution network that is used for routing content lookup messages to a storage node that hosts the desired item. The routing of the advertisement and lookup messages may be logically *coupled* or *decoupled* to the routing protocol of the architecture.

When advertisement and lookup are coupled to the routing protocol, the corresponding messages directly shape (and follow) the routing table entries of all routers all over the network. Content advertisements are flooded to the

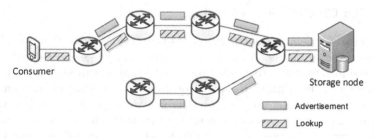

Fig. 1. Advertisement and lookup coupled to the routing protocol. All network routers act as resolvers.

whole network and create the routing state. Lookup messages are routed using this state to an appropriate storage node. When this design choice is used, the resolution network is formed by all network routers. Figure 1 gives an example of an ICN network, where advertisement and lookup are coupled to the routing protocol.

When advertisement and lookup are decoupled to the routing protocol the resolution network is implemented as a new overlay network. Content advertisements are routed in the overlay network until they reach a specific resolver that is responsible for handling the advertised content name; this resolver acts as the *rendezvous point* for this content name. The advertisement messages create state only in the rendezvous points. Content lookup messages are routed in the resolution network until they reach an appropriate rendezvous point; when a content lookup reaches the rendezvous point, the latter *notifies* a storage node. Figure 2 gives an example of an ICN network, where advertisement and lookup are decoupled from routing protocol.

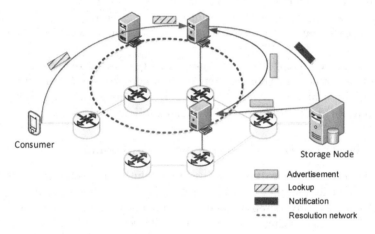

Fig. 2. Advertisement and lookup decoupled to the routing protocol. Resolvers are seperated entities organized in an overlay network.

3.4   Design Choices for Forwarding

A successful advertisement/lookup match leads to the desired content item being forwarded to the consumer. An ICN architecture can be geared towards using source-based forwarding or towards using hop-by-hop forwarding. In the former case, a storage node "learns" the path towards the consumer(s), and encodes it in a format that can be used by the intermediate nodes in order to take the appropriate forwarding decisions. The forwarded content items therefore should include this encoding in the header. When hop-by-hop forwarding is used data items are forwarded back to the consumer using the state that has been created during the lookup process: in this case every node that routes a lookup message maintains state that indicates the direction towards which the corresponding response should be forwarded. In this case, the forwarded content items should include in their header the same identifier as the one used during the lookup phase, and they should follow the same path as the lookup message.

4 Privacy Threat Analysis

In this section we present our privacy threat model. In this model two information containers are of importance *data flows* and *data pools*. A data flow concerns the data traversing the network in order to reach some endpoint(s) whereas a data pool concerns the data stored in a single node, usually used for facilitating networking operations and applications. Examples of data flows are advertisement messages, lookup messages, notifications, and forwarded items. Example of data pools is the state created in a resolver by the advertisement messages.

4.1 Adversaries

Adversaries may act on their own or collude with other entities. Adversaries in our framework are grouped by their *location, role,* and *mode of operation.*

With respect to the location an adversary can be *arbitrary* or *local.* An arbitrary adversary launches a privacy attack from an arbitrary point in the network. On the other hand a local adversary is located "close" to the target in terms of physical, network, or even social proximity. A malicious mobile phone in the same room as the target's laptop, a malicious default gateway, and a malicious consumer sharing the same interests with the target, all are examples of local adversaries.

An adversary can hold one or more of the following roles: *owner, consumer, storage node, resolver, observer,* or *authority.* The first four roles concern ICN roles and refer to ICN entities acting maliciously. An adversary holding the role of an observer is a third party that cannot actively participate in the defined procedures but has access to the data flows and data pools. An eavesdropper listening to the communication between a consumer and a resolver is an example of an adversary that has the role of the observer. An adversary that holds the role of the authority reflects an entity that either can administrate network elements of the architecture, or it is in position to dictate to some network elements how to behave. A resolver provider and a state government are two examples of adversaries that hold the role of the authority.

Finally adversaries may be *active, passive* or *honest-but-curious.* Active adversaries may change an information flow and/or a record in a data pool or completely remove it. Depending on the architecture and the particular implementation choices the actions of an active adversary may be *detectable* or *undectable.* As an example, if digital signatures are used in every information flow the manipulation of a data flow will be detectable with high probability. Passive and honest-but-curious adversaries simply observe data flows, and/or data pools, and/or *side channel* information (such as response times). The difference between a passive and honest-but-curious adversary is that the latter does not deviate from the specified protocols, whereas the former may violate them in order to achieve her goal (e.g., she may *impersonate* another entity).

How effective an adversary is into launching a privacy attack is highly affected by the number of the data flows and pools to which he has access, as well as, by the amount of information that is revealed by these flows and pools. Clearly this depends on the characteristics of the adversary, as well as, on the design choices that have been made.

4.2 Privacy Attacks

The terminology of the attacks considered in our framework is borrowed from Solove [13]. However, the taxonomy of the attacks has been modified (compared to [13]) and has been adapted to the context of ICN.

Privacy attacks can be grouped into *monitoring* attacks, *decisional interference* attacks and *invasion* attacks. An attack may belong to multiple groups.

Monitoring. Monitoring attacks aim at learning the preferences and interests of particular consumers, or the consumers interested in a particular content item (or group of items), or the types of content a particular owner offers, or the owners of a particular content item (or group of items). This goal can be achieved using the *surveillance* and *interrogation* attacks, the *identification* attack, and the *breach of confidentiality* and *disclosure* attacks.

Surveillance aims at collecting as much information about a target as possible. This information includes lookup messages, advertisements, forwarded items, as well as, side-channel information. Surveillance can be performed by passive or honest-but curious attackers (of any role) simply by monitoring data flows and pools or by active attackers that probe data pools (e.g., by requesting content from caches) or insert new data flows (e.g., repeat a lookup message). A surveillance attack can be supported (or amplified) by the interrogation attack. Interrogation aims at forcing targets into giving information in order to receive or take part in a service. Interrogation can be achieved for example by a resolver that requires owners to digitally sign their advertisements in order to be accepted. Malicious resolvers can potentially collect information using interrogation from specific owners and consumers, whereas malicious owners can potentially collect information using interrogation from specific consumers. An interrogation attack is more effective when the adversary behaves in an honest-but-curious manner.

Identification aims at linking collected information to a particular target. An identification attack aims at linking: a data flow to a consumer or to an owner, or data flows to each other (e.g., a lookup to a response). An identification attack can be launched by any attacker capable of collecting information.

Breach of confidentiality and disclosure are both related to the revelation of information regarding a target by a third party. Breach of confidentiality refers to the revelation of information about a target, stored in a (previously) trusted entity. The impact of this attack is dual: it reveals information about the target and it breaks a trust relationship. Revealing a list of consumers of a content item by a resolver constitutes such an attack. The entity that reveals this information may be the trusted entity itself, or another third party. A breach of confidentiality attack can be performed by an active attacker that interacts with the target trusted entity, or by any attacker that holds an ICN entity role.

Disclosure occurs when certain information about a target is revealed to others. The revealed information is in transit or stored in an untrusted entity (e.g., a cache). Therefore a disclosure attack does not involves the break of a trust relationship. An example of disclosure attack is the revelation that a consumer is interested in a particular content item, by an attacker that monitors the the communication channel between a consumer and a resolver. Disclosure attacks can be performed by an active or passive observer.

Decisional Interference. Decisional interference attacks may aim at one or more of the following: (i) preventing a particular consumer from accessing certain content items, (ii) preventing the advertisement or forwarding of content items belonging to certain owners, (iii) preventing the advertisement or forwarding of content items that have certain characteristics (e.g., censorship based on content identifiers or filtering based on file types). This goal can be achieved using the identification attack followed by the *insecurity* or the *distortion* attack.

The insecurity attack refers to the manipulation of a data pool that is possible due to the inefficiencies or vulnerabilities of the way it is maintained. In other words the insecurity attack exploits the fact that a data pool is not properly secured and therefore illegitimate information can be added, or legitimate information can be removed. An example of this attack is the manipulation of the state of a resolver in order to erase advertisements of certain content items. Insecurity attacks can be performed by active attackers that exploit weaknesses in the implemented protocols.

Distortion, on the other hand, aims at manipulating or deleting an information flow in order to hide a consumers lookup, or an advertisement or a forwarded content item. Therefore this attack "distorts" the profile of a consumer and presents her as she is not interested in a content item, or "distorts" the profile of a storage node and presents it as it does not "serve" an item. Any active attacker can launch this type of attacks.

Invasion. Invasion attacks affect privacy related information of a target in order to cause (not necessarily privacy related) harassment. In particular they aim at luring a consumer into requesting particular content items, force the forwarding of a content item to a consumer (not necessarily interested in that item), make a resolver associate a content item with a particular owner or storage node. Invasion is possibly using the *insecurity* and the *distortion* attacks, described previously, as well as using the *exclusion* and the *secondary use* attacks.

The insecurity attack is used in order to make a resolver believe that a consumer is interested in a particular content item, or that a storage node offers an item, or that an item belongs to a owner. The distortion attack is used in order to modify a lookup, or an advertisement or a forwarded item in order to refer to another content item, or consumer, or storage node, or owner.

Exclusion prevents a target from modifying or deleting an entry stored for him in a data pool. As an example if a consumer is not able to withdraw his interest on a specific content item, this may result in receiving items in which he is not interested in. Malicious resolvers maintain information about both consumers and owners therefore they may prevent them from modifying it. Similarly malicious owners may maintain information about consumers. Finally, active attackers, may *block* messages that aim at modifying stored information.

Secondary use, is the use of collected information for purposes unrelated to the purposes for which the information was initially collected without the target's consent. An example of this attack is the repetition of a lookup message. Any adversary that is able to collect information can potentially perform this attack.

Figure 3 illustrates the identified privacy threats.

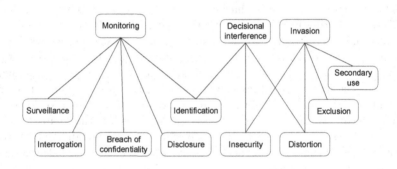

Fig. 3. ICN Privacy threats

4.3   Analyzing Threats

The ultimate goal of a privacy analysis is to identify and document privacy threats. The prerequisites for this step are: a model of the ICN architecture that specifies the design choices, a list of considered privacy attacks and a list of adversary types. Given this information threats can be ranked based on their feasibility and impact. The DREAD model [9] can be used to achieve this goal. DREAD is a threat ranking model, developed by Microsoft, that ranks threats based on their **D**amage, **R**eproducibility, **E**xploitability, **A**ffected users and **D**iscoverability.

Before proceeding with an example, we revisit the design choices, presented in Section 3, and for each choice we identify some properties that may affect a DREAD factor. This list is not exhaustive and does not consider combinations of choices.

Table 1. Privacy related properties of the design choices

Naming	
Direct security binding	Content items can be tracked more easily
Indirect security binding	Additional entities are required (therefore more potential adversaries)
Human readable	Names reveal more information
Human unreadable	Additional entities may be required
Mutable	Additional entities may be required
Immutable	Content items can be tracked more easily
Single name per item	Content items can be tracked more easily
Multiple names per item	Additional entities may be required
Advertisement, Lookup	
Coupled	Lookups and forwarded content may traverse the same nodes, any network router can be a potential resolver for a specific item
Decoupled	Resolvers have greater power, lookups should contain a consumer specific location identifier
Forwarding	
Source-based	Forwarded items contain information about how can a consumer be reached
Hop-by-hop	Forwarded items usually contain the content identifier

Let us now illustrate how DREAD model can be used in our framework using an example.

For each DREAD factor we use a scale from 1 to 5. Our setup is the following

- **Privacy threat:** Surveillance of the consumers of a specific content item
- **Design choices:** Advertisements and lookups are decoupled to the routing protocol, names are immutable, each content item is identified by a single name
- **Adversaries:** Arbitrary, honest-but-curious resolver

In this setup all lookups for a specific content identifier will end up in the same resolver. Since the content item is identified by a single name there will be a resolver for handling all requests for this content item. If the adversary happens to be that resolver then it is able to monitor *all* lookups for that content item. The **Damage** factor of this threat will receive therefore the highest rank (5). On the other hand, generally, it is not very easy for an attacker to make the resolution network to believe she is responsible of a particular content name (of course this is implementation specific, but we base this assumption considering how DNS and secure DHTs are organized), therefore the `Reproducibility` of the attack will not receive a high rank (1). In order for a malicious resolver to perform this attack it has simply to observe incoming lookups. Moreover lookups should contain a location identifier of the consumer therefore they can be relatively easily linked the to particular consumers. So `Exploitability` will also receive a high rank (4). This attack may potentially affect all the consumers of the content item. The number of these consumers depends on the popularity the item. Therefore `Affected users` will receive an indicative rank (3). Since this is a passive attack, it cannot be easily discovered. However if it is discovered, it is easy to decide which resolver performed it. Therefore, `Discoverability` will receive a medium rank[3] (2). The following table summarizes our assessment.

Table 2. DREAD ranking

Damage	Reproducibility	Exploitability	Affected users	Discoverability
5	1	4	3	2

Let's now modify the design choices of the ICN architecture and examine how the ranking is of this privacy threat is affected. We now consider a setup with the same threat and adversary model but with the following design choices:

– `Design choices`: Advertisements and lookups are **coupled** to the routing protocol, names are immutable, each content item is identified by a single name

When advertisements and lookups are coupled, lookups use the routing plane. Therefore, in contrast to the previous scenario it is not likely that all lookups for a specific content will be routed through the same resolver. The `Damage` factor of this threat will receive a lower rank (2). On the other hand, compared to the previous setup, it is easier for a resolver to make the resolution network to believe that it knows a route to a particular content name therefore the `Reproducibility` of the attack will receive higher rank (3). As in the previous setup, in order for a malicious resolver to perform this attack it has simply to observe incoming lookups. However in this setup lookups contain only the next hop to the consumer, so additional information is required in order to link a lookup to a consumer. Therefore `Exploitability` will receive a lower rank (3). The design choices do not affect the popularity of the item, therefore `Affected users` will receive the same indicative rank (3) . Finally, again this attack cannot be easily discovered. However even if it is discovered, it is not easy to detect which resolver performed it. Therefore, `Discoverability` will receive higher rank (3). Table 3 summarizes the assessment for this setup.

---

[3] The Discoverability rank indicates how hard is to detect a threat: the higher the rank the harder is to detect a threat.

Table 3. DREAD ranking

Damage	Reproducibility	Exploitability	Affected users	Discoverability
2	3	3	3	3

Although subjective, the DREAD ranking gives an indication how the design choices affect the privacy properties of an ICN architecture. In the studied case, if it is assumed that all DREAD factors are equally wighted it can be concluded that the second design choice has better privacy properties w.r.t. to the specific threat model.

5   ICN Privacy Research

Various research efforts have highlighted privacy issues in ICN architectures and they have proposed solutions to address them.

DiBenedetto et al. [5] proposed a Tor-like *anonymization* network for the NDN ICN architecture [10] code-named ANDaNA. In ANDaNA, before sending a lookup request, a consumer selects two "anonymizing routers", the entry router and the exit router, and distributes different symmetric encryption keys to each of them. The consumer encrypts her request using the public keys of the routers, and sends the request to the entry router, which then forwards it to the exit router. When the exit router receives a response, it encrypts it using the symmetric key has been provided by the consumer, and forwards it to the entry router. Then the entry router encrypts once more the received ciphertext with its own symmetric key (that has been provided by the consumer) and forwards the response to the consumer. Finally, the consumer decrypts the response. ANDaNa protects consumers against *surveillance* and *distortion* attacks, since their lookups and the corresponding responses are encrypted and their integrity is checked (although additional measures are required in order to detect deleted lookups or forwarded items). The proposed scheme offers protection against malicious storage nodes and observers. A malicious resolver that happens to be the entry router learns the identity of the consumer and the identifier of the item in which she is interested in, whereas a malicious resolver which happens to be the exit router learns the content item identifier and potentially its data. The former resolver is able to perform distortion and possible surveillance, whereas the latter resolver is able to perform decisional interference.

Arianfar et al. [2] proposed a solution that offers *pseudonymity* of content names for the PURSUIT [6] architecture. In their approach an owner splits the file she wants to protect into n blocks, t_1, t_2,..., t_n, and creates a "cover file" with n blocks (c_1, c_2, ..., c_n). All file blocks, and the corresponding cover file blocks, are assumed to have the same length. Then, the owner applies a reversible randomizing function r() to every block and advertises all the (randomized) blocks of the cover file (i.e., $r(c_1)$, $r(c_2)...r(c_n)$) as well as chunks that are created by XORing a (randomized) file block with a (randomized) covered file block (e.g., $r(t_1)$ XOR $r(c_2)$, $r(t_3)$ XOR $r(c_1)$). For a consumer to receive a file block she has to lookup for to the appropriate cover file blocks and chunks (e.g., in order to receive t_1 she must perform a lookup for to $r(c_2)$ and to $r(t_1)$ XOR $r(c_2)$, and then she will be able to compose t_1, simply by XORing the received packets). The name used for the ith advertised block of the cover file c is $H(H(c), i)$, where H is a well known function. The name used for an advertised chunk, composed by XORing the kth block of the cover file with the lth file block of a file t is $H(H(c), k, H(t), l)$. A consumer learns through a secured channel the function $H()$ and the number of blocks, therefore she is able to perform lookups for any combination of files. An attacker on the other hand, is not able to determine the file that in which a consumer is interested in. Providing that the cover file is updated often enough, the proposed solution protects consumers and owners from *surveillance* by malicious observers, since the content identifiers used for both advertisement and lookup are scrambled. Moreover, this solution offers protection against *insecurity* and *distortion* attacks, targeting specific content item identifiers. However a malicious resolver is able to determine the owner with which a consumer interacts and vice versa.

Fotiou et al. [7] proposed a solution that offers *unobservability* of data flows for the PURSUIT architecture. The unobservability property assures that it is not possible to associate a data flow with a particular content item. The proposed solution is based on the homomorphism property of the Paillier cryptosystem [12], which allows operations over encrypted data by a 3rd party without revealing to that 3rd party any information associated with this data. The approach is based on a query/response model in which a consumer defines a linear equation over a set of content item identifiers and a resolver solves this equation. The result of this equation is the location identifier of the item in which the consumer is really interested in. Nevertheless, the resolver is unable to interpret the result as it is encrypted with a key that is known only to the consumer. The solution completely hides consumer preferences from observers and resolvers, therefore, it protects consumers from *surveillance*. Moreover the proposed scheme performs integrity checks and prevents lookup repetitions, thus protecting consumers from *distortion* and *secondary use* attacks.

Many recent works, study the problem of consumer *surveillance* by malicious observers using as a side-channel information the response time of a content lookup. Lauinger et al.[11] as well as Acs et al.[1] assess this problem in the context of NDN. In NDN a local cache in an access network is often populated with the items accessed by a few users in its vicinity. In this case if an adversary can figure out which items have been cached, it can easily associate those items with a certain group of local consumers. Chaabane et al.[3] point out that specific protocol details can increase the chances of cache tracing in NDN. Specifically, NDN's prefix-based content request and delivery means that an adversary can just ask for a certain prefix and the cache would return any available item with that prefix. There are different solutions suggested in [11,1,3] to overcome the problem of tracing the cache access pattern. These solutions can be divided into two different categories: first, affecting the access pattern or the cache structure, and second, changing the content or its name and affecting the cacheability of each item. Access patterns can be obfuscated for privacy considerations, e.g. through adding random delay to the data that is served from a cache, or through caching only the items that have been accessed at least K times. The cache structure can be affected using collaborative caching and by increasing the size of the user-set for each cache. The cachebility of private items can be affected by creating new, user-specific, names or by flagging the content item as being private and not cacheable.

6 Conclusions

ICN is an intriguing networking paradigm receiving growing attention. However, being name oriented, ICN raises privacy concerns, which unfortunately have not been tackled by the research community. Privacy analysis of ICN is impeded by the lack of a privacy analysis framework, which is mainly due to the departure from the traditional end-host oriented communication model, as well as to the multitude of different ICN architectures.

In this paper we developed a generic, solution independent, model of an ICN architecture and we highlighted the design choices that can be made for implementing its functions. We believe that most ICN architectures can be mapped onto this model. Moreover, we presented a thorough list of categories of privacy attacks, as well as a comprehensive adversary model. These tools can be used for identifying and ranking privacy risks in existing and future ICN architectures.

Future work in this domain includes the expansion of our model in order to include even more design choices, threats and adversary types, as well as the application of our model to evaluate the privacy properties of specific ICN proposals.

Acknowledgment. This research was supported by a grant from the Greek General Secretariat for Research and Technology, financially managed by the Research Center of AUEB.

References

1. Acs, G., Conti, M., Gasti, P., Ghali, C., Tsudik, G.: Cache privacy in named-data networking. In: The 33rd International Conference on Distributed Computing Systems, ICDCS (2013)
2. Arianfar, S., Koponen, T., Raghavan, B., Shenker, S.: On preserving privacy in content-oriented networks. In: Proc. ACM SIGCOMM Workshop on Information-Centric Networking (ICN), pp. 19–24 (2011)
3. Chaabane, A., De Cristofaro, E., Kaafar, M.A., Uzun, E.: Privacy in content-oriented networking: threats and countermeasures. SIGCOMM Comput. Commun. Rev. 43(3), 25–33 (2013)
4. Deng, M., Wuyts, K., Scandariato, R., Preneel, B., Joosen, W.: A privacy threat analysis framework: supporting the elicitation and fulfillment of privacy requirements. Requirements Engineering 16(1), 3–32 (2011), http://dx.doi.org/10.1007/s00766-010-0115-7, doi:10.1007/s00766-010-0115-7

5. DiBenedetto, S., Gasti, P., Tsudik, G., Uzun, E.: Andana: Anonymous named data networking application (2012)
6. Fotiou, N., Nikander, P., Trossen, D., Polyzos, G.C.: Developing information networking further: From psirp to pursuit. Tech. rep. (2012)
7. Fotiou, N., Trossen, D., Marias, G., Kostopoulos, A., Polyzos, G.C.: Enhancing information lookup privacy through homomorphic encryption. Security and Communication Networks (2013)
8. Ghodsi, A., Shenker, S., Koponen, T., Singla, A., Raghavan, B., Wilcox, J.: Information-centric networking: seeing the forest for the trees. In: Proceedings of the 10th ACM Workshop on Hot Topics in Networks, HotNets 2011, pp.1:1–1:6. ACM, New York (2011), http://doi.acm.org/10.1145/2070562.2070563, doi:10.1145/2070562.2070563
9. Howard, M., LeBlanc, D.: Writing Secure Code, 2nd edn. Microsft Press (2002)
10. Jacobson, V., Smetters, D.K., Thornton, J.D., Plass, M.F., Briggs, N.H., Braynard, R.L.: Networking Named Content. In: Proc. ACM CoNEXT (2009)
11. Lauinger, T., Laoutaris, N., Rodriguez, P., Strufe, T., Biersack, E., Kirda, E.: Privacy risks in named data networking: what is the cost of performance? SIGCOMM Comput. Commun. Rev. 42(5), 54–57 (2012)
12. Paillier, P.: Public-key cryptosystems based on composite degree residuosity classes. In: Stern, J. (ed.) EUROCRYPT 1999. LNCS, vol. 1592, pp. 223–238. Springer, Heidelberg (1999)
13. Solove, D.J.: A taxonomy of privacy. University of Pennsylvania Law Review, pp. 477–564 (2006)
14. Trossen, D., Särelä, M., Sollins, K.: Arguments for an information-centric internetworking architecture. SIGCOMM Computer Communication Review 40(2), 26–33 (2010)
15. Xylomenos, G., Ververidis, C., Siris, V., Fotiou, N., Tsilopoulos, C., Vasilakos, X., Katsaros, K., Polyzos, G.C.: A survey of information-centric networking research. IEEE Communications Surveys Tutorials 99, 1–26 (2013)

Auctioning Privacy-Sensitive Goods:

A Note on Incentive-Compatibility

Nicola Jentzsch

DIW Berlin, Mohrenstrasse 58, 10117 Berlin

Abstract. One mechanism to obtain valuations of personal data from individuals is the reverse second-price Vickrey auction (RVA), which is assumed to be an incentive-compatible mechanism. Herein, it is analyzed whether conditions for RVA incentive-compatibility exist, once personal data is sensitive and induces privacy costs. In the experiment subjects could sell the result of a logic test together with their name as privacy-sensitive good using an auction mechanism. The winner's identity and result was revealed to the group. The key result is that a significant 'identification effect' exists that acts as auction entry barrier. Thus, the RVA is not an incentive-compatible mechanism for obtaining valuations of privacy-sensitive goods.

Keywords: Privacy, information sharing, data protection.

1   Introduction

The right price for personal data is a field of much controversy. There is a trend in the privacy economics literature to increasingly use the reverse Vickrey auction (RVA) in order to obtain valuations of personal data from individuals. In a RVA, bidders submit sealed bids, where the lowest bid is the clearing price. As the presented auction is a second-price procurement auction, the winner is paid the price reflected in the second lowest bid, which ensures a premium for the seller. This mechanism is claimed to be incentive-compatible (IC) under specific conditions, meaning that the revelation of truthful valuations is a dominant strategy of the player. If the mechanism is not IC it is a biased estimate of the valuation. Obtaining truthful valuations of personal data profiles is an important question in today's Internet business, because an increasing number of platforms on the Internet allow the sale of personal data profiles to firms. Some of these platforms involve the data subjects directly (such as mint.com, Personal, Allow Ltd.).[1] Some, such as myID.com, allow people to create lockers, i.e. accounts with personal data, which can be sold to interested parties. The Belgium platform Jini provides a direct auction mechanism, where consumer can sell personal data.

Others only indirectly involve consumers, among them BlueKai, an auction-based exchange platform in the U.S., which aggregates user data from surfing and shopping

---

[1] The websites are www.mint.com; https://www.personal.com/; and http://i-allow.com/. See also Brustein, J. (2012). Start-Ups Seek to Help Users Put a Price on Their Personal Data, New York Times, February 12, 2012, https://www.nytimes.com/2012/02/13/technology/start-ups-aim-to-help-users-put-a-price-on-their-personal-data.html?_r=0

B. Preneel and D. Ikonomou (Eds.): APF 2014, LNCS 8450, pp. 133–142, 2014.

activities and sells these to ad networks and marketers.[2] In the U.S., it is reported that privacy groups already started to petition the Federal Trade Commission to establish some oversight over data auctions.[3] In 2012, Congress started to investigate data brokers. Moreover, at the European level, the new Horizon 2020 calls ask for additional research on the valuation of personal data.

These trends aside, there is an increasing number of research works in the area of the economics of privacy that use second price RVAs in order to obtain valuations of individuals. In general, it is assumed that the RVAs are IC and thus render truthful valuations of personal data. This question is analyzed empirically in this paper with the main focus on auction entry barriers.

The main motivation is to evaluate whether basic conditions for IC exist and are reflected empirically once the data concerned is in fact personal, private and sensitive, i.e. if it is a privacy-sensitive good. These are necessary conditions for the creation of privacy costs (i.e. costs associated with the disclosure of personal data), which may impact on auction participation whenever the data owner is the data subject. This is of interest insofar as detailed consumer profiles allow social comparisons and these are at the very core of filtering (financially) worthy individuals in micromarketing. For Internet platforms in the real world auction entry barriers may evolve into a self-selection mechanism.

I present a reverse second-price Vickrey auction in which individuals can sell the result of a logic test they conducted in the laboratory together with their name (the so-called personal profile). The comparison of treatments shows a robust 'identification effect': as soon as all participants need to identify themselves before entering the auction, information sensitivity impacts on participation.[4]

Moreover, most of the conditions for IC in RVA do not hold, because of the good sold is inherently different from traditional auction goods. Linked with the above discussion on market places, it is doubtful whether an auction mechanism can be introduced for a market place involving consumers and sensitive data directly. At the broader scale, this research refutes claims that individuals do not value their privacy.

2   Literature Discussion

In economics, there is virtually no experimental literature on auctions of personal profiles, while there is a lot on revelation of private valuations and bidding mechanisms. The main and obvious difference to the canonical auction literature is that in an auction of personal data, the sellers sell information about their identity, i.e. personal information and the valuation of that personal data. Thus, the auction object is not an economic good in the traditional sense (like a painting): In fact it is a differentiated good, because personal information varies qua definition from person to person.

Information in general has public good features (non-excludability and non-rivalry). Moreover, personal data is not even like traditional information goods:

---

[2] See http://www.bluekai.com/

[3] Worley, B. (2010). Cyberspace Wild West? Advocates Want Limits on Online Personal Info Profiling, April 16, 2010, http://abcnews.go.com/GMA/ConsumerNews/restrictions-sought-internet-data-profiling/story?id=10389313

[4] The impact on price-setting behavior is part of a separate follow-up research project.

identification and thus personalization gives rise to a variety of psychological effects, one of which is the concern about reputation. This concern does not exist for information goods such as newspapers, DVDs, etc. Therefore, it is more precise to speak about *privacy-sensitive goods*. In the privacy economics literature, there are a number of papers that use RVAs to obtain valuations of individuals with respect to such goods ([1, 2, 3, 4]).

One of the first papers (to the knowledge of the author) implementing an IQ test in the laboratory was [5]. In an economics setting, another implementation was conducted later by [6]. In [3] the logic tests are associated with verified personal names of subjects, who then could sell the data. However, the most closely related experimental papers are [1], [4]. In [1] the researchers lead participants to believe that they take part in a sealed-bid second price auction of having their location monitored (via mobile phone) over a month's time. The researchers were interested in the valuation individuals attached to locational privacy. The study worked with a sample of 74 students and showed that the median bid was £10 with a distribution from less than a pound to £400. The bids were higher for those more often travelling outside of Cambridge, where the study was conducted. This indicates some sensitivity of the locational information.

In [4] a reverse second price auction is used to obtain the private value for weight and age information. Note that the participants in that experiment remained anonymous. However, neither age nor weight are entirely private information, both can be derived approximately by looking at a person. Still this work was a motivator for the present paper: the authors show that deviation from the group's mean (in age and weight) asymmetrically impacts the price demanded for the information.

In the theoretical literature, the most closely related works are those of [7] and [8]. In the former, it is discussed that bidding in an auction comes with privacy costs, which emerge with the revelation of individual valuations (bids) to the auctioneer. Privacy costs also emerge if the bidder does not win the auction such that it introduces negative payoffs for losing bidders. We will see that in the experiment presented herein, identification constitutes exactly such costs.[5] The authors model a reverse first-price and a RVA with privacy costs. They show that if (a) bidders are risk-neutral, (b) valuations are i.i.d.,[6] (c) privacy costs are monotonically increasing functions of estimated valuations; and (d) bidding strategies are monotonically increasing, no dominant strategy for a bidder exists in either auction. Further, privacy costs influence the Nash equilibrium strategies and result in lower bids and lower expected revenue. It depends on the situation, who is ending up with bearing the privacy costs. If bidders behave like in a standard auction, privacy costs are absorbed into their payoffs. If the bidder, however, decreases the value of the bid due to privacy costs, then the seller bears the costs; therefore, the equilibrium strategies will determine distribution of privacy costs.

There is a more technical stream of literature on cryptographic auctions devoted to ensure secure design through privacy-preserving mechanisms [8] and differential privacy.[7] As example only one paper will be mentioned here for reference. In [8] a protocol for a sealed-bid second price auction is suggested, where the auctioneer obtains a minimum of

---

[5] This means that both identification and revelation of valuation are privacy costs.

[6] Independent and identically distributed.

[7] See also the works of [9] and [10].

information: the identity of the winner and the clearing price.[8] To obtain a privacy-preserving auction, the authors suggest a protocol, where an auction issuer computes the auction. The aforementioned identity and clearing price aside, the auctioneer neither obtains the identity of the second-highest bidder nor of all other (loosing) bids.

3   Theoretical Considerations

Traditional auctions involve physical, private goods that are undifferentiated and indivisible. RVA is then IC for private goods with valuations i.i.d. and risk neutral bidders. Moreover, the valuations of bidders are not correlated, meaning that a bidder's valuation of the auction object does not depend on what others know.

If the auctioneer is blindfolded as typical in sealed-bid auctions, no privacy costs arise. Under these circumstances RVA is an IC mechanism and the same holds for the well-known Becker-DeGroot-Marschak mechanism. In the latter, people bid against a random price generator. If the price submitted is greater than the randomly drawn price, they obtain the good and pay the price drawn. If the counter-case occurs, the individual does not receive the good and makes no payment.

Unfortunately, an auction involving privacy-sensitive goods is a completely different animal. As noted above, in such an auction information is traded, which contains public good features, some of which might be reduced through a specially designed auction protocol. Moreover, it is a differentiated good that is divisible at the same time. It is also not a single-unit good, but often contains personally identifiable information (identity) and additional information creating an information bundle. In order to be able to ascertain that it is a seal-bid auction, the auctioneer needs to be blindfolded. But in this case, no personal information is created, because participants are anonymous. If identity information is generated, the auctioneer is not blindfolded anymore. Thus, theory needs to take the information revelation structure into account: with respect to the auctioneer and the group in the lab. This again, makes privacy-sensitive goods special. Finally, it is questionable whether valuations of such goods that at the same time allow social comparisons are drawn from a symmetric distribution and can be considered i.i.d.

In addition to the above, if the auction object is a lottery the price paid for it is uncertain. Neither BDM nor RVA are IC under the latter [11].

The experimental design gives rise to the following expected utility function,

$$EU = \begin{cases} p(v_k(i^t) - c_k^t) \\ 1 - p(-c_k^t) \end{cases} \tag{1}$$

where p is the probability of winning the auction rendering $v_k(i^t) - c_k^t$ as the valuation of subject k with respect to the information on type i^t with t being the relative ranking in the group minus the costs of subject k. In the case the auction is not won by the subject, the payoff is $1 - p(-c_k^t)$. The latter term denotes the privacy costs as explained in [7]. Herein, privacy costs can be assumed to be differentiated and depend

---

[8]   In a reverse second price auction it is the second lowest price.

on the result of the logic test. It may be assumed that c_k^t increases with the relative performance of the subject.

While there is the problem of over-bidding, once people have to bid against others, they behave more rationally [12].

4   Experimental Design

In the following, I describe the experimental design, where subjects were fully informed about the procedures through the instructions they obtained. The subjects' first task in the experiment was the conduct of a logic test, similar to an intelligence test. The information is sensitive insofar as it is correlated with academic performance [13]. We used questions from an intelligence test, though, but did not conduct a full-fledged IQ test as it would have taken much longer and an IQ score is a complex calculation based upon age of peers, etc.

After conducting the test, individuals were privately informed about their test result and the distribution of results in the group. This allows social comparison. The latter information was common knowledge, anonymous and the same for all subjects. The test was incentivized, were subjects obtained 50 Euro Cents per correct answer.[9] Next the participants could sell their result together with their name in a RVA. Note, again, that the test result is connected to the name of a person and only both can be sold together. Therefore, it constitutes personalized information.[10] The winner of the auction was revealed to the group with his/her name and the test result. The auction used the mechanism of selecting of the lowest bid as winner, where the second lowest bid is paid to the winner. If two winners had submitted the same price, a random draw selected the winner. Thus, the auction offered the possibility to obtain an extra monetary amount.

4.1   Identification and Privacy Concerns

Privacy costs introduced in an auction (typically because of the auctioneer obtaining all valuations) lead to the problem that losing bidders have a negative payoff. In this case, theory preliminarily holds that there is no dominant strategy [7]. So privacy costs arise under the following conditions:

    (a) Subjects cannot lie about their identity;
    (b) Subjects cannot lie about the information involved; and
    (c) The information concerned is sensitive.

All of these conditions were fulfilled in the experimental design. The experimental protocol was such that the lab assistants checked all names of individuals, once typed into the respective field on the computer screen. Subjects were instructed that they

---

[9] The test had 22 questions, which needed to be answered within 17 minutes. Subjects could obtain 11 Euros from the test by answering all questions correctly. Wrong answers were not punished.

[10] I use the legal definition of personal information based upon the EU Data Protection Directive, Art 2 (a).

would not obtain the payoff once they lied about their information. Moreover, individuals could not manipulate the test score. Only personal data that is truthful allows identification of individuals and creates privacy concerns. Thus, secure identification is a precondition for raising privacy concerns. As the results show below, the typing of the name renders the test result as sensitive information for bad performers. It is an accomplishment of the experimental design presented herein (originally developed for setting discounts in [3] to create information that is not useful outside the laboratory, but still sensitive for the participants.[11]

4.2   The Treatments and Payoffs

In order to test for identification effects, and thus existence of privacy costs (c_k^t), the following treatments were used. The stimulus is the variation of the identification mechanism.

Treatment 1: First, the subjects conducted the test. They received truthful information about their result and the distribution of the results. Next, they could sell this information linked to their name in the auction. The auction winner had to type his/her name into a field on the computer screen. Lab assistants verified the name by comparing it with the subject's national identity card or student card. Subjects were informed that if they lied about their name they would not obtain the gain from the auction.[12]

Treatment 2: The procedures were exactly the same as in treatment 1, except for one modification. This time all auction participants had to type their name into a field when participating in the auction. Just as above, only the auction winner was identified.

We informed the subjects that after the end of the experiment, their names would be erased from the files and data would be kept anonymously.

Altogether subjects could earn a show-up fee (5 Euros), the profit from the logic test (11 Euros at maximum) as well as the profit from the auction in case of winning it. We also used entry and exit questionnaires in order to obtain demographic information on our subjects. Moreover, we tested with a quiz, whether they had understood the instructions, especially the auction. For example, they were asked under what conditions they would win the auction. We also collected a number of other variables such as motivation to perform well on the test, and how strongly they cared for the result of the test.

5   Econometric Evidence

The sample consists of 216 students and University employees drawn randomly from the experimental pool of the Technical University of Berlin. The sessions were run over several months during 2012. Subjects were randomly assigned to their places

---

[11] For example, the author could have not collected credit card numbers or verifiable health information.

[12] Both types of cards carry the picture of the person. Participants bring such documentation to the lab sessions as it is part of the procedure to check who showed up for the experiment.

and they were fully informed about the procedures through instructions. Table 1 in the Appendix presents the summary statistics of our sample. Of particular interest is the explanation of the variation of the entry into the auction (variable termed *'Logic test result sold'*), which acted as dependent variable.

5.1   Bivariate Analysis

Bivariate correlations show that there is a weak positive correlation of the test result and the sale of the name and test result, i.e. the participation in the auction. The Point Biserial Correlation (PBIS) is Coef. = 0.2670 at $p>|t|= 0.0001$ based upon the whole sample, containing observations from both treatments. This correlation becomes stronger, if only treatment 2 observations are considered (PBIS Coef. = 0.3699 at $p>|t|= 0.0001$). In treatment 2, all subjects participating in the auction, not only the winner, had to identify themselves by typing their name into a field on the computer screen. Next, we explore multivariate relationships at the individual level through regression analysis.

5.2   Logit Model: Test Performance and Auction Entry

First a logit model is used to explore the relationship of test performance and auction participation, where intuition holds that good performers ought to have a greater inclination to participate in the auction. The intuition is that for good performers type information is less sensitive. The dependent variable is a dummy (participation or not), violating common OLS conditions. We estimated various specifications of the baseline logit model with and without treatment effects (see Table 2), also exchanging predictors (not reported). The result that the test outcome is significantly and positively associated with auction entry is robust. The parameter estimate shows an increase in the predicted log odds of *Logic test result sold*, which is predicted by a one unit increase in the *Logic test result* variable holding all other factors constant. If the coefficients are exponentiated, they can be interpreted as odd-ratios (output not extra displayed). So for a unit-increase in the test result the odds of participation in the auction (versus non-participation) is raised by a factor of roughly 1.23.

The comparison with the robust models shows that parameter estimates on the coefficient of *Logic test result* do not change much. Such re-estimation of the model with the robust option is a test of whether the correct functional form has been chosen.

In the whole sample, the subjects' test results are positively and significantly related to the increase in the odds of entering the auction. If we only take the sample of treatment 1, where only the winner was identified, this relationship disappears. This is intuitive insofar as the identification of the winner only (in the auction) does not raise privacy concerns of (all) participants, *which an identification of all in turn does*.

We are aware that the identification in treatment 2 is for most only towards the experimentalist and not the public, because subjects knew that only the winner is 'called out'. However, this does not lower the informativeness of the result that at the individual level, where an increase in test performance raises the inclination to enter the auction and sell the data. Identification for private data that yields a 'bad picture' in a social comparison, however, acts as an entry cost for auction participation.

It has been stated that the incentives for an individual to bid optimally in a second-price auction are rather weak due to the low probability of winning the auction, which reduces the expected payoff to virtually zero [14]. However, the same authors show that such a weak incentive is not the case if valuations are extreme or individuals bid against others with valuations drawn from particular distributions, such as the right-skewed distribution. This distribution is the case for the bids submitted in this experiment.[13]

All in all, the experimental results show that identification in fact can constitute a barrier for entering the auction as discussed in the theoretical part. At the more general level, in the market for privacy-sensitive goods market segments are missing, if individuals can opt-out of participation. From this research it cannot be concluded that individuals do not care about their privacy, as such considerations even guide auction participation decisions. In a later work, it will be tested how such sensitivity influences not only participation, but also price-setting.

5.3   Model Diagnostics

Visual inspection of correlation coefficients among explanatories did not render any concern about multi-collinearity, except for the aforementioned expectation variable. The robust option for the logit model indicates that the right model was chosen.

6   Conclusions

In this auction experiment, privacy considerations and costs not only play a role for price-setting behavior, but also for market participation. Identification with the real identity of individuals introduces privacy costs. One can find robust effects that information allowing social comparisons is sensitive. If sensitive personal and private data is compiled into an information bundle, we can speak of a privacy-sensitive good. As stated, if market participation is voluntary, persons with a bad reflection on their identity might not participate, i.e. some segments in the market for privacy-sensitive goods might be lacking due to self-selection.

This confirms theoretical models, which assume positive privacy costs associated with identification. It can be preliminarily concluded that no dominant strategy exists, if there are positive privacy costs. It also sheds a light on the IC of RVA for obtaining personally sensitive data. Valuations in this auction are not drawn from symmetric distributions, but are skewed and depend on the type (i.e. test result). Moreover, it can be assumed that social comparison renders those valuations correlated.

These results are informative for online platforms that plan to directly involve consumers for data sales. Although field evidence would be needed to underpin the observations presented herein, one can speculate that such marketplaces mainly attract those with 'good signals.' Finally, this research shed doubts on the use of RVA as IC mechanism for obtaining valuations of personally sensitive information from individuals, as there is an absence of valuations by those who do not participate in the auction and the distribution of valuations itself in the auction is skewed as a consequence.

---

[13] Results are not shown as they are part of a following research project.

Acknowledgements. The author acknowledges funding under the Google Research Award for the project "Incentive-compatible Mechanism Design for Privacy". This research was not commissioned and not influenced by Google, Inc. The author is in particular thankful to Professor Dorothea Kübler for laboratory access and Ludwig Ensthaler. The author also thanks four reviewers for constructive remarks for the version submitted to the Annual Privacy Forum 2014.

References

1. Danezis, G., Lewis, S., Anderson, R.: How Much is Location Privacy Worth? Working Paper presented at WEIS (2005),
   http://infosecon.net/workshop/pdf/location-privacy.pdf
2. Egelman, S., Porter Felt, A., Wagner, D.: Choice Architecture and Smartphone Privacy: There's A Price for That, Working Paper presented at WEIS (2012),
   http://weis2012.econinfosec.org/papers/Egelman_WEIS2012.pdf
3. Feri, F., Giannetti, C., Jentzsch, N.: Disclosure of Personal Data under Risk of Privacy Shocks, Quaderni DSE Working Paper N° 875 (2013),
   http://ideas.repec.org/p/bol/bodewp/wp875.html
4. Huberman, B., Adar, E., Fine, L.: Valuating privacy. IEEE Security & Privacy 3(5), 22–25 (2005)
5. Dijksterhuis, A., van Knippenberg, A.: The relation between perception and behavior, or how to win a game of Trivial Pursuit. Journal of Personality and Social Psychology 74, 865–877 (1998), doi:10.1037/0022-3514.74.4.865
6. Ariely, D., Norton, M.: Self-deception: How we come to believe we are better than we truly are. Working Paper, Sloan School of Management. MIT (2005)
7. Joshi, S., Sun, Y.-A., Vora, P.L.: The Influence of Privacy Cost on Threshold Strategies in Sealed-bid First and Second-price Auctions (2005),
   http://www.seas.gwu.edu/poorvi/auctions.pdf
8. Naor, M., Pinkas, B., Sumner, R.: Privacy preserving Auctions and Mechanism Design. In: Proceedings of the First ACM Conference on Electronic Commerce, pp. 129–139. ACM Press (1999)
9. Gosh, A., Roth, A.: Selling Privacy at Auction, Working Paper,
   http://arxiv.org/abs/1011.1375 (November 29, 20011)
10. McSherry, F., Talwar, K.: Mechanism Design via Differential Privacy, In: Proceedings of the 48th Annual Symposium on Foundations of Computer Science (2007),
    http://research.microsoft.com/apps/pubs/default.aspx?id=65075
11. Horowitz, J.K.: The Becker-DeGroot-Marschak mechanism is not necessarily incentive compatible, even for non-random goods. Economics Letters 93(1), 6–11 (2006)
12. Shogren, J.F., Cho, S., Koo, C., List, J., Park, C., Polo, P., Wilhelmi, R.: Auction Mechanisms and the Measurement of WTP and WTA. Resource and Energy Economics 23, 97–109 (2001)
13. Azmat, G., Iriberri, N.: The importance of relative performance feedback information: Evidence from a natural experiment using high school students. Journal of Public Economics 94(7-8), 435–452 (2010)
14. Lusk, J.L., Alexander, C., Rousu, M.C.: Designing Experimental Auctions for Marketing Research: The Effect of Values, Distributions, and Mechanisms on Incentives for Truthful Bidding. Review of Marketing Science 5(3) (2007), http://www.researchgate.net/

Appendix

Table 1. Summary Statistics

Variable	Obs	Mean	Std. Dev.	Minimum	Maximum
Gender	195	0.6	0.4911589	0	1
Age (years)	195	25.97436	6.055104	2	62
Logic test result sold	216	0.837963	0.3693407	0	1
Logic test result	216	14.30093	3.695025	2	21
Pressure test	195	3.179487	2.28703	0	7
Motivation	195	5.415385	1.973215	0	7
Risk attitude	216	4.236111	1.399266	1	7
Privacy compromised	195	0.1846154	0.3889839	0	1
Offer	179	4.206592	6.846117	0	50

Table 2. Logit Models: Participation in the Auction (Logic Result sold)

Variable (options)	Logit Model	Logit Model (Treatment effect)	Logit Model (robust)	Logit Model (Treatment effect, robust)
Gender	0.41258738	0.41774195	0.41258738	0.41774195
Age (years)	-0.03410595	-0.033877	-0.03410595	-0.033877
Logic test result	0.20342138***	0.20440379***	0.20342138***	0.20440379***
Pressure test	0.01118043	0.01256177	0.01118043	0.01256177
Risk attitude	0.30356332*	0.30395066*	0.30356332*	0.30395066*
Privacy compromised	0.74065701	0.745609	0.74065701	0.745609
Treatment dummy		0.06145622		0.06145622
_cons	-1.9067208	-2.038415	-1.9067208	-2.038415

Legend: * $p<0.05$; ** $p<0.01$; *** $p<0.001$, DV: offer variable with outliers removed

Privacy-ABCs to Leverage Identity Management as a Service

Ahmad Sabouri[1] and Ronny Bjones[2]

[1] Goethe University Frankfurt,
Deutsche Telekom Chair of Mobile Business & Multilateral Security,
Grueneburgplatz 1, 60323 Frankfurt, Germany
Ahmad.Sabouri@m-chair.de
[2] Microsoft Corporate, Belgium
Ronny.Bjones@microsoft.com

Abstract. Along with the rapid growth in adoption of cloud services, there have been developments towards a new emerging concept, called Identity Management as a Service. As the internal IT systems were not designed for externals, the IT solutions from the cloud can solve the challenges of connecting the enterprises to the outer world and consequently, bring all the benefits of the cloud-based services to them.

However, the other side of the coin of moving towards outsourcing identity infrastructure is a set of privacy and security challenges that cannot be neglected. In this paper, we propose an architectural model based on Privacy Preserving Attribute-based Credentials, and show how we can benefit from the advantages of Privacy-ABCs to help the concept of Identity Management as a Service, and address the privacy concerns that it raises.

Keywords: Identity Management as a Service, IdMaaS, Privacy Preserving Attribute-based Credentials.

1 Introduction

The US National Institute of Standards and Technology (NIST) defines Cloud Computing to be a model for enabling ubiquitous, convenient, on-demand network access to a shared pool of configurable computing resources (e.g., networks, servers, storage, applications, and services) that can be rapidly provisioned and released with minimal management effort or service provider interaction [1]. In another perspective, cloud services give organizations the opportunity to outsource the parts of their IT infrastructures that they do not have adequate skills, and therefore focus more on their own expertise to increase their productivity and lower their costs.

Researchers have conduced various studies, like [2], to investigate the economics of the cloud and justify how migrating to cloud platforms will reduce the infrastructure and the labour cost while increasing the security and reliability. A more comprehensive list of the drivers and the blockers to uptake cloud services has been surveyed in [3]. Their results show that the drivers extend well

B. Preneel and D. Ikonomou (Eds.): APF 2014, LNCS 8450, pp. 143–153, 2014.

beyond cost savings; In addition to the lower cost of ownership, over 50% of their respondents have recognized better working practices for the employees, improved efficiency, easier external interactions, and access to specialized and affordable applications to be *significant* or *very important* drivers. On the other hand, according to [3], it seems that each industry has its own bug-bears: governments organizations are more concerned about privacy and data protection, financial services worry about regulation and compliance, commercial organization consider storage of personal identifiable data to be a barrier, while telcos see intellectual properties as the most important blocker on their way.

In spite of all the barriers, a considerable number of services are offered as cloud services and enterprises and governments are rapidly adopting them. For example, Office 365 [4] and Google Apps [5] are making a good progress in the market. Therefore, we are in the stage where the cloud paradigm is building its concrete shape. The statistics by [6] shows that Software-as-a-Service is in use in 63% of organizations and it had a growth of 15% from 2012 to 2013. Therefore, cloud-based services can be considered as a mainstream way of delivering certain aspects of the IT requirements of many organizations.

As explained by [7], cloud computing is an amalgamation of various technologies to meet the demands of an interdependent maze of software and services. This necessitates several Identity Management Systems (IdMs), based on various technologies, to interoperate and function as one consolidated body. Hence Identity Management in the cloud is sufficiently more complex problem than the traditional IdM and consequently more expensive to implement. That is why cloud IdMs need to be built by specialized organizations to deal with the compliance, security and privacy complexities. Still hiding those complexities from its users to allow easy adoptance of cloud IdMs. This justifies the move towards outsourcing the IdM infrastructure to cloud services similar to other application services. Nowadays, a majority of enterprises are using Identity Management Systems and many of the deployed IdMs are onpremise, but increasingly they are being supplemented by the use of on-demand IdM service (IdMaaS) [8].

In this paper we present an architectural model based of Privacy Preserving Attribute-based Credentials (Privacy-ABCs) to leverage Identity Management as a Service and address some of the privacy concerns that has been identified for different deployment models of IdMaaS. The rest of this paper is organized as follows. Section 2 provides a brief overview of Identity Management in the cloud environment. Section 3 introduces Privacy-ABCs and shows their significant potential in addressing IdMaaS privacy requirements. Then we propose and analyze our model for IdMaaS based on Privacy-ABCs in Section 4. Later we close the discussion and conclude in Section 5.

2   Identity Management in the Cloud Environment

There has been an interesting survey reported in [8] based on over three hundred interviews with senior IT managers in medium size to large organizations in a range of business sectors across Europe. It shows a growth of 45% in the number of deployed IdMs in any from (on-premise, hybrid or on-demand). The report claims that the majority of businesses are opening up at least some of their application to external users and almost 58% transact directly with the users from other businesses or customers. In addition to that, their findings show that social media is emerging as key source of identity, particularly for the consumers, which has basically led to the emergence of the concept "Bring Your Own Identity". These two trends along with the rising use of cloud services and increasingly complex mix of identity sources are mentioned as the main drivers behind the growing use of Identity Management Systems.

Cloud Security Alliance [9] considers Cloud Identity as a Service (IDaaS) to be a broad term that covers the management of any part of the Identity, Entitlement, and Authorization/Access Management in the cloud environment. Based on this, [10] introduces IdMaaS as outsourcing the identity management service by companies and organizations from their internal infrastructures and deploy it on the cloud providers in order to benefit from the innovative offer by the cloud for externalizing the workload.

According to [8], IdMaaS is the provision of IdM capabilities on-demand over the Internet, which include the capabilities of an on-premise IdM Systems as well as the additional benefits specific to IdMaaS. Looking closely at the listed benefits, one could see that there is a high degree of overlap with the aforementioned drivers: IdMaaS eases provisioning of external users as it is designed for remote access, certain IdMaaS systems have pre-configured links to many social media sites supporting the concept of "Bring You Own Identity", IdMaaS enables easy federation of applications from different cloud service providers for all types of users, IdMaaS is easily scalable and can be expanded or contracted based on the need, and IdMaaS improves productivity of employees as it provides easy access to wide range of resources for all employees, including those working remotely. More interestingly, their findings show that the potential of IdMaaS is widely recognised even by those with pure on-premise IdM deployments, which gives hope to see further transitions towards IdMaaS in future.

Considering the case where internal policies of an enterprise do not allow some sensitive information to reside outside of the enterprise premises or the case where legacy system might cause interoperability problems, a Hybrid Model can be employed to bring agility to the enterprise to benefit from the full capabilities of IdMaaS while minimizing the cost of the on-premise IdM to the scale of that sensitive data or the legacy systems.

Whether IdM is deployed in the public cloud or in a private data center operated by a partner or on-premise; the great news is that this is all transparent to the user. Today there are still differences in the technologies deployed in the cloud or on-premise but this will all fade away turning the question where to run the IdM services into a pure compliance and deployment task. Services will be moved between the different deployment environments by means of a mouse click.

Besides all the benefits and motivations mentioned about IdMaaS, Identity Management in the cloud comes with a set of challenges with regard to its security and privacy. These problems has been studied and investigated to some extend in various research works including [11] [12] [13] [14] [15]. Although security has been identified as the most important concern in using cloud services, in this work we focus more on the problem of Privacy. In this regard, [16] proposes an Identity Management System called SPICE for cloud environments whose main goal is to preserve users' privacy. The authors claim a set of properties for Identity Management Systems in the cloud environments, which we take as the basis for our analysis. Using a different set of cryptographic tools, [17] proposes another approach to the verification of digital identity for cloud platforms. This work utilizes zero-knowledge proofs to enable the user to prove the knowledge of a set of attributes without revealing their value. In our work, we do not employ any specific cryptographic solution and base our model on the abstract definitions of Privacy-ABCs' features. Therefore, any concrete implementation of Privacy-ABCs would fit in this model.

As it is shown in Figure 1, having Identity Management of an enterprise outsourced to the cloud, we suggest to consider a four-corner model where User, Enterprise, IdMaaS Provider and Cloud Service Provider (CSP) are the involved entities. This reflects the basic difference with the traditional three-corner model where IdMaaS and Enterprise were represented by a single entity called Identity Service Provider (IdSP). There are several privacy concerns in the new model that must be addressed. But before moving to this discussion, it is important to understand that the trust relationships have changed compared to the case of on-premise deployment of services (e.g. applications) and IdM Systems. In a full on-demand deployment of IdMaaS, IdM capabilities and cloud services are being operated by external entities and not the enterprise itself. Therefore, additional measures are needed to deal with the emerging privacy issues. More specifically, these privacy issues are the followings:

1. *IdMaaS must not learn about the services that the users are authenticating to:* Due to the fact that IdMaaS Provider is not the same entity as the enterprise, tracking the services accessed by the enterprise's users might introduce threats to the enterprise's business.
2. *CSPs must not be able to link a user to her identity:* The CSPs are not operating in the domain of the enterprise and therefore minimal disclosure implies that they should be provided only with the necessary information. In this regard, the CSP only needs to ensure that the user is authorized by the enterprise to access the licensed service.
3. *CSPs must not be able to profile a user based on her different accesses:* Similar to the case of IdMaaS Provider, building profile of the users by an external entity is not desired for the enterprise and can be considered as the threat.
4. *Enterprise should be able to audit the use of resources and services while the CSPs are blinded to these information:* To avoid misuse and fraud cases, the enterprises demand for mechanisms to monitor the access to the resources. However, the minimal disclosure principle requires these mechanisms to limit monitoring capabilities only to the enterprise and avoid leaking extra information to the external parties operating the resources and services on the cloud.

Fig. 1. The four corner model of IdMaaS setup

3   Privacy Preserving Attribute-Based Credentials

Strong authentication and authorization techniques used nowadays are double edged swords: while they can protect service providers by offering a satisfactory level of resilience against unauthorized accesses, most of these technologies have the drawback of threatening the clients' privacy. Privacy Preserving Attribute-based Credentials (Privacy-ABCs) are elegant techniques to cope with these problems. They can offer strong authentication and a high level of security to the service providers, while users' privacy is preserved [18]. Existing privacy preserving authentication mechanisms are based on advanced cryptographic primitives [19] [20] [21] [22] [23]. In these schemes, users obtain certified credentials for their attributes from trusted issuers and later derive, without further assistance from any issuer, unlinkable tokens that reveal only the required attribute information yet remain verifiable under the issuer's public key [24].

[24] refers to the unification of concepts and features of the different privacy preserving authentication mechanisms such as Microsoft's U-Prove [25] and IBM's Identity Mixer [26], as privacy preserving attribute-based credentials or Privacy ABCs. Their definitions abstract away from the concrete cryptographic realizations but are designed in a way that instantiation with different cryptographic protocols is feasible.

A detailed description of all these concepts and features has been defined in Chapter 2 "Features and Concepts of Privacy-ABC" of [27]. Here we briefly quote the described entities and their interactions from [27] and [24].

As it is shown in Figure 2, Users, Issuers, Verifiers, Revocation Authorities and Inspectors are the five different involved roles in the ecosystem. The Users obtain "Credentials" containing certified "Attributes" from the Issuers. They can present the tokens derived from these credentials to the "Verifiers" to prove their eligibility for accessing a resource as long as their credentials are not marked as revoked in the corresponding "Revocation Authority". Furthermore, there is a possibility for the Users to encode their attribute values in such a way that can only be read by a specific Inspector.

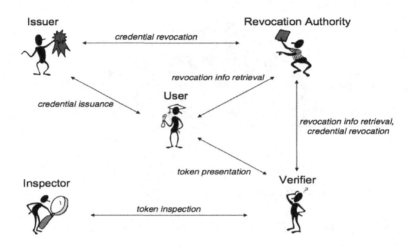

Fig. 2. Entities and interactions diagram [27]

As [24] says, "a secure realization of a Privacy-ABC system guarantees that (1) users can only generate a valid presentation token if they were indeed issued the corresponding credentials that have not been revoked, (2) that attributes encoded in the presentation token for an inspector can indeed be retrieved by that inspector, and (3) that the presentation tokens do not reveal any further information about the users other than the attributes contained in them."

4   Modeling IdMaaS Using Privacy-ABCs

In this section we propose an architectural model that represents the mapping between the Privacy-ABCs roles to the four-courner model explained earlier and demonstrated in Figure 1 in order to address the privacy concerns of IdMaaS. In a quick look, the proposed model for a full on-demand IdMaaS results in the setting shown in Figure 3.

In this setting, IdMaaS Provider will take the role of Issuer since identity information is residing on the cloud and they are available to the IdMaaS. Therefore it can issue credentials to the users based on the attributes and relationships that have been defined for the users in the user store (e.g. Directory). Theoretically, whoever is the Issuers can play as Revocation Authority as well. Even though it is possible to introduce a fifth party to perform as the revocation authority, a proper revocation scheme can give the opportunity to assign this role to the IdMaaS without any major risk. It is worth noting, that the request for revoking a credential always initiates by the Enterprise. On the other side of the story, the Cloud Service Providers (CSPs) are the entities that require to authenticate users before offering their services according to the predefined policies. Therefore, CSPs are acting as Verifier in this setting. Furthermore, another important required feature is Accountability and Auditing. The Enterprise needs to be able

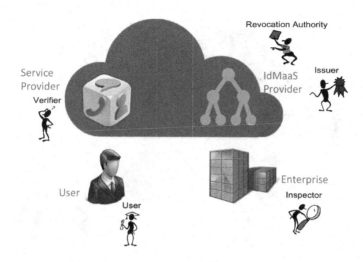

Fig. 3. Mapping of Privacy-ABCs' roles to on-demand IdMaaS four corner model

to monitor access to the resources and services in certain cases, in such a way that the Cloud Service Provider would not be able to profile the users. This is possible via the Inspection feature of Privacy-ABCs. The Enterprise becomes the Inspector and every access to the services on the cloud must be accompanied with a token, which is inspectable by the Enterprise when needed. Table 1 summarizes the role mappings.

Table 1. Mapping of the roles for full on-demand IdMaaS

Privacy-ABCs Role	Entity in the Cloud Setting
User	User
Issuer	IdMaaS Provider
Verifier	Cloud Service Provider
Revocation Authority	IdMaaS Provider
Inspector	Enterprise

The four-corner model needs to be adjusted a bit to reflect the Hybrid deployment of IdMaaS. Furthermore, the role assignment will also experience a change when Enterprise puts limited trust on IdMaaS Provider, which consequently requires on-premise hosting of attribute values. In this case, the IdMaaS Provider cannot issue credentials on its own for the users due to lack of access to the attributes. As a result, the Enterprise should be equipped with certain modules to play the role of Issuer and can be proxied by the IdMaaS to be reachable in the cloud environment. Figure 4 depicts the four-corner model for a Hybrid deployment and Table 2 summarizes the role mappings.

Fig. 4. Mapping of Privacy-ABCs' roles to Hybrid IdMaaS four corner model

Table 2. Mapping of the roles for Hybrid IdMaaS

Privacy-ABCs Role	Entity in the Cloud Setting
User	User
Issuer	Enterprise
Verifier	Cloud Service Provider
Revocation Authority	IdMaaS Provider
Inspector	Enterprise

4.1   Does the Model Fulfil the Privacy/Security Properties?

In [16], the authors list the following desirable security/privacy properties for authentication in the cloud. We consider this list as the basis for our analysis of the interactions between Users, IdMaaS Provider, Cloud Service Providers (CSPs) and the Enterprise.

– Unlinkability: In cloud computing, a user may access multiple services associated with the same or different CSPs. Unlinkability ensures that no CSPs, even if they collude, can link different transactions, whether they are of the same service or different services, of the same user. In addition to this definition by [16], another type of unlinkablity is needed, which concerns the IdMaaS learning about the services that a user accesses. This type of unlinkability is also known as untraceability in the literature and it is required in our model because the IdMaaS Provider is considered as an external entity for the Enterprise. The Enterprise might not be content if IdMaaS Provider profiles its employees or users.

One of the key properties of Privacy-ABCs is that the Presentation sessions are not linkable. Therefore none of the verifiers can profile a user or link different transactions of the same user even if they collude. In addition to that, the IdMaaS is not involved in the presentation process at all; therefore it will not learn about the presentation sessions and the services a user gets access to.

– Delegatable Authentication: In case that the service offered by a CSP, is a combination of services by some other CSPs, the authentication should be delegatable such that the CSP behind the scene can authenticate a user without a direct communication with either the user or the IdMaaS Provider, and without fully trusting the CSP in front.

In our model, the CSP in front can easily act as an intermediate proxy between the user and the CSP behind the scene and help them to exchange the Presentation protocol messages. The secondary CSP can perform the authentication using only the public information available about the IdMaaS.

– Anonymity: The users should be able to anonymously authenticate themselves, as authorized users to the CSP, without letting the CSP know about their real identity or exact attributes.

Another key feature of the Privacy-ABCs is minimal disclosure. If there presentation token does not include identifiable information, the anonymity of the user is preserved.

– Accountability: The users may abuse their anonymity. If needed, a trusted party can revoke the anonymity so the users can be held accountable for their malicious actions. As we mentioned in the previous section, the Inspection feature of Privacy-ABCs enables the Enterprises to securely log and audit the access to the resources. Using this feature, the CSPs can force the users to include encrypted identifiable information in the authentication token. Since nobody else than the actual user can create such a token, the user will be responsible in case of a misuse.

– User Centric Access Control: Users should be able to control what information they want to reveal about themselves over the cloud or to a CSP, and to control who can access that information, and how this information would be used in order to minimize the risk of identity theft and fraud.

Users of Privacy-ABCs are in control of their credentials. Before any presentation takes place, users get notified about the information that the access policy requires them to disclose. They can fully control what kind of information they are giving out. Furthermore, since the user is actively involved in the presentation phase, nobody else (not even the IdMaaS Provider or the Enterprise) can impersonate the user.

– Single Registration: The users need to register themselves only once for getting the credentials without the need of contacting the IdMaaS every time authentication is needed. Once the users obtained their credentials, they can perform authentication until their credentials are revoked. However, for some concrete realization of Privacy-ABCs like U-Prove, the credential consists of a bunch of unlinkable U-Prove tokens. When the user runs out of tokens, she has to somehow reload the credential with more tokens.

5   Conclusion

The trend is to move towards cloud services and replace on-premise infrastructures that are managed by non-specialists with cloud services that are offered by professionals. Identity Management is the underlying layer of every IT platform and can be also counted as the backbone of the cloud environment. Along with the growth in use of cloud services, there have been efforts to also offer Identity Management as a cloud service to bring agility to enterprises and facilitate their better integration with the cloud-based applications. In this paper we suggested an architectural model based on Privacy Preserving Attribute-based Credentials for the concept Identity Management as a Service. Our analysis shows that Privacy-ABCs can deal with the privacy concerns that have been identified for Identity Management in the cloud while providing a high level of assurance for authentications.

Acknowledgements. The research leading to these results has received funding from the European Community's Seventh Framework Programme (FP7/2007-2013) under Grant Agreement no. 257782 for the project Attribute-based Credentials for Trust (ABC4Trust).

References

1. The NIST Definition of Cloud Computing,
   http://csrc.nist.gov/publications/nistpubs/800-145/SP800-145.pdf
2. Harms, R., Yamartino, M.: The economics of the Cloud,
   http://www.microsoft.com/en-us/news/presskits/
   cloud/docs/the-economics-of-the-cloud.pdf
3. The adoption of cloud-based services, http://www.ca.com/es/~/media/files/
   industryanalystreports/the-adoption- of-cloud-based-services-
   increasing-confidence-through-effective-security.pdf
4. Office 365, http://www.office365.com/
5. Google Apps, http://www.google.com/apps
6. The future of cloud computing, 3rd annual survey (2013),
   http://www.northbridge.com/2013-cloud-computing-survey
7. Gopalakrishnan, A.: Cloud computing identity management. SETLabs briefings 7(7), 45–54 (2009)
8. Digital identities and the open business, http://www.ca.com/cn/~/media/files/
   industryresearch/quocirca-digital-i dentities.pdf
9. Alliance, C.: Security guidance for critical areas of focus in cloud computing v3.0. Cloud Security Alliance (2011)
10. Nunez, D., Agudo, I., Lopez, J.: Integrating openid with proxy re-encryption to enhance privacy in cloud-based identity services. In: 2012 IEEE 4th International Conference on Cloud Computing Technology and Science (CloudCom), pp. 241–248 (2012)
11. Brodkin, J.: Gartner: Seven cloud-computing security risks (2008)
12. Pearson, S., Benameur, A.: Privacy, security and trust issues arising from cloud computing. In: 2010 IEEE Second International Conference on Cloud Computing Technology and Science (CloudCom), pp. 693–702 (2010)

13. Takabi, H., Joshi, J., Ahn, G.-J.: Security and privacy challenges in cloud computing environments. IEEE Security Privacy 8(6), 24–31 (2010)
14. Angin, P., Bhargava, B., Ranchal, R., Singh, N., Linderman, M., Ben Othmane, L., Lilien, L.: An entity-centric approach for privacy and identity management in cloud computing. In: 2010 29th IEEE Symposium on Reliable Distributed Systems, pp. 177–183. IEEE (2010)
15. Architecture serving complex Identity Infrastructures,
    http://www.trustindigitallife.eu/actor/tdl-publications.html
16. Chow, S., He, Y.-J., Hui, L., Yiu, S.: Spice simple privacy-preserving identity-management for cloud environment. In: Bao, F., Samarati, P., Zhou, J. (eds.) ACNS 2012. LNCS, vol. 7341, pp. 526–543. Springer, Heidelberg (2012),
    http://dx.doi.org/10.1007/978-3-642-31284-7_31
17. Bertino, E., Paci, F., Ferrini, R., Shang, N.: Privacy-preserving digital identity management for cloud computing. IEEE Data Eng. Bull. 32(1), 21–27 (2009)
18. Sabouri, A., Krontiris, I., Rannenberg, K.: Attribute-based credentials for trust (ABC4Trust). In: Fischer-Hübner, S., Katsikas, S., Quirchmayr, G. (eds.) TrustBus 2012. LNCS, vol. 7449, pp. 218–219. Springer, Heidelberg (2012)
19. Chaum, D.L.: Untraceable electronic mail, return addresses, and digital pseudonyms. Communications of the ACM 24(2), 84–90 (1981)
20. Belenkiy, M., Camenisch, J., Chase, M., Kohlweiss, M., Lysyanskaya, A., Shacham, H.: Randomizable proofs and delegatable anonymous credentials. In: Halevi, S. (ed.) CRYPTO 2009. LNCS, vol. 5677, pp. 108–125. Springer, Heidelberg (2009)
21. Brands, S.A.: Rethinking public key infrastructures and digital certificates: building in privacy. MIT Press (2000)
22. Camenisch, J.L., Lysyanskaya, A.: An efficient system for non-transferable anonymous credentials with optional anonymity revocation. In: Pfitzmann, B. (ed.) EUROCRYPT 2001. LNCS, vol. 2045, pp. 93–118. Springer, Heidelberg (2001)
23. Camenisch, J.L., Lysyanskaya, A.: Signature schemes and anonymous credentials from bilinear maps. In: Franklin, M. (ed.) CRYPTO 2004. LNCS, vol. 3152, pp. 56–72. Springer, Heidelberg (2004)
24. Camenisch, J., Dubovitskaya, M., Lehmann, A., Neven, G., Paquin, C., Preiss, F.-S.: Concepts and languages for privacy-preserving attribute-based authentication (2013)
25. Microsoft U-Prove, http://www.microsoft.com/uprove
26. Identity Mixer, http://idemix.wordpress.com/
27. D2.1 Architecture for Attribute-based Credential Technologies Version 1,
    https://abc4trust.eu/download/ABC4Trust-D2.1-Architecture-V1.pdf

My Data, Your Data, Our Data: Managing Privacy Preferences in Multiple Subjects Personal Data[*]

Stefania Gnesi[1], Ilaria Matteucci[2], Corrado Moiso[3], Paolo Mori[2],
Marinella Petrocchi[2], and Michele Vescovi[4]

[1] ISTI– CNR – Pisa – Italy
stefania.gnesi@isti.cnr.it
[2] IIT– CNR – Pisa – Italy
{ilaria.matteucci,paolo.mori,marinella.petrocchi}@iit.cnr.it
[3] Future Centre– Telecom Italia–Torino – Italy
corrado.moiso@telecomitalia.it
[4] Semantic&Knowledge Innovation Lab– Telecom Italia–Trento –Italy
michele.vescovi@telecomitalia.it

Abstract. The evolution of mobile devices, the success of social networks, and the digitalization of business/personal services have resulted in a huge and continuous production of Personal Data (PD). The creation of a balanced ecosystem of PD, where data act as the fuel for novel application scenarios, may drive the shift toward a user-centric paradigm, in which constraints should be imposed on the data usage, to protect the individuals' privacy. The possibility for people to directly collect, manage and exploit PD introduces both technical and regulatory new issues in PD management. Uncertainty especially arises in the case of PD related to multiple subjects, *e.g.*, containing identifiers referring to more than one person, each of which holds rights to control how these PD are treated. In this paper, we refer to this kind of valuable data as Multiple Subjects Personal Data (MSPD). The protection of MSPD in a user-centric paradigm is an undeniable requirement to ensure privacy to all MSPD right-holders. We discuss the relevance of MSPD, providing a technical approach to regulate their trusted management in a user-centric model context.

Keywords: Multiple Subjects Personal Data, Personal Data Management, Privacy policies management, User-centric Privacy-aware architecture.

1   Introduction

Nowadays data are becoming the fuel of the innovation and an essential resource for the design and development of new, or better, services and products for Society and Business and they are at the basis of all the modern applications, ranging from personal applications and social networks to the future "smart cities" and "smart spaces"

---

[*] The research leading to these results has received funding from the European Union Seventh Framework Programme (FP7/2007-2013) under grant no 610853 (CoCo-Cloud) and the Registro.it funded project MobiCare.

B. Preneel and D. Ikonomou (Eds.): APF 2014, LNCS 8450, pp. 154–171, 2014.
© Springer International Publishing Switzerland 2014

solutions. They are the ingredient that is driving the evolution of the technology and the spark inspiring novel business. Moreover, data are also a source of information in order to better understand the behaviour of communities and of individuals, by means of data mining and social mining techniques.

The Directive 95/46/EC of the European Parliament and of the Council defines **Personal Data (PD)** as *"any information relating to an identified or identifiable natural person (the data subject)"* [13, 2]. Even if PD can (directly or indirectly) relate to an individual in several ways, in this paper we focus on PD intended to be pieces of digital information containing a Personal Identifier. In this paper, **Personal Identifiers (PIs)** are considered sequences of digital chars that uniquely identify a (natural) person within a domain[1]. Some examples are: names, phone numbers, e-mail addresses, passport numbers, driver's license number, credit card numbers, etc.

The amount of PD that nowadays is available and generated on a daily basis is rapidly growing due to:

- the increasing number of activities performed online or with a digital representation, due to a wide-spreader adoption of new types of personal devices (*e.g.,* smartphones, tablet), which enable people to access online services in an ubiquitous way and to interact with the real-world service (*e.g.,* payment, ticketing, check-in) in an innovative way (*e.g.,* by means of NFC solutions);
- the pervasiveness of sensors, either in the surrounding environment or integrated in the mobile devices, which enable the collection of contextual information in a transparent way with respect to people.

Gathering and processing PD enable organizations to a deeper understanding of people' needs and behaviour, while individuals can benefit from the creation of novel personalized applications with enhanced user's experience and improve their quality of life. Unfortunately, the current models of managing PD do not fully allow a rights-respecting, controlled, and effective exploitation of such benefits. In fact:

- PD are often spread and fragmented in the data centres of a multitude of organizations that an individual interacts with, either in the real or in the digital world. In this scenario, it is not possible to have a holistic view of individuals, as PD are collected and stored in several independent silos, each of which includes only the data concerning a specific domain.
- Individuals are almost excluded from the lifecycle of the PD which include the identifiers referring them (for the sake of brevity, hereafter we will refer to PD including the personal identifier of a data subject as "her" PD). Usually, they have a (very) limited possibility to manage their PD and exploit them according to their needs and wills, being mostly relegated to the role of producers of PD. This generated a lot of concerns in the users, leading to a loss of trust with respect to the collection and granting of their PD.
- As PD are mainly collected/stored by organizations, the focus of authorities has been more on PD protection, to reduce risks of uncontrolled use, than on the promotion of their full usage when paired with a higher control from data subjects.

---

[1] This concept, adopted in this paper, is not necessarily related to a legal terminology.

These factors imply a deadlock between the opportunities for exploiting PD in order to enable novel application scenarios and the constraints imposed on their usage to protect the individuals' privacy.

In order to overcome this situation, the shift towards a user-centric model for PD management has been promoted by several initiatives [42, 43], in particular by the WEF, in order to increase trust, to enable a higher control of individuals over the life-cycle of their PD [43], and encourage the creation of a balanced ecosystem of PD.

In the context of user-centric models, one of the undeniable requirement is to guarantee the right control and protection of PD also related to multiple subjects, *i.e.,* in which a subject can be the responsible of the storage of PD which refer to her and to other subjects Hereafter, we refer to this kind of data as **Multiple Subjects Personal Data (MSPD)**. Examples of MSPD are records of phone calls, co-location logs or reports of medical examinations. Hereafter, if one of the PIs of a user is in a MSPD, we refer to "her" MSPD, meaning that this user holds some rights on this MSPD.

Switching back to PDS services, if on one side a PDS should be able to collect and manage MSPD, on the other side such a service should adopt solutions for preventing and avoiding abuses performed by the "PDS-owner" *i.e.,* the PDS service subscriber, possibly damaging other individuals referred in the stored data. In this way, the PDS service is compliant to the Directive 2009/136/EC of the European Parliament and of the Council [14], and with the recommendation of an ENISA study [37].

Contribution. This paper aims at providing a technical solution to protect the privacy of the PDS-owners with respect to the other PDS-owners. The solution is based on privacy policies and it adopts a technical approach to regulate the storage, disclosure, and use of MSPD within a PDS model. In particular, we face the problem of personal data referring to more subjects. In general a *subject* could be a "single natural person", or simply a *person* that we refer in this work also with the terms *user* or *individual*, but it could be also a "legal person", *i.e.,* an organization (private or public) or a person acting in the name of the organization. In the following, we consider the case in which the subjects are natural persons. Furthermore, the protection of the privacy of the PDS-owners with respect to the PDS manager (and, in general, with respect to attackers) is not covered by this paper, and it is left as future work, although is a fundamental issue to be solved in order to design a real PDS system. The paper describes a PDS-based architecture that implements the proposed approach, detailing the interactions with the user and among the components of the architecture.

Structure of the paper. In Section 2, we discuss relevant aspects concerning PD and MSPD in the context of their storage and usage within PDSs. In Section 3, we describe a MSPD privacy-preserving architecture based on privacy policies. Section 4 analyses how the proposed solution could also apply to handle PD released back by organizations. Section 5 recalls related work in the area. Section 6 discusses about some pros and cons of the proposed approach. In particular, it provides an analysis of different privacy issues that may occur when we deal with not only natural persons but also legal persons, and when the PDS service provider is not a trusted party. In Section 7, we conclude with final remarks.

2 PD and MSPD in PDS Context

2.1 Personal Data in a Personal Data Store

A PDS is defined as a secure digital space, owned and controlled by an individual, acting as repository for PD, providing to her a set of services for the collection, management and the exploitation of her PD. PD can be collected from several sources and through different procedures. Some examples are:

- PD voluntarily introduced by the user, *e.g.*, uploading files in a personal cloud storage service (such as Dropbox), changing/filling the attributes of a user profile (*e.g.*, Facebook), content/information uploaded on particular Apps or services.
- PD automatically collected in mobility (from Apps or sensing platforms on personal devices of the user) or during online activities (*e.g.*, search/browsing history).
- PD uploaded (possibly in an automatic way) from organizations' data centers and returned in a digital, reusable format (*e.g.,* connectors to the social networks' APIs), as according to the "right of copy"/ "right of access".

PD are organized in records, grouping all the information related to the same object, action or event. We assume that distinct kinds of records stored in the PDS are predefined and, consequently, the format of each of these records is predefined too. In other words, for each kind of PD, a specific record type is defined. A record type declares its fields, each of which is characterized by type of its values (*e.g.,* a location, time, a sensor measure, etc.). For each record type, some fields store personal identifiers (PI). For instance, the records representing phone calls will include (at least) four fields: the phone number of the caller, the phone number of the callee, the call starting time and its duration. The values of the fields of the caller and the callee numbers are personal identifiers. The fields of the record which are not PIs, instead, become critical when they are stored in the record, because they can be refereed to (or have particular relevance/value for) the other subject(s) whose PIs are stored in the record. Roughly speaking, in the case of a phone call record including both the caller's and the callee's PIs, all the other information included in the record, such as the timestamp and the duration, become critical. They, in fact, may reveal personal information (such as actions, behaviours, etc.) concerning both the speakers.

A PDS provider manages an ecosystem of PDSs. A PDS subscriber (owning a PDS) can decide which PD have to be collected and stored in her PDS, can be passed as input to personal applications, or can be disclosed to other individuals or organizations. A PDS provider operates on behalf of its subscribers and should not perform any action on the stored PD according to autonomous decisions (unless these decisions have been authorised by subscribers). It is worth noticing that an individual can decide to store her PD in multiple PDS: this has the advantage to avoid a single point of failure on her privacy, but has the disadvantage of not having an integrated view of her digital footprint and of both increasing the complexity of data management and the data fragmentation and/or replication. For the scope of this paper, we concentrate hereafter on PDS owners storing their PD in a single PDS.

2.2   Multiple Subjects Personal Data

If a PD record includes PI fields referring to different subjects, this PD record is a **Multiple Subjects Personal Data (MSPD)** record: in this case, more than one subject could have control rights on (some fields of) such a record. It is worth noticing that MSPD are critical by itself whenever associated to other information; for instance, the exact time of an interaction coupled with one individual GPS location could reveal also the other individual location.

A simplified (possibly non-exhaustive) categorization of MSPD involving "natural persons" subjects includes *Interactions* and *Co-location*. In the following we provide definitions and examples of these two categories of MSPD.

Interactions. MSPD that contain parameters that identify two or more mutual individuals interacting, but also implicitly describe their relations, their social network, behaviour, and habits are classified as Interactions MSPD.

Examples of such MSPD are SMS, e-mails or messages exchange on social networks (which may involve simultaneously many actors and include sensitive content such as messages/mails' text). One of the most common is the Call Data Record (CDR), *i.e.,* the log of phone call. A CDR includes data such as: the speakers' (caller and callee)'s phone numbers, the time when the call was made, its duration, its type (received, unanswered, ..), etc. Therefore, a CDR includes PIs, *i.e.,* their phone numbers of (at least) two individuals, the caller (Speaker A) and the callee (Speaker B).

Co-location. We classified as Co-location MSPD those data that not only describe a relation (or, at least, a physical proximity) among two or more individuals, but also "benefit" of the property of being stackable with other personal information increasing the risks correlated to PD abuses. For instance if an individual A is co-located with B and this information is disclosed and combined with the location of B, the location of A is also inferred.

Examples of such category of MSPD are, *e.g.,* the logs of device-to-device interactions via Bluetooth (including the device name or univocal device id) as far as mutual tagging (*e.g.,* "I'm here with...") on social networks such as Facebook or Foursquare.

Let us consider more into detail the case in which an individual A (the PDS owner) wants to store in her PDS all the log records of the device-to-device interactions occurred via Bluetooth between her device and other Bluetooth devices in her physical proximity. In particular, using Bluetooth, A can continuously "scan" the area surrounding her device and monitor the presence of other visible Bluetooth devices (including personal devices like mobile phones or tablets). For every device-to-devices logged interaction, a record containing the two devices' MAC addresses, assigned names, and classes of devices can be stored together with the date and time of the interaction. In this case, the MAC addresses of the two involved devices are PIs, because the MAC address uniquely identifies the device and, thus, it might identify the device owner. Critical information contained in this kind of MSPD are, moreover, the name assigned to the device (which further can tell –but not uniquely identify– the identity of its owner) and the class of the device.

Thanks to the collected records, A can, *e.g.,* ask to some application to build the graph of her "face-to-face" interactions, to reckon her more frequent interactions (in proximity) or, even more, to keep track of "where I met whom", by combining these information with her precise geographical location (e.g., from GPS sensor or Wi-Fi connections).

2.3   Rights and Permissions on MSPD

As shown in previous examples, in several cases, the PD stored in the PDS of a PDS owner contains PIs related to other subjects and thus they are MSPD. We think that the concept of "ownership" of MSPD should be considered as for the case of PD. As discussed in [42], "the debate over who owns PD has proven to be complex and a key source of tension. It is an emotionally charged debate in which stakeholders have radically different and valid points of view." In line with the Data Protection Directive 95/46, we will refer to "control rights", instead of "data ownership", also for MSPD.

Thus, each of the subjects, whom PIs are into the MSPD, has some rights on defining preferences on how those MSPD are managed, such as: how they are stored, processed, and disclosed.

Uncontrolled usage of MSPD could result in a violation of the privacy of some of the (right-)holders, for example caused by the disclosure of the MSPD with 3rd parties or by allowing applications to process them. A recent remarkable case is the one involving WhatsApp: the Office of the Privacy Commissioner of Canada and the Dutch Data Protection Authority, in a joint report, said the app violated privacy laws because users have to provide access to all phone numbers in their address book, including both users and non-users of the app [36].

To give an example of the kind of preferences that could be expressed for managing MSPD, we consider here the case of the Interactions MSPD Call Data Record (CDR), introduced in Section 2.2. If one speaker would like to store the CDRs related to her calls in her PDS, she needs the permission of the other involved speakers. Suppose, for example, that the subject owner of the PDS is the caller, *i.e.*, Speaker A (the other case is absolutely symmetric, thus equivalent). In this scenario, different cases may occur, such as:

- the callee (*i.e.*, Speaker B) allows the (specific or every) PDS owner to store the CDRs, including her PI, (*i.e.*, Phone Number);
- Speaker B grants the permission to the Speaker A to store such records, but with her phone number encrypted;
- Speaker B does not grant any permission to Speaker A to store the record including her PI.

In the previous example, we are focusing on the privacy between subjects of the PI. Whenever B required storing her PI not in clear, PI could be pseudo-anonymized. We assume that pseudo-anonymization is achieved through an irreversible hash function taking as input the PI referring to B and a key associated to A (*e.g.*, her internal ID). In this way, A can correlate records referring to B, but a 3rd party is not able to correlate records referring to B disclosed by different PDS owners. Even if this does not prevent the possibility that an entity can de-anonymize B by means of an inference attack, it reduces the risk. Moreover, B could also increase the level of protection by denying to A the possibility to disclose MSPD about B, without having previously removed all the B's pseudo-anonymized PI or other fields critical for B.

The PDS owner could then define further rules defining how the CDR should be stored in her PDS (*e.g.*, she could require that only the calls to people in a "white list" should be either stored or excluded).

Moreover, the callee (*i.e.*, Speaker B in the previous example) must be able to control how her MSPD are used. Indeed, the CDRs can be used by the PDS owner for several purposes, such as input to applications which, *e.g.*, determine her social graph, check the interaction level with a given person (possibly in combination with other interaction-related PD, such as SMS or e-mails exchanges), or determine the phone user specific usage profile.

Also in this case the callee can determine, *e.g.*, the level of detail according to which her identifier or other information are disclosed; these rules could be different according to the usage scenario (*e.g.*, processing performed by a "personal application" run by the caller, or the exchange). The rules of the callee can contribute to determine (jointly with the rules defined by the caller) the format of the disclosed CDR, for instance:

- <PhoneNumA, PhoneNumB, *null*, duration,...>: if the Callee does not want to disclose when a call is performed
- <PhoneNumA, PhoneNumB, day, duration,...>: if the Callee wants to reduce the level of resolution for data on time
- <PhoneNumA, *null*, time, duration,...>: if the Callee does not give the permission to disclose PhoneNumB(in this case, the record includes only information which are under the control of the caller)

Other options could be to define rules for disclosing CDR information in aggregated form (*e.g.*, number of calls between caller and callee in a given time interval).

Coming back to Section 2.2 and the example of the Co-location MSPD, we remind that an individual A can scan the area surrounding her device, monitor the presence of other visible Bluetooth devices, and store every device-to-devices logged interaction. However, in terms of rights and permissions, another individual B could choose to deny the storage in a PDS of the proximity interactions of his Bluetooth device, in order to avoid of being unconsciously "scanned" (and thus being co-located to other devices) when he activates and sets to visible his device. This should be also the default policy defined by the PDS provider. In a different case, the individual B could grant to the other users the right of storing and using (for personal applications) these data or, even more, to disclose them to third parties.

The PDS should implement mechanisms to enforce controls on the managed MSPD, according to the preferences defined by those subscribers of the PDS service which have rights on those MSPD, but also in protection of the privacy of all the other data subjects which have rights on MSPD too, and not necessarily are subscribing the service. Relying on such mechanisms, the subscribers of a PDS service (*i.e.*, the individuals that own a PDS) will be able to control which of their PIs, or, in general any of the data on which they have some right, can be stored in other PDS, used by other PDS owners, and disclosed to 3rd parties. Such kinds of control imply the capability for the subscribers to define preferences on how their PIs can be stored in MSPD, and how the MSPD on which they have some right can be stored, given as input to applications, or disclosed to 3rd parties. We propose here to express these preferences with privacy policies, and each time a PDS owner requests to perform an action concerning a record and his data space, *e.g.*, store, give as input, or disclose, the set of people who have some rights on this record must be determined to enforce the proper privacy policies to decide whether the action on the record can be executed or not.

The PIs stored in the record (*e.g.*, the phone numbers and MAC addresses in the previous examples) are exploited to determine the ID of the referred person through the list of the PIs managed by the PDS manager and, consequently, to determine the privacy policy to be enforced. We assume that a default privacy policy is paired to individuals that are not subscribers of the PDS service, such that their PIs cannot be disclosed to the PDS service subscribers.

3   Architecture

We propose a framework for the privacy-preserving management of MSPD in a PDS context. The main goal is to define and enforce the privacy policies that regulate the storage, usage, and disclosure of MSPD within a PDS-based infrastructure.

Before introducing the privacy-preserving policy-based architecture, we present the actors involved in our framework. It is worth noticing that, hereafter, we concentrate on the storage of MSPD. A simple extension of the framework applies to manage the control on the usage and the disclosure of the MSPD already stored in a PDS.

The main actors of our framework are:

- *The PDS owner* that subscribed the PDS service and wants to store some PD records in her PDS. These records could be MSPD.
- *The MSPD right-holders*, *i.e.*, the individuals that have rights on the record the PDS owner wants to store in her PDS. The MSPD's right-holders are all the entities that are referred by some of the identifiers included in the record.
- *The PDS manager*, that is the entity that provides to individuals a PDS service; it is also contributes for the definition and the enforcement of the policies enabling people to control the collection, usage and disclosure of their MSPD. Moreover, it manages the registry for associating PIs to PDS subscribers.

When a new user subscribes the PDS, she can set her own preferences that regulate the storage of her data in the PDSs of other users (and the subsequent usage and disclosure to 3rd parties). However, since the subscriber does not know, at registration time, the exact set of subjects to whom she wants to disclose her data, she can set (or modify) her general and/or specific (*i.e.*, referred to one –group of– subject) privacy preferences at any time. The new preferences should be enforced both on the new MSPD that will be stored in her PDS or in the PDS of other users from that moment on, and on the existing MSPD, *i.e.*, the ones that have been already stored in PDSs. In the reference scenario, we protect the privacy of the PDS-owner w.r.t. the other PDS-owners only. Since all the accesses to the PDS are mediated by the authorization system (including the accesses of the PDS-owner to read the already stored MSPD) the right to execute an action on a MSPD is determined according to the current privacy preferences of all the subjects having some rights on this MSPD. Hence, in the case where the privacy preferences of one of the involved data subjects changed, the updated preferences are always used to determine the access right.

In order to identify its subscribers in the context of a PDS service, the PDS provider must assign to each of them a unique ID. An internal Id, or an hash of the user's phone number, or of another unique identification code (*e.g.*, the SSN in US, or the Fiscal Code in Italy and the National Insurance Number issued in the United Kingdom) could be chosen as unique ID.

Moreover, in order to easily determine the subjects referred by each MSPD, the PDS provider exploits a User Registry that manages a list of PIs of its subscribers. The PDS User Registry pairs each user ID with all the PIs of the user (and vice versa).

We also assume that "unknown" MSPD right-holders (*i.e.*, identified by PIs not included in the PDS manager registry) have associated the most restrictive policy, *i.e.*, that completely denies the disclosure of their PIs in the subscribers' PDS.

We focus on MSPD phone call data records (CDR). The caller A wants to store the CDR in her PDS. Both the caller and the callee B have rights on part of the CDR.

Let us suppose that B is registered to the PDS: she has not set any privacy preference at registration time and A calls her. A wants to save the CDR concerning this call in her PDS, but this record includes a PI of B (*i.e.*, her phone number). The PDS manager retrieves from the registry the unique ID of B from her phone number, evaluates B's privacy policy and finds out that it does not allow A to store B's data since no policy has been explicitly set to authorize that storage. Hence, A receives a notification that the CDR was stored with partial information (the CDR is stored without B's phone number). In the case where the record includes other data fields on which B holds some rights, these will not be stored as well. In the case where B is not registered to the PDS, instead, a default policy states that her PIs cannot be saved in the PDS of A. It is worth noticing that A is able to use the PDS. Indeed, A can store the fields in the MSDP that are only under her control. Hence, as soon as a bunch of people interacting one another starts to use the PDS, the amount of data stored in each PD starts to grow up. Finally, it is worth noticing that notifications are not stored in PDS.

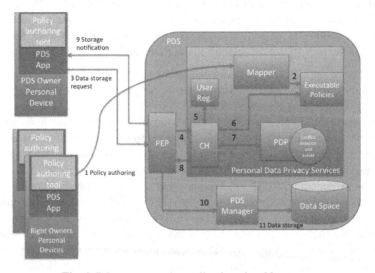

Fig. 1. Privacy-preserving policy-based architecture

3.1 Description of the Architectural Components

Figure 1 shows the policy-based architecture that we propose. The components of the architecture are the following:

1. The PDS App runs on user's device or machine and provides the user an access to the functions of her PDS. The PDS App allows users to control which types of PD are collected and stored in their PDS, to search, retrieve, and visualize the collected data, to delete some of them, and to control which data disclose to applications and the level of disclosure with other users or 3rd party organizations.
2. The Policy Authoring Tool (PAT) runs on user's device as well, allowing the user to edit her privacy preferences, on if and how MSPD referring to her can be accessed in the PDS of the other referred data subjects. The tool we consider is tailored for users not familiar with technical policy write up. To the best of our knowledge, there is a few works on privacy policies authoring tool tailored for non expert users. Some of them, *e.g.,* [19,22,7,35,8], study different aspects on the capability of common users to use such tools. Here, we consider the authoring tool we proposed in [11]. It has been designed and implemented in a customized way, in order to provide different levels of granularity when specifying the preferences. The graphical interface provides i) an easy and quick way for a common user to set privacy preferences on her MSPD in a few click; ii) the capability to set privacy preferences using a device of common use, such as a smartphone or a tablet; iii) an advanced mechanism to compose fine-grained privacy preferences for users that want to set up which MSPD category could be disclosed into which PDS, or could be used by which PDS owner applications, or could be disclosed to which 3rd parties. For example, users would simply like to set their preferences in few clicks, just giving a broad consent to sharing MSPD about them in other PDS, whatever the nature of such MSPD is. Instead, other kind of users would like to set, *e.g.,* the category of MSPD whose disclosure is allowed, or the period of time over which their preferences should be considered applicable.
3. The PDS Manager is the service that manages the functions of the PDS on PD (such as, storage). This paper does not describe this service in detail; for specific insights, the interested reader is referred to [31].
4. The Data Space, the database where the PD collected by the PDS owner, including the MSPD, are securely stored in a structured way.
5. The Policy Enforcement Point (PEP) is the component embedded in the PDS that intercepts all the requests concerning the storage or the accesses to the MSPD. The PEP invokes the Personal Data Privacy Service to perform the decision process, and enforces the decision. The PEP must be tamper proof and non by-passable, *i.e.,* all the attempt to access the PDS are intercepted by the PEP and forwarded to the Personal Data Privacy Service.
6. The Personal Data Privacy Services in the PDS includes several components:
    - The Mapper from Preferences to executable policies. The privacy preferences are mapped to an executable format, such as, *e.g.,* XACML, the well-known policy language constituting the "de facto" standard for defining access control rules [33]. The Mapper enables automatic translation between users preferences, edited in natural language, and the executable policies.

- The User Registry (UR) that pairs the unique ID of each user with all the PIs related to him (phone numbers, email addresses, and so on).
- The Context Handler (CH) receives the storage (or access) request from the PEP, retrieves the policies concerning the subjects that have some rights on the record that is being stored, along with other subjects' attributes that could be evaluated by the PDP and asks the PDP to perform the decision process evaluating the access request with the selected policies.
- The Policy Decision Point (PDP) performs the decision process by evaluating a set of privacy policies to decide whether the storage (or access) request should be granted or not. The PDP response could also include some obligation that must be performed by the PEP as the result of the decision process *e.g.*, request to pseudo-anonymize, reduce the precision scale or aggregate data before storing or using it.
- The Conflict Detector and Solver (CDS) component determines when two (or more) policies applicable to the same storage request returns conflicting results (*i.e.*, one policy allows the storage of a record while the other denies it) and decides the final result, *i.e.*, the decision that will be enforced by the PEP. The XACML authorization framework comes with a native conflict detector. For solving the detected conflicts, the XACML comes with a set of native *combining algorithms* that define the strategy for solving conflict. Usually, it adopts standard rules, such as, Deny-Override, Permit-Overrides, First-Applicable, and Only-One-Applicable. Other approaches have been proposed in the literature, see, *e.g.*, [26,18,1,16,27,38,29,15]. In particular, here we propose the approach we have designed and implemented in [26,18]. It is based on a multi-criteria decision process that allows to prioritize the conflicting policies by considering the degree of specificity of the elements constituting each conflicting policy. The elements of a policy are the subject, the object, the action, and the environmental conditions. Each of the elements can be characterized by several attributes. As an example, the attributes "category" and "Identification Number" can characterized the element "object" (in our context, the MSPD). To solve a conflict, we evaluate the specificity of the policy attributes. As an example, in [26,18], the category of the MSPD has been considered to be less specific than the Identification Number of the MSPD. Thus, the strategy that ranks the conflicting policies privileges that policy having specified the MSPD Identification Number rather than the one having specified the MSPD category.

Components 1 and 2 are deployed on users' devices, while the other components are generally deployed on servers in the network or "in the cloud".

3.2   Description of Logical Workflow

We concentrate on the logic workflow for storage operations. Similar workflow could be applied for authorizing other operations, such as the MSPD elaboration by user applications or the disclosure of MSPD with 3rd parties. It is important to remark that the storage operation is as representative as elaboration and disclosure to 3rd parties..

Overall, we assume that the MSPD right-holders have composed their privacy preferences through the authoring tools installed in the PDS App on their mobile devices (as indicated by arrow 1 in Fig. 1). The privacy preferences are automatically translated to executable policies by the mapper (arrow 2, Fig. 1). Then, the logic workflow concerning the storage of a new record in a PDS is described hereafter.

a. The PDS owner requests to store a new record in his PDS. Let us suppose that this record represents a phone call performed by the PDS owner. The PDS owner sends the storage request to the PDS (arrow 3, Fig. 1) toward his PDS App instance.
b. The PEP installed in the PDS intercepts the incoming request, and it creates a storage request message that is sent to the CH (4). This message includes both the data extracted from the incoming request and other data that are collected by the PEP because they are required to perform the decision process.
c. The CH retrieves the relevant privacy policies from the policy repository. In particular, it exploits the User Registry to identify the IDs of the MSPD right-holders from the PIs stored in the record (5). Policies are supposed to be indexed in the repository by the unique ID of the MSPD right-holders. Recalling the CDR running example, suppose that the caller would like to store the record of the call. He is not the only MSPD right-holder, since the callee identifier is owned by the callee herself. Thus, the CH retrieves from the repository both the policies defined by the caller and by the callee (6). Overall, we assume that a default policy exists that allows PDS owners to store data they have rights on in the PDS they own. However, the PDS owners can change this default policy whenever desired.
d. The PDP evaluates the privacy policies selected by the CH to decide whether the storage request can be executed or not. If more than one policy is applicable to the storage request, the Conflict Detector finds out whether the related results are conflicting, and the Conflict Solver is invoked to determine the final response. In our example, a conflict would exist, *e.g.,* if the caller authorizes himself to store the CDR, while the callee denies that storage. The conflict solver will take its final decision based on, *e.g.,* a strategy considering the level of specificity of each conflicting policy, as modeled in [30].
e. The PDP sends the final response to the CH (7), which forwards it to the PEP (8).
f. The PEP enforces a positive (respectively, negative) response by performing the storage request, (respectively, by skipping the request and sending back a notification to the PDS owner) (33,26,18).

4   Related Work

The existing literature refers to "multi owner" data whenever data can be exchanged among several entities that can perform some kind of action on them, with a particular eye to cloud storage. In [21], the authors deal with the sharing of data by considering the untrusted relation between the user and the data center provider. Due to this fact, they mostly rely on the CP-ABE schema. In [25], the authors propose a secure multi-owner data-sharing scheme able to efficiently support dynamic groups and guarantee privacy and anonymity to users. The approach is focused on a cryptographic model for sharing data of a data set among users belonging to a group.

Both these works do not refer directly to PD and PDS but treat the challenge of managing the access to data shared among different entities. Furthermore they propose solutions specific for some aspects related to the sharing of data. Here, instead, we presented an architecture that aims at being general enough to sustain any specific implementation of the single components, where the PDS is one of the main ones.

For what concerns Personal Data Stores, several platforms and solutions are already implementing PDS-based services. Most of them provide features for enabling the "owner" of a PDS account to control how the stored data can be disclosed or shared with 3rd parties. Here below we review the more relevant ones. None of these PDS platforms, however, considers the MSPD: the owner of the PDS is the only who has the right to control which PD are stored, in which way they are used or disclosed. They do not implement mechanisms to prevent and avoid possible abuses performed by the "PDS-owner" person possibly damaging the other individuals and organizations referred in the stored data.

The open source project *Danube* (*http://projectdanube.org/*) adopts XRI and XDI technology for controlling data access: relationships with individuals and organizations are defined by using XDI (XRI Data Interchange), through which a user can define rules for sharing, linking, importing and synchronizing data.

Higgins (*http://eclipse.org/higgins/*), another PDS-related open source project, gives user control over the information stored in her account, by allowing her to share selected subsets of it with 3rd parties. Relationships with external parties are established as bi-directional data flows to share/synchronize a set of attributes.

The PDS open source platform *ZXID* (*www.zxid.org*), developed inside the IST TAS3 Project (*http://www.tas3.eu*), extends the specification defined by Liberty Alliance related to the access of users' data attributes in the context of an Identity Management framework. It introduces a policy management architecture to make authorization decisions regarding data accesses according to the users' defined policies. The policy enforcement function is enhanced with a notification mechanism used to inform a user about the accesses to the data stored in her PDS.

The *OpenPDS* developed at MIT, instead, provides mechanisms to protect users' privacy by providing a query-based interface so as to enable only the sharing of anonymous and aggregated data (according to users' choices), and not of raw data [12].

A very preliminary approach to MSPD is implemented in the current setting of the PDS developed by Telecom Italia in the context of the *Mobile Territorial Lab (MTL) project* (*www.mobileterritoriallab.eu*), and exploited in its experimentations. The MTL's PDS implements features empowering people with full control over the lifecycle of their PD, from the data collection to the deletion of single/bunches of PD. In particular, a user of this PDS can choose whether to disclose or not the data of a specific type with other users or 3rd parties, and with which level of detail (*e.g.,* in an anonymous or "nominal" way) [40]. In order to avoid the privacy issues arising from MSPD, the *MTL*'s PDS does not include in its records information directly referring to other individuals different from the specific PDS owner.

Some companies, moreover, are starting providing commercial PDS-like services. For example *Personal* (*www.personal.com*) offers a "vault", where a person can store the "details of her life". Data are stored encrypted through a key under the control of the user, therefore, they cannot be accessed by the provider. *Personal* provides features to control the sharing of the stored information, and to improve the user experience in filling web forms, through data stored in user's vault. Analogously the platform developed by *Mydex* (*mydex.org*) implements features to enable users to control which data can be disclosed to another person or accessed by an application.

As previously mentioned in the introduction, user-centric identity management approaches exists [24]. These solutions aim at placing administration and control of identity information directly in the hands of individuals. In this way people have the control on the (certified) attributes to disclose to a provider when they are accessing a service, so as to fulfill the data minimization requirements. Examples of solutions are those based on attribute-based credential technologies [9]. Even if these solutions share with PDS-based approaches the same objective of give more control in the hands of individuals, the addressed scenarios differ: in fact, these solutions aim at performing secure transactions in the digital world, where strong authentication and according authorization based on certified attributes of the requester is paramount for protecting critical information and infrastructures online. Moreover, users' identity is mainly abstracted as a set of (certified) attributes to be passed in a privacy-preserving way to the service providers. Instead PDS-based solutions aims at offering to individuals an environment for the controlled collection, management, exploitation, and disclosure of the PD produced by them or about them.

5   Discussion

As discussed in [23], "there are many requirements for achieving the privacy needs as expressed as law. Currently there is no commonly accepted technical approach for meeting these privacy requirements".

For example, international regulations, such as the European Directive 95/46/EC [13] and its recent reform, give a definition of personal data and attempt to clarify how their privacy should be addressed. However, at the lower level of the single countries, both definitions and methodologies enabling a privacy-aware data management are often in contrast one with each other. To cite a singular example, ``pseudo-anonymity" is a different concept from the 95/46/EC Recital 26 and the UK/IE recommendations points of view. As an attempt to solve contradictions at various country level, the Article 29 Working Party has produced a set of Opinions and Recommendations concerning data protection, with an effort to shed light on how to deploy and implement effective solutions compliant with regulatory normative. In particular, Opinion 04/2007 [2] clarifies the definition of personal data, while Opinions 01/2012 [3] and 08/2012 [5] provides guidelines on their protection.

In this section, we briefly discuss some open issues deserving more investigation, in order to fill the gap between technological solutions and regulatory directives, and achieve a common vision for preserving privacy of shared personal data. This paper has focused on a user-centric model based on Personal Data Stores (PDS) platforms [12], enriched with a privacy policy-based architecture, in part covering some legal issues. However, there is still several questions worth to be addressed. We list them hereafter, and we leave a deeper investigation for future work.

In line with the Directive 2009/136/EC of the European Parliament and of the Council (stating that personal data must be protected against unauthorized management because personal data breach could have very dangerous consequence for data subjects, such as the identity theft [14]), we focus on controlled storage, use and disclosure of PD and MSPD. One possible way to foster the user-centric paradigm is to enable individuals to have a copy of PD (and MSPD). This is claimed to be sufficient to "create a liquid, dynamic new asset class" [34]. Individuals also achieve the opportunity to combine the data with information from other sources and to set permissions about how others can use data [42]. However, to have a copy of their PD is not enough to create value for people, if not combined with quality services for their collection, control (*e.g.,* on disclosure) and exploitation (*e.g.,* through an ecosystem of applications). A PDS platform provides a person with a data space, where she can collect her PD and access a set of services enabling her to manage and use her PD according to her wills and needs. In some cases, PDSs are built on top of innovative Identity Management platforms [24, 17] and their model supports the guidelines on the minimization of asserted/certified attributes necessary to access digital services [20], enhancing them with new application and business scenarios [32]. Actually, the deployment of PDS-based approach would enable new business opportunities with several advantages to all the actors involved in a PD ecosystem [32].

In the organization-centric model, organizations collect and process the data related to their customers/users according to the terms and conditions agreed with them. There are laws and recommendations that determine "guidelines" on the definition of these conditions and on how the users should express their consent on their application (*e.g.,* the rules on the informed consent) [41]. Unfortunately, there are not clear rules for a user-centric model. In fact, even if the PD Regulation should not apply to exclusively personal or domestic processing of PD (related to other data subjects) by a natural person, the exemption does not apply to actors which provide the means for processing PD for such personal or domestic activities. Moreover, analyses on the impacts of cloud-based services on PD treatment mainly addresses cloud services offered to enterprises and not to individuals [4]. Therefore, a regulation on PD in the context of personal cloud services, such as the PDS-based ones, it seems still missing.

In this paper we tackle with the privacy protection of the PDS owner PD against other PDS owners. We propose a solution based on privacy policies, whose management infrastructure is provided by the PDS manager. However, enabling inexperienced users with even an appropriate technology could not be sufficient. Indeed, especially in non trivial user-centric solutions, the probable low level of users' expertise may prevent individuals to manage (*e.g.,* edit and analyze) complex privacy policies to define fine-grained access rights or to frequently update these policies to fit new needs. Also, a noticeable study in [28] shows "privacy policies are hard to read, read infrequently, and do not support rational decision making". This makes worth to better investigate the comprehensibility of the kind of policies individuals are willing to accept. Also, an interesting study in [6] reveals "how technologies that make individuals feel more in control over the release of personal information may have the unintended consequence of eliciting greater disclosure of sensitive information". This paves the way for further investigation towards benefits and drawbacks of the adoption of privacy-enhancing technologies to protect PD and MSPD.

Finally, we are aware that other critical aspects to be dealt with are: how to protect PD from 1) the PDS manager itself, maliciously acting, *e.g.,* to sell PD of their PDS customers to third organizations; 2) the so called "malicious insider" attacker, *e.g.,* an employee at the PDS manager provider that could access PD of the PDS customers for activity of doubtful legality, and 3) a totally external attacker, able to break the security measures of the PDS manager and accessing in such a way to PD of PDS customers. In the literature some partial solutions able to guarantee privacy properties between the PDS owner and PDS service providers exist. They are mostly based on cryptographic protocols such as blind signatures [10] and 0-knowledge protocols [39]. However, they do not exhaustively accomplish with all the issues we have listed above leaving space for further investigations.

6   Conclusion and Future Work

This paper describes a technical approach to regulate the storage of MSPD within a user-centric PD management model. Even if we concentrate on the logic workflow required for storage operations, similar workflows can be easily derived for authorizing other PDS operations, such as the MSPD elaboration by personal applications or the disclosure of MSPD with 3rd parties (either other people or organizations).

An area for future work is to extend the solution in order to deal with multiple PDS managers. This is a fundamental requirement in order to enable a person to freely choose her preferred provider. We are considering several options on how the functions in the proposed architecture can be invoked in a multi-PDS context. Moreover we are investigating on how to transform the interfaces internal to the proposed architecture into open protocols, which, in the future, could be object of a standardization process. The integration of the components of our architecture is an ongoing work.

References

1. Al-Shaer, E.S., Hamed, H.H.: Firewall policy advisor for anomaly discovery and rule editing. In: IFIP/IEEE Integrated Network Management, pp. 17–30 (2003)
2. ARTICLE 29 DATA PROTECTION WP136, Opinion 04/2007 on the concept of Personal Data, http://goo.gl/8hO9m (last checked February 21, 2014)
3. ARTICLE 29 WP191, Opinion 01/2012 on data protection reform proposals (2012), http://goo.gl/9tMKa (last checked February 21, 2014)
4. ARTICLE 29 WP196, Opinion 05/2012 on Cloud Computing (2012), http://goo.gl/tvKNG (last checked February 21, 2014)
5. ARTICLE 29 WP199, Opinion 08/2012 providing further input on the data protection reform discussion (2012), http://goo.gl/1AJXB (last checked February 21, 2014)
6. Brandimarte, L., Acquisti, A., Loewenstein, G., Babcock, L.: Privacy concerns and information disclosure: An illusion of control hypothesis. In: CIST (2010)
7. Brodie, C., et al.: An Empirical Study of Natural Language Parsingof Privacy Policy Rules using the SPARCLE Policy Workbench. In: SOUPS. ACM (2006)
8. Brodie, C., et al.: The Coalition Policy Management Portal for PolicyAuthoring, Verification, and Deployment. In: POLICY, pp. 247–249 (2008)
9. Camenisch, J., Dubovitskaya, M., Lehmann, A., Neven, G., Paquin, C., Preiss, F.-S.: Concepts and Languages for Privacy-Preserving Attribute-Based Authentication. In: Fischer-Hübner, S., de Leeuw, E., Mitchell, C. (eds.) IDMAN 2013. IFIP AICT, vol. 396, pp. 34–52. Springer, Heidelberg (2013)
10. Chaum, D.: Blind signatures for untraceable payments. Advances in Cryptology Proceedings of Crypto 82(3), 199–203 (1983)
11. Conti, R., Matteucci, I., Mori, P., Petrocchi M.: An Expertise-driven Authoring Tool of Privacy Policies for e-Health. Technical Report IIT TR-02/2014

12. de Montjoye, Y.A., Wang, S.S., Pentland, A.: On the trusted use of large-scale personal data. IEEE Data Eng. Bull. 35(4), 4, 5–8

13. Directive 95/46/EC of the European Parliament and of Council, Official Journal of the European Union, L281/31 (November 23, 1995)

14. Directive 2009/136/EC of the European Parliament and of the Council. Official Journal of the European Union, L337/11 (November 25, 2009)

15. Dunlop, N., et al.: Methods for conflict resolution in policy-based management systems. In: IEEE Enterprise Distributed Object Computing, pp. 98–109 (2003)

16. Hall-May, M., Kelly, T.: Towards conflict detection and resolution of safety policies. In: Intl. System Safety Conf. (2006)

17. Hardjono, T., Greenwood, D., Pentland, A.: Towards a Trustworthy Digital Infrastructure for Core Identities and Personal Data Stores. Global Forum on Identity (2013)

18. Jin, J., Ahn, G.-J., Hu, H., Covington, M.J., Zhang, X.: Patient-centric authorization framework for electronic healthcare services. Computers & Security 30(2-3), 116–127

19. Johnson, M., et al.: Optimizing a policy authoring framework for security and privacy policies. In: SOUPS, pp. 8:1–8:9. ACM (2010)

20. Jøsang, A., Pope, S.: User centric identity management. In: AusCERT Asia Pacific Information Technology Security Conference (2005)

21. Kan, Y., Jia, X., Ren, K.: DAC-MACS: Effective Data Access Control for Multi-Authority Cloud Storage Systems. IACR Cryptology ePrint Archive, 419 (2012)

22. Karat, J., Karat, C.-M., Brodie, C., Feng, J.: Designing Natural Language and Structured Entry Methods for Privacy Policy Authoring. In: Costabile, M.F., Paternó, F. (eds.) INTERACT 2005. LNCS, vol. 3585, pp. 671–684. Springer, Heidelberg (2005)

23. Korba, L., Kenny, S.: Towards Meeting the Privacy Challenge: Adapting DRM. In: Feigenbaum, J. (ed.) DRM 2002. LNCS, vol. 2696, pp. 118–136. Springer, Heidelberg (2003)

24. Leenes, R., Schallaböck, J., Hansen, M.: PRIME White Paper, Version 3. PRIME Project (2008)

25. Liu, X., Zhang, Y., Wang, B., Yan, J.: Mona: Secure Multi-Owner Data Sharing for Dynamic Groups in the Cloud. IEEE Trans. Parallel Distrib. Syst. 24(6), 1182–1191

26. Lunardelli, A., Matteucci, I., Mori, P., Petrocchi, M.: A Prototype for Solving Conflicts in XACML-based e-Health Policies. In: Proc. 26th IEEE International Symposium on Computer-Based Medical Systems, pp. 449–452 (2013)

27. Lupu, E.C., Sloman, M.: Conflicts in policy-based distributed systems management. IEEE Trans. Softw. Eng. 25(6), 852–869 (1999)

28. McDonald, A., Cranor, L.: The cost of reading privacy policies. ISJLP 4, 543 (2008)

29. Masoumzadeh, A., Amini, M., Jalili, R.: Conflict detection and resolution in context-aware authorization. In: IEEE SNDS, pp. 505–511 (2007)

30. Matteucci, I., Mori, P., Petrocchi, M.: Prioritized Execution of Privacy Policies. In: Di Pietro, R., Herranz, J., Damiani, E., State, R. (eds.) DPM 2012 and SETOP 2012. LNCS, vol. 7731, pp. 133–145. Springer, Heidelberg (2013)

31. Moiso, C., Antonelli, F., Vescovi, M.: How do I manage my Personal Data? – A Telco-perspective. In: Proc. Data 2012, pp. 123–128 (2012)

32. Moiso, C., Minerva, R.: Towards a User-Centric Personal Data Ecosystem – The Role of the Bank of Individuals' Data. In: Intelligence in Next Generation Networks (2012)

33. OASIS, eXtensible Access Control Markup Language (XACML) Ver. 3.0 (January 2013)

34. Pentland, A.: Society's Nervous System: Building Effective Government, Energy, and Public Health Systems. IEEE Computer 45(1), 31–38

35. Reeder, R.W., Karat, C.-M., Karat, J., Brodie, C.: Usability challenges in security and privacy policy-authoring interfaces. In: Baranauskas, C., Abascal, J., Barbosa, S.D.J. (eds.) INTERACT 2007. LNCS, vol. 4663, pp. 141–155. Springer, Heidelberg (2007)
36. Reuters.com, WhatsApp violates privacy laws over phone numbers: report, `http://goo.gl/9tJzF` (last checked February 21, 2014)
37. Roussopoulos, M., et al.: Technology-induced challenges in Privacy & Data Protection in Europe. A report by the ENISA Ad Hoc Working Group on Privacy & Technology (2008)
38. Syukur, E.: Methods for policy conflict detection and resolution in pervasive computing environments. In: Policy Management for Web (WWW 2005), pp. 10–14. ACM (2005)
39. Uriel, F., et al.: Zero-knowledge proofs of identity. Journal of Cryptology 1(2), 77–94 (1988)
40. Vescovi, M., Moiso, C., Antonelli, F., Lepri, B., Clippinger, J.-H.: Toward Personal Big Data passing through User Transparency, Control and Awareness: A Living-Lab experience. In: Proc. European Data Forum (to appear, 2014)
41. Whitley, E.: Towards effective, consent based control of Personal Data. In: Hildebrandt, M., O'Hare, K., Waidner, M. (eds.) The Value of Personal Data, pp. 165–176 (2013)
42. World Economic Forum, Rethinking Personal Data: Strengthening Trust (2012), `http://www.weforum.org/reports/rethinking-personal-data-strengthening-trust`
43. World Economic Forum, Unlocking the Value of Personal Data: From Collection to Usage (2013), `http://www.weforum.org/reports/unlocking-value-personal-data-collection-usage`

Towards Electronic Identification and Trusted Services for Biometric Authenticated Transactions in the Single Euro Payments Area

Nicolas Buchmann, Christian Rathgeb, Harald Baier, and Christoph Busch

da/sec – Biometrics and Internet Security Research Group
Hochschule Darmstadt, Darmstadt, Germany
{firstname.lastname}@h-da.de

Abstract. On 14th October 2013 the European Parliament Committee on Industry, Research and Energy (ITRE) paved the way on the regulation and harmonisation for electronic identification, authentication and trust services (eIDAS) between EU member states. This upcoming regulation will ensure mutual recognition and acceptance of electronic identification across borders, which also provides an opportunity to establish trusted electronic transactions in the Single Euro Payments Area (SEPA). The contribution of the presented paper is twofold: on the one hand we discuss the adaption of the upcoming eIDAS standard towards trusted banking transactions and outline resulting security and privacy enhancements; on the other hand we extend the eIDAS standard by biometric authenticated transactions which not only boost user convenience, trust and confidence towards eBanking and eBusiness, but suggest to integrate state-of-the-art privacy compliant biometric technologies into the security ecosystem, which is promoted by both, the European Payment Council (EPC) and the European Banking Union (EBU). As a result we identify eIDAS as highly suitable for banking transactions since it is solely based on security protocols and infrastructure which have been for more than ten years proven secure in the civil aviation domain.

1 Introduction

The European Parliament Committee on Industry, Research and Energy (ITRE) initiated the regulation and harmonisation for electronic identification, authentication and trust services (eIDAS) between EU member states [11]. The eIDAS security protocols and infrastructure are based on standards which have been successfully adapted in the civil aviation organisation for a long time [5,6]. More than a hundred states actively issue ePassports, 54 of which store face and fingerprint biometrics on their ePassports and in total nearly 490 million ePassports have been issued (status: Nov. 2012) [19]. The upcoming EU regulation will ensure mutual recognition and acceptance of electronic identification across borders, which also provides a significant opportunity for trusted electronic transactions in the Single Euro Payments Area (SEPA).

Currently, 33 SEPA countries process over 80 billion electronic payment transactions annually [15]. Therefore a security protocol responsible for protecting

B. Preneel and D. Ikonomou (Eds.): APF 2014, LNCS 8450, pp. 172–190, 2014.

such a vast number of transactions has to be based on a standard which has been proven secure and functional in practice. These pre-conditions apply to the upcoming eIDAS standard, i.e. building a bridge between the upcoming eIDAS standard and SEPA transactions provides a mutual gain for both sectors. On the one hand the ongoing process of the eIDAS regulation is strengthened by new use cases targeted at millions of users (e.g. secure home eBanking and skimming prevention at ATMs). On the other hand SEPA transactions could rely on standards which have been proven secure in another high-security domain.

A study in 2010 [2] identified the harmonisation of the diverse regulatory regimes across Europe as one of the main obstacles for cross-border financial service profit. Despite the fact, that eIDAS is an upcoming standard, which will eliminate the aforementioned obstruction, it will rely on existing infrastructure. Belgium, Estonia, Germany, Italy, Latvia, the Netherlands, Portugal, Romania, and Spain are the EU member states which already operate eID systems, in addition, France, Hungary and Slovakia announced to establish their own eID system in the near future [33]. The harmonisation of these eID systems by the EU with eIDAS yields significant potential and a new level of security for eBanking in the SEPA. Furthermore, incorporation of biometric technologies is conceded to provide protection against phishing, eBanking fraud, as well as identity theft. Additionally, features extracted from biometric characteristics generally exhibit higher entropy than regular numeric PINs applied in current standards.

The contribution of the presented paper is twofold:(1) we discuss the adaption of the upcoming eIDAS standard towards trusted banking transactions and outline resulting security and privacy enhancements; (2) the first extension of the eIDAS standard regarding privacy compliant biometric authenticated transactions is given, which enhances user convenience, trust and confidence towards eBanking and eBusiness.In contrast to the very limited amount of existing proposals on the integration of biometrics into trusted banking transactions, e.g. [16], the proposed system fully relies on standardised and provable secure protocols, infrastructure, and technologies, which is vital for any kind of banking transaction application.

This paper is organised as follows: Section 2 presents the proposed overall system. Section 3 summarises the state-of-the-art of privacy compliant biometric technologies and discusses the entropy of common biometric characteristics. To augment the eIDAS standard by biometric authentication we extend the well-established PACE protocol to the BioPACE protocol in Section 4. Section 5 introduces the used security protocols and infrastructure. Section 6 evaluates the overall security and privacy properties of the proposed system. Finally, conclusions are drawn and future perspectives are given in Section 7.

2   System Architecture

The proposed system comprises four constituting processes, which are schematically depicted as part of Figure 1 and Figure 2, and combines three key components, (1) electronic identification, authentication and trust services (eIDAS) which are currently harmonised by the EU, (2) biometric template protection,

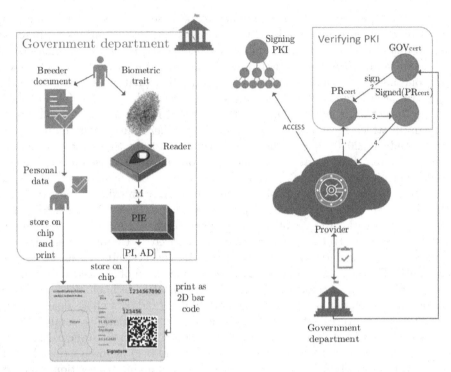

(a) eIDAS token issuing and enrolment   (b) eIDAS provider activation

Fig. 1. Wrap-up of (a) token issuing, enrolment, and (b) provider activation

(3) and the BioPACE protocol. These three components together provide a trusted service with electronic identification and biometric authenticated transactions (see: section 6).

2.1 System Hardware Requirements

A user needs a specific set of hardware in order to use an eIDAS-enabled eBanking application. The vast majority of users will most likely possess a subset of the required hardware. The primary device can either be a notebook, smartphone or tablet with a browser and Internet access. This user device, which is assumed to be free of any kind of malware, additionally needs a camera which is common for all three mentioned device families. An eIDAS token can either be contact based or contactless, but due to easier handling and less abrasion, most eIDAS tokens will be contactless. In case of smartphones or tablets Near Field Communication (NFC) is necessary in order to communicate with a contactless eIDAS token. Focusing on notebooks the user most likely needs an external eIDAS token reader or a notebook with NFC support. To capture the user's biometric characteristic he either needs a device with an integrated biometric reader or an external device which could be a feature set of the external eIDAS token reader. Since a user might also use eGovernment services with his eIDAS token it is even more likely that he already possesses the appropriate hardware.

2.2   eIDAS Token Issuing and Biometric Enrolment

Within the proposed system a user is required to possess an eIDAS token which can either be a separate token or, in the common case, an integrated functionality of a national ID card or driver's license. As usual, the citizen applies for the national ID card (with eIDAS functionality), e.g. by presenting a breeder document, at a local government department and performs a supervised trusted biometric enrolment.

At the time of biometric enrolment a citizen presents a biometric characteristic, e.g. a fingerprint or iris, based on which biometric data is extracted. Biometrics create a strong link between the subject and the eIDAS token. It is important to note state-of-the-art biometric capturing devices, e.g. fingerprint readers, include liveness detection technologies which prevent from presentation attacks [32]. Biometric data M serves as input for a biometric template protection scheme [31] which permanently protects the privacy of the data subject in accordance with the ISO/IEC IS 24745 [21] on biometric information protection. Based on this standardized architecture a *pseudonymous identifier encoder* (*PIE*) generates a pseudonymous identifier PI and auxiliary data AD out of M in the enrolment process, $[PI, AD] = PIE(M)$. PI represents a protected identity of an individual and AD is user-specific data, which assists in reproducing PI in an authentication process. In the proposed system AD is stored via a visual 2D barcode, see Fig. 1a, PI is stored in the internal memory of the eIDAS token chip and is therefore only available to the chip itself, and the unprotected biometric data M is deleted after the enrolment. The incorporation of biometric data is suggested to be implemented throughout the ongoing harmonisation of eID cards.

2.3   eIDAS Provider Activation

The eIDAS provider, e.g. a bank, requires access to the so-called *Signing* Public Key Infrastructure (PKI) [17] in order to check the originality of the eIDAS token presented by the user and to verify the authenticity and integrity of the personal data read from the eIDAS token (see: section 6).

Additionally, the eIDAS provider registers its service at the appropriate government department which handles the so-called *Verifying* PKI [7,27] in order to receive a service provider certificate. This certificate can be verified by the eIDAS token and also contains the eIDAS provider's access rights, i.e. the eIDAS token will only allow access to data groups granted by the service provider certificate, as shown in Figure 1b.

2.4   Entity Authentication: Token – Reader

At authentication the user presents his biometric characteristic and the eIDAS token, which comprises AD in form of a visual 2D barcode, to the user's device.

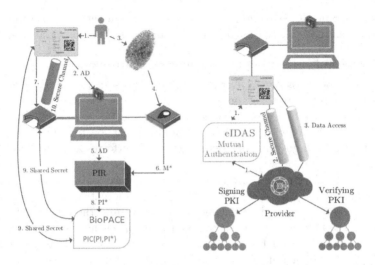

(a) Entity auth.: Token – Reader (b) Entity auth.: Token – Provider

Fig. 2. Wrap-up of authentication of token and (a) reader, and (b) provider

The *pseudonymous identifier recorder* (PIR) takes a queried biometric datum M^* and AD as inputs and calculates a pseudonymous identifier PI^*, $[PI^*] = PIR(M^*, AD)$. This PI^* is transferred from the reader to the eIDAS token as part of the BioPACE [8] protocol which also performs the comparison of protected templates. Within a conventional template protection scheme the *pseudonymous identifier comparator* (PIC) compares PI^* with the stored PI, $v = PIC(PI, PI^*)$. Depending on comparators, the comparison result v is either a hard decision (yes/no) or a similarity score v which is then compared against a threshold t, in order to obtain a binary decision. Based on this static shared secret PI the eIDAS token and the eIDAS reader agree on an ephemeral shared secret authenticated with PI during the BioPACE protocol and establish a secure channel which provides authenticity, integrity and confidentiality for all data which is sent afterwards (see: section 6), as shown in Figure 2a.

2.5   Entity Authentication: Token – Provider

After the secure channel between eIDAS token and eIDAS token reader has been established, the eIDAS provider and the eIDAS token mutually authenticate with the help of the eIDAS protocols, the *Signing* PKI and the *Verifying* PKI. In case this step is performed successfully, it can be assured that(1) the eIDAS token communicates with a trusted eIDAS provider and knows its access rights, (2) the eIDAS provider knows that it communicates with a genuine eIDAS token, and (3) during this process both parties establish a secure channel.

Subsequently, the eIDAS provider can now access the eIDAS token's data over this secure channel to authenticate the user. Since now both parties are completely authenticated the user can perform an online banking transaction. This transaction is two-factor authenticated since the user proofed possession of the eIDAS token by holding it up to the camera and placing it on the reader, and by presenting his biometric characteristic to the reader. Due to the separation of possession (eIDAS token) and being (biometric characteristic) the eIDAS provider can be certain that the user performed the transaction himself. The entire process is illustrated in Figure 2b.

3   Incorporation of Biometrics

The term biometrics is defined as *"automated recognition of individuals based on their behavioural and biological characteristics"* (ISO/IEC JTC1 SC37). Physiological as well as behavioural biometric characteristics are acquired applying adequate sensors and distinctive features are extracted to form a biometric template in an enrolment process. At the time of verification or identification the system processes another biometric input which is compared against the stored template, yielding acceptance or rejection [26]. From a privacy perspective most concerns against the common use of biometrics arise from the storage and misuse of biometric data. Biometric template protection schemes [31] which are categorized as biometric cryptosystems [34] and cancellable biometrics [28] address these concerns and improve public confidence and acceptance of biometrics.

Both technologies are capable of generating AD and PI out of a given biometric input M. In case, PIs are applied within further applications, e.g. data encryption, it is required that generated PIs exhibit sufficient entropy. The entropy of biometric input data M directly relates to the entropy of the corresponding PI. Since biometric features cannot be expected to be mutually independent, different techniques of how to measure entropy provided by biometric characteristics have been suggested.

3.1   Template Protection

Biometric cryptosystems are designed to securely bind a digital key to a biometric characteristic or generate a digital key from a biometric characteristic [9] offering solutions to biometric-dependent key-release and template protection [10,25]. Replacing password-based key-release, biometric cryptosystems bring about substantial security benefits. It is significantly more difficult to forge, copy, share, and distribute biometrics compared to passwords [26]. Further, most biometric characteristics provide an equal level of security across a user-group. Due to biometric variance, see Fig. 3, conventional biometric systems perform "fuzzy comparisons" by applying decision thresholds which are set up based on score distributions between genuine and non-genuine subjects. In contrast, biometric cryptosystems are designed to output stable keys which are required to match a hundred percent at authentication. Biometric templates are replaced through biometric-dependent public information (AD) which is used in order to release a key (PI).

Cancelable biometrics consist of intentional, repeatable distortions of biometric signals based on transforms (AD) which provide a comparison of protected

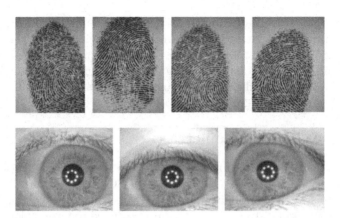

Fig. 3. Biometric variance (images taken from FVC'04, CASIAv3 database)

templates (*PIs*) in the transformed domain [28]. The inversion of such transformed biometric templates must not be feasible for potential imposters. In contrast to templates protected by standard encryption algorithms, transformed templates are never decrypted since the comparison of biometric templates is performed in transformed space which is the very essence of cancelable biometrics. Obviously, cancelable biometrics are closely related to biometric cryptosystems. In accordance with the ISO/IEC IS 24745, both technologies aim at meeting the two major requirements of irreversibility and unlinkability preventing from identity fraud and privacy violation:

- *Irreversibility*: knowledge of the protected template cannot be used to determine any information about the original biometric sample, while it should be easy to generate the protected template.
- *Unlinkability*: different versions of protected biometric templates can be generated based on the same biometric data, while protected templates should not allow cross-matching.

In past year numerous approaches to biometric template protection have been designed with respect to different biometric characteristics and application scenarios, see [25, 31]. In addition, various approaches to multi-biometric template protection schemes, i.e. systems which incorporate biometric data extracted from different biometric characteristics, have been proposed [30]. Nonetheless, the vast majority of template protection schemes report a reasonable decrease in recognition accuracy, yielding a trade-off between security and biometric performance.

3.2   Entropy of Biometric Data

As previously mentioned, biometric features must not be expected to be mutually independent, e.g. fingerprints underlie distinct structures. Focusing on data storage, binary biometric templates represent a favourable representation, enabling compact storage and rapid comparison. So far, numerous approaches have been

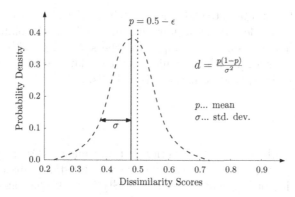

Fig. 4. Binomial distribution of scores between different pairs of vectors

Table 1. Entropy reported in literature for different biometric characteristics

Biometric characteristic	Feature extractor	Entropy (in bits)	Ref.
Fingerprint	Minutia-based	84	[29]
Iris	2D Log-Gabor wavelets	249	[13]
Face	Fusion of FLD and PCA	56	[1]

FLD ... Fisher linear discriminant   PCA ... Principal component analysis

proposed to extract binary feature vectors from diverse biometric characteristics, i.e. without loss of generality we will restrict to analyse entropy of biometric data according to a binary representation of biometric features.

A common way to estimate the average entropy ($\simeq$ amount of mutually independent bits) of biometric feature vectors is to measure the provided "degrees-of-freedom" which are defined by $d = p(1 - p)/\sigma^2$, where p is the mean Hamming distance (HD) and σ^2 the corresponding variance between comparisons of different pairs of binary feature vectors, shown in Fig. 4. In case all bits of each binary feature vector of length z would be mutually independent, comparisons of pairs of different feature vectors would yield a binomial distribution, $\mathcal{B}(z, k) = \binom{z}{k}p^k(1 - p)^{z-k} = \binom{z}{k}0.5^z$ and the expectation of the HD would be $1/z \cdot \mathbb{E}(X \oplus Y) = zp \cdot 1/z = p = 0.5$, where X and Y are two independent random variables in $\{0, 1\}$. In reality p decreases to $0.5 - \epsilon$ while HDs remain binomially distributed with a reduction in z in particular, $\mathcal{B}(d, 0.5)$ [35]. Reported entropy in literature of relevant biometric characteristics are summarised in Table 1. Estimated entropy can be directly transferred to AD and PIs which are applied in further application. However, techniques which are employed to overcome biometric variance, e.g. severe quantisation, may reduce the entropy of resulting protected templates [1].

In addition the amount of degrees-of-freedom can be directly derived from the false match rate (FMR) provided by a biometric (template protection) system. According to the ISO/IEC IS 19795-1 [24] the FMR defines the proportion of zero-effort impostor attempt samples falsely declared to match the compared non-self template. At a targeted false non-match rate (*FNMR*), the proportion of genuine attempt samples falsely declared not to match the template of the same characteristic from the same user supplying the sample, provided entropy (in bits) is estimated as $\log_2(FMR^{-1})$, which directly relates to entropy estimations which are frequently applied to passwords or PINs.

4   (Bio)PACE

The Password Authenticated Connection Establishment (PACE) protocol was first introduced in the German electronic ID card and standardised by the German Federal Office for Information Security (BSI). It has become an international standard in form of the PACE-based Supplemental Access Control (SAC) [18] which will be added to ePassports by the end of 2014 as a supplementing access control protocol and will replace the current ePassport access control protocol Basic Access Control (BAC) by 2018 [20]. The BioPACE protocol utilises PACE as its basic building block, but instead of using a knowledge-based shared secret like PACE, it uses a biometric-based secret instead.

The idea of BioPACE was first introduced in [14] and later extended in [8] in the form of BioPACE version 2. Since version 2 fixes a tracking issue and adds some useful security properties relevant for the eIDAS context, in this work we will from now on refer to BioPACE version 2 as BioPACE.

In the eIDAS system the PACE protocol is used to mutually authenticate the eIDAS token and the eIDAS token reader, and to establish a secure channel between the two entities which provides authenticity, integrity and confidentiality of the transferred data by means of the *Secure Messaging* sub-protocol.

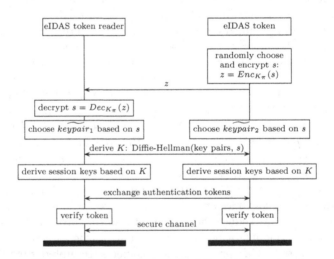

Fig. 5. Basic operation mode of the PACE protocol

4.1   Password Authenticated Connection Establishment

PACE is patent-free, provides strong session keys even in the presence of low-entropy passwords, and is resistant against off-line brute-force attacks [5]. The shared password is denoted by π and can either be received from the Machine Readable Zone (MRZ), a PIN, or the Card Access Number (CAN), which is printed on the eIDAS token and consists of a six digit number. Since eIDAS tokens can be contactless or contact-based both variants have different requirements in the eIDAS standard. The contactless version must support a CAN and a PIN, and the contact-based version requires only the PIN, the CAN is optional. For our eIDAS system only the PACE variant which derives π from a six digit numeric PIN is relevant. PACE is based on symmetric and asymmetric cryptography, depicted in Fig. 5, details are summarised in Appendix A.1.

Fig. 6. The eIDAS token with AD printed as data matrix code

4.2   BioPACE

BioPACE is a pre-processing step to the PACE protocol which replaces the commonly used knowledge-based shared secret by a biometric-based secret. In [14] the idea to make use of biometric template protection based on the ISO/IEC 24745 standard for biometric information protection is introduced (see Section 3). BioPACE does not favour a biometric characteristic, i.e. BioPACE may be implemented using the facial image, fingerprints, iris, etc. The BioPACE protocol consists of two phases:(1) initialisation phase and (2) regular use phase.

For every eIDAS token the initialisation phase has to be conducted before the manufacturer can personalise the eIDAS token. During the application of an eIDAS token a user is enrolled and feature extraction is applied to the captured biometric sample, resulting in a biometric reference consisting of a pseudonymous identifier PI and auxiliary data AD.

After the biometric enrolment AD is printed on the eIDAS token in form of a 2D barcode (e.g., a QR code [23] or a Data Matrix code [22]), which is shown as part of Fig. 6. *PI* is not publicly available, instead it is stored in the internal memory of the eIDAS token chip and is therefore only available to the chip itself, but not to the eIDAS token reader.

After initialisation BioPACE is ready for the regular use phase which consists of a new feature extraction from a biometric sample and an optical scan of previously enrolled *AD*. An eIDAS token reader requires optical access to the eIDAS token in order to scan the 2D barcode and receive *AD* to calculate *PI**, which equals *PI* if and only if the same person provided the biometric sample and therefore a biometric match occurs, this phase is depicted in Fig. 7.

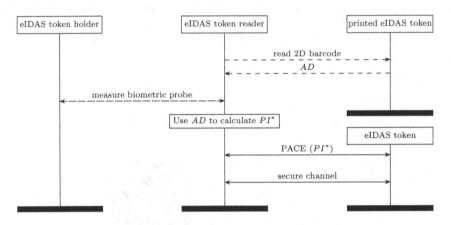

Fig. 7. Basic operation mode of the BioPACE protocol

After this pre-processing step *PI** is used as input for the PACE protocol. *PI** is implicitly compared to *PI* by the completion of the PACE protocol, because if *PI** and *PI* do not match the PACE protocol will fail. With respect to provided entropy biometric-based *PI*s exhibit sufficient entropy, cf. Table 1, compared to a PACE-based six digit numeric PIN which provides $\log_2(10^6) \simeq 20$ bits entropy.

5   eIDAS

eIDAS heavily relies on protocols and infrastructure introduced for electronic machine readable travel documents (eMRTD) [4]. Currently, eIDAS token functionality exists solely as feature of national identity cards which represent eMRTDs. Nevertheless, an eIDAS token does not necessarily have to be an eMRTD, but could also be a standalone token or part of a driving license.

5.1   eIDAS Security Goals

Between two entities (e.g. a user and a bank with an eID enabled service) eIDAS provides mutual authentication and key agreement to establish a secure channel. On the one hand the user can be certain that he is communicating with his bank and the bank can be assured to communicate with a user in possession of a valid eIDAS token. On the other hand, during the eIDAS procedure, user and bank agree on an ephemeral common secret to create a secure channel between the two parties which provides authenticity, integrity and confidentiality for further communication (see: section 6).

5.2   eIDAS Infrastructure

The infrastructure of eIDAS consists of two PKIs which are both common in the eMRTD domain [7, 17, 27], i.e. the *Signing* PKI and the *Verifying* PKI. Every eID service provider requires an authorisation certificate which regulates his access control rights for the information stored on the eIDAS token and serves as means of authentication towards the eIDAS token. The authorisation certificate belongs to the *Verifying* PKI and must be part of a certificate chain which has the eIDAS token's issuing country's Country Verifying Certificate Authority for eID (CVCA-eID) root certificate as trust anchor. This is crucial because the CVCA-eID certificate is stored on the eIDAS token and used during *Terminal Authentication* (TA) by the token in order to authenticate the service provider and validate its access rights.

The *Signing* PKI fulfils the opposite role for the eID service provider. On the one hand it can check the originality of the eIDAS token, i.e. it communicates with a genuine uncloned eIDAS token. On the other hand the eID service provider needs the *Signing* PKI to check the authenticity and integrity of the personnel data send by the eIDAS token. Therefore, every country which issues eIDAS tokens needs a Country Signing Certificate Authority (CSCA) which constitutes the root anchor of the *Signing* PKI and signs a certificate of the domestic eIDAS token manufacturer. During the eIDAS token personalisation process the manufacturer digitally signs a hash list of all data groups stored on the eIDAS token. The CSCA certificate and the certificate of the eIDAS token manufacturer enable the eID service provider to verify the digital signature stored on the eIDAS token to ascertain the origin and the genuineness of the data.

5.3   eIDAS Operation Mode

The regular operation mode of eIDAS starts with a mutual authentication and key agreement between the eIDAS token chip and the local eIDAS token reader of the user. Therefore, the entities either perform the PACE or, as in the proposed system, the BioPACE protocol which is described in Section 4. Focusing on PACE the user ensures his willing to use the eIDAS service and the token reader to transfer his private data by placing the eIDAS token on the reader and entering a PIN. For BioPACE the user provides his declaration of consent by scanning the eIDAS token's 2D barcode with the device's camera, placing the eIDAS token on the reader and disclose his biometric characteristic to the eIDAS reader. Subsequently, PACE/ BioPACE establishes a secure channel between the eIDAS token chip and the user's eIDAS token reader.

eIDAS Provider Authentication. The next step in eIDAS process is the authentication of the eID service provider towards the eIDAS token and its holder with the TA protocol. After TA, the eIDAS token holder can be assured about the authenticity of the eID service provider he is communicating with as well as about the communication partner's access rights. Additionally, he receives an authentic ephemeral public key from the eIDAS provider. TA is depicted in Fig. 8a, detailed steps are summarized in Appendix A.2.

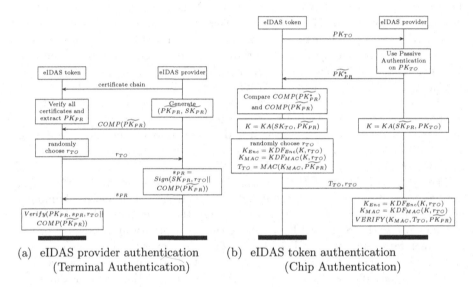

(a) eIDAS provider authentication
(Terminal Authentication)

(b) eIDAS token authentication
(Chip Authentication)

Fig. 8. Basic operation mode of the eIDAS mutual authentication

After successful TA the eIDAS provider's name is extracted from its authorisation certificate and presented to the user either on the eIDAS token reader or on the user's client device. The user has to manually accept that he wants to share his personal data according to the eIDAS provider's access rights by pressing a specified button on the eIDAS token reader or by accepting a dialog on the client device.

eIDAS Token Authentication. The closing protocol prior to the actual personal data transfer is called *Chip Authentication* (CA), which ensures originality of the eIDAS token and establishes session keys between the eIDAS token and the service provider.

In order to proof its originality an eIDAS token possesses a static Diffie-Hellmann key pair of which the corresponding private key is safely stored in the inaccessible internal memory of the eIDAS token. The public key has been signed by the eIDAS token manufacturer during personalisation, i.e. the public key can be verified with the help of the *Signing* PKI via Passive Authentication. CA is depicted in Fig. 8b, detailed steps are summarized in Appendix A.3.

eIDAS Data Access and User Authentication. Both parties restart *Secure Messaging* with the derived session keys. The eIDAS provider can now be assured that it is communicating with a genuine eIDAS token, but it cannot yet uniquely identify the user, because the eIDAS token's static Diffie-Hellman key is not unambiguous among eIDAS tokens. The ambiguity of the static Diffie-Hellman keys exists to prevent tracking based on the CA keys. To uniquely identify the eIDAS token holder the eIDAS provider is required to read the actual data from the chip over the established secure channel.

6 System Security Properties

Table 2 presents an overview of security properties provided by applied technologies and protocols. The majority of listed security property contributions have already been outlined in the corresponding technology sections. Biometric technologies create a strong bond between the eIDAS token holder and the token, thus preventing identity theft and mitigating eBanking fraud. Since BioPACE relies on a biometric-based secret, in contrary to PACE's knowledge-based secret it cannot be forgotten, lost, stolen, shared or duplicated by the user which enhances usability and reduces user frustration. The eIDAS standard unambiguously proves the authenticity of the service provider to the user. This process does not only protect eBanking customers from fraud, but, by presenting them with the access rights granted to the service provider, also protects their privacy.

Table 2. Summarized security properties of applied technologies and protocols

Properties	Biometrics	PACE	BioPACE	eIDAS	Proposed
Authenticity$_{token \leftrightarrow reader}$		✓	✓		✓
Authenticity$_{token \leftrightarrow provider}$				✓	✓
Access rights control				✓	✓
Data integrity		✓	✓	✓	✓
Confidentiality		✓	✓	✓	✓
Privacy preserving	✓		✓	✓	✓
Identification	✓		✓	✓	✓
Fraud detection	✓			✓	✓
Identity theft protection	✓				✓
Usability enhancing	✓		✓		✓
Phishing protection	✓			✓	✓
High entropy key seed	✓		✓	✓	✓
Standardised	✓	✓	(✓)	✓	(✓)

All security protocols which comprise the upcoming eIDAS standard are openly standardised and have been proven secure in the civil aviation domain [4]. These protocols have been standardised for the EU, since no international standardised protocol fulfilled the high security and privacy requirements which were demanded by the EU to protect sensitive user data, i.e. eIDAS builds upon carefully crafted security protocols. BioPACE has not been standardised but builds upon standardised components, i.e. biometric template protection and the PACE protocol.

6.1   Trusted Hardware and Trusted Enrolment

eIDAS tokens can be standalone tokens, but much more likely they will be part of a sovereign document such as a national ID card. Therefore they will be manufactured and personalised under highest government security regulations and certified using information technology evaluations. Therefore, eIDAS tokens can be considered trusted hardware which nearly any citizen will own in the near future.

The biometric enrolment is conducted in a supervised, trusted environment by trained operatives. In comparison to other systems, e.g. [16], the user has to present a valid breeder document before he is allowed to enrol for the new document. That is, there exists a strong, trusted link between the eIDAS token and the eIDAS token holder.

6.2   Security Assumptions

The PACE protocol has been formally proven in [3]. A detailed security discussion of Chip Authentication and Terminal Authentication can be found in [12]. Technologies of biometric template protection are standardised in the ISO/IEC IS 24745 [21] and have been reported to provide biometric-based secret which exhibit sufficient entropy to be applied in the proposed system architecture.

7   Conclusion and Future Work

In this work the eIDAS standard, which has been harmonized and regulated on 14th October 2013 by the ITRE, is(1) adapted towards trusted eBanking and eBusiness, and (2) extended with respect to privacy compliant biometric authenticated transactions. The proposed system fully relies on standardised and provable secure protocols, infrastructure, and technologies, which is vital for any kind of banking transaction application. Based on a detailed description and investigation of constituting system components we identify a significant improvement of user convenience, trust, and confidence towards eBanking and eBusiness. Compared to other systems involved costs are considered negligible for both parties since users can rely on hardware which, for the most part, already available. Furthermore, service providers can employ an already established infrastructure and, more importantly, delegate expensive hardware support to government departments. Based on presented investigations we identify eIDAS as an appropriate key driver in future eBanking services. In order to underline the potential of the proposed infrastructure future work will be focused on providing a formal proof of the BioPACE protocol.

Acknowledgment. This work was supported by the European Commission through the FIDELITY EU-FP7 project (Grant No. SEC-2011-284862) and CASED.

References

1. Adler, A., Youmaran, R., Loyka, S.: Towards a measure of biometric information. In: Canadian Conference on Electrical and Computer Engineering (CCECE 2006), pp. 210–213 (2006)
2. Ahlswede, S., Gaab, J.: eIDS in Europe – Not (yet) yielding profits for the cross-border financial services sector. Deutsche Bank Research (September 2010)
3. Bender, J., Fischlin, M., Kügler, D.: Security analysis of the pace key-agreement protocol. In: Samarati, P., Yung, M., Martinelli, F., Ardagna, C.A. (eds.) ISC 2009. LNCS, vol. 5735, pp. 33–48. Springer, Heidelberg (2009)
4. BSI: Technical Guideline TR-03110-1 Advanced Security Mechanisms for Machine Readable Travel Documents - Part 1 – eMRTDs with BAC/PACEv2 and EACv1, 2.10 (March 2012)
5. BSI: Technical Guideline TR-03110-2 Advanced Security Mechanisms for Machine Readable Travel Documents and eIDAS Token - Part 2 – Protocols for electronic IDentification, Authentication and trust Services (eIDAS), 2.20 beta edn. (September 2013)
6. BSI: Technical Guideline TR-03110-4 Advanced Security Mechanisms for Machine Readable Travel Documents and eIDAS Token - Part 4 – Application and Profiles, 2.20 beta edn. (September 2013)
7. BSI: Technical Guideline TR-03139 Common Certificate Policy for the Extended Access Control Infrastructure for Passports and Travel Documents issued by EU Member States, 2.1 edn. (May 2013)
8. Buchmann, N., Peeters, R., Baier, H., Pashalidis, A.: Security considerations on extending PACE to a biometric-based connection establishment. In: 2013 International Conference of the Biometrics Special Interest Group (BIOSIG), pp. 1–13 (2013)
9. Cavoukian, A., Stoianov, A.: Biometric encryption. In: Encyclopedia of Biometrics. Springer (2009)
10. Cavoukian, A., Stoianov, A.: Biometric encryption: The new breed of untraceable biometrics. In: Biometrics: Fundamentals, Theory, and Systems. Wiley (2009)
11. Committee on Industry, Research and Energy: EU e-signature plan to make electronic deals safer and easier (October 2013), http://www.europarl.europa.eu/pdfs/news/expert/infopress/20131014IPR22239/20131014IPR22239_en.pdf
12. Dagdelen, Ö., Fischlin, M.: Security analysis of the extended access control protocol for machine readable travel documents. In: Burmester, M., Tsudik, G., Magliveras, S., Ilić, I. (eds.) ISC 2010. LNCS, vol. 6531, pp. 54–68. Springer, Heidelberg (2011)
13. Daugman, J.: Probing the uniqueness and randomness of iriscodes: Results from 200 billion iris pair comparisons. Proc. of the IEEE 94(11), 1927–1935 (2006)
14. Deufel, B., Mueller, C., Duffy, G., Kevenaar, T.: BioPACE – Biometric passwords for next generation authentication protocols for machine-readable travel documents. Datenschutz und Datensicherheit - DuD 37(6), 363–366 (2013)
15. European Payments Council (EPC): SEPA - Key Figures, http://www.europeanpaymentscouncil.eu/ (November 2013)

16. Hartung, D., Busch, C.: Biometric transaction authentication protocol: Formal model verification and "Four-eyes" principle extension. In: Danezis, G., Dietrich, S., Sako, K. (eds.) FC 2011 Workshops 2011. LNCS, vol. 7126, pp. 88–103. Springer, Heidelberg (2012)

17. ICAO: Doc 9303 Part 1 Machine Readable Passports Volume 2 Specifications for Electronically Enabled Passports with Biometric Identification Capability. International Civil Aviation Organization (ICAO), sixth edn. (2006)

18. ICAO: Supplemental Access Control for Machine Readable Travel Documents. International Civil Aviation Organization (ICAO), 1.01 edn. (November 2010)

19. ICAO: Technical Advisory Group on Machine Readable Travel Documents (TAG/MRTD) – Twenty-First Meeting – Montreal. International Civil Aviation Organization (ICAO) (November 2012)

20. ICAO: SUPPLEMENT to Doc 9303. International Civil Aviation Organization (ICAO), 13 edn. (October 2013)

21. ISO/IEC JTC 1 /SC 27 Security Techniques: ISO/IEC 24745:2011. Information Technology - Security Techniques - Biometric Information Protection. International Organization for Standardization (2011)

22. ISO/IEC JTC 1/SC 31 - Automatic identification and data capture techniques: Information technology – Automatic identification and data capture techniques – Data Matrix bar code symbology specification. ISO/IEC 16022:2006 (2006)

23. ISO/IEC JTC 1/SC 31 - Automatic identification and data capture techniques: Information Technology – Automatic Identification and Data Capture Techniques – QR Code 2005 Bar Code Symbology Specification. ISO/IEC 18004:2006 (2006)

24. ISO/IEC TC JTC1 SC37 Biometrics: ISO/IEC 19795-1:2006. Information Technology – Biometric Performance Testing and Reporting – Part 1: Principles and Framework. International Organization for Standardization and International Electrotechnical Committee (March 2006)

25. Jain, A.K., Nandakumar, K., Nagar, A.: Biometric template security. EURASIP J. Adv. Signal Process 2008, 1–17 (2008)

26. Jain, A.K., Ross, A., Prabhakar, S.: An introduction to biometric recognition. IEEE Trans. on Circuits and Systems for Video Technology 14, 4–20 (2004)

27. NORMA, C.T.: CSN 36 9791 ed. A – Information technology - Country Verifying Certification Authority Key Management Protocol for SPOC (December 2009)

28. Ratha, N.K., Connell, J.H., Bolle, R.M.: Enhancing security and privacy in biometrics-based authentication systems. IBM Systems Journal 40, 614–634 (2001)

29. Ratha, N.K., Connell, J.H., Bolle, R.M.: An analysis of minutiae matching strength. In: Bigun, J., Smeraldi, F. (eds.) AVBPA 2001. LNCS, vol. 2091, pp. 223–228. Springer, Heidelberg (2001)

30. Rathgeb, C., Busch, C.: Multibiometric template protection: Issues and challenges. In: New Trends and Developments in Biometrics. pp. 173–190. InTech (2012)

31. Rathgeb, C., Uhl, A.: A survey on biometric cryptosystems and cancelable biometrics. EURASIP Journal on Information Security 2011(3) (2011)

32. Sousedik, C., Busch, C.: Presentation attack detection methods for fingerprint recognition systems: A survey. IET Biometrics (January 2014)

33. Tractis – Negonation: World Map of eID deployments, https://www.tractis.com/help/?p=3670 (December 2012)

34. Uludag, U., Pankanti, S., Prabhakar, S., Jain, A.K.: Biometric cryptosystems: issues and challenges. Proc. of the IEEE 92(6), 948–960 (2004)

35. Viveros, R., Balasubramanian, K., Balakrishnan, N.: Binomial and negative binomial analogues under correlated bernoulli trials. The American Statistician 48(3), 243–247 (1984)

A Appendix – Detailed Protocol Steps

A.1 Password Authenticated Connection Establishment

1. The eIDAS token chip randomly chooses a nonce s and encrypts it with K_π which is derived from the shared password π. The eIDAS token sends the ciphertext $z = Enc_{K_\pi}(s)$ to the eIDAS token reader.
2. The reader recovers s with π and receives $s = Dec_{K_\pi}(z)$.
3. Chip and reader create ephemeral key pairs, and perform a Diffie-Hellman key agreement protocol and s. By performing Diffie-Hellman both entities agree on a new shared secret K.
4. Based on K both parties derive session keys.
5. Chip and reader exchange and verify authentication tokens based on a MAC.
6. *Secure Messaging* sub-protocol is started with the derived session keys to establish a secure channel, which provides authenticity, integrity and confidentiality.

A.2 eIDAS Terminal Authentication

1. The eIDAS provider sends a certificate chain to the eIDAS token starting with its authorisation certificate and ending with a certificate signed with the private key which corresponds to the CVCA-eID certificate stored on the eIDAS token.
2. The eIDAS token's chip verifies the signatures of all received certificates, checks their validity periods, and extracts the access rights and public key of the eIDAS provider PK_{PR} from its authorisation certificate.
3. The eIDAS provider generates an ephemeral Diffie-Hellman key pair $\widetilde{PK_{PR}}, \widetilde{SK_{PR}}$ and sends the compressed public key $COMP(\widetilde{PK_{PR}})$ to the eIDAS token.
4. Based on PK_{PR} the eIDAS token checks if the eIDAS provider is in possession of the private key SK_{PR} with a simple challenge-response protocol. Therefore the eIDAS token chooses a random challenge r_{TO} and sends it to the eIDAS provider.
5. The eIDAS provider signs r_{TO} and the compressed ephemeral Diffie-Hellman key $COMP(\widetilde{PK_{PR}})$ with its private key SK_{PR} and sends the digital signature $s_{PR} = Sign(SK_{PR}, r_{TO} || COMP(\widetilde{PK_{PR}}))$ back to the eIDAS token.
6. The eIDAS token verifies the signature $Verify(PK_{PR}, s_{PR}, r_{TO} || COMP(\widetilde{PK_{PR}}))$ with PK_{PR}.

A.3 eIDAS Chip Authentication

1. The eIDAS token sends its static Diffie-Hellman public key PK_{TO} to the eIDAS provider which checks the public key for authenticity via Passive Authentication.
2. The eIDAS service provider sends its ephemeral Diffie-Hellman pubic key $\widetilde{PK_{PR}^*}$ to the eIDAS token.
3. Based on the received public key the eIDAS token computes the compressed public key $COMP(\widetilde{PK_{PR}^*})$ and compares it to the compressed public key $COMP(\widetilde{PK_{PR}})$ received during TA.
4. Next the eIDAS token and the eIDAS provider both compute their shared secret K via the Diffie-Hellman key agreement employing the exchanged public keys $K = KA(SK_{TO}, \widetilde{PK_{PR}}) = KA(\widetilde{SK_{PR}}, PK_{TO})$.

5. The eIDAS token derives session keys $K_{Enc} = KDF_{Enc}(K, r_{TO})$ and $K_{MAC} = KDF_{MAC}(K, r_{TO})$ with K and a random chosen nonce r_{TO}. To prove possession of the private key SK_{TO} the eIDAS token derives an authentication token $T_{TO} = MAC(K_{MAC}, \widetilde{PK_{PR}})$ with the just derived MAC session key K_{MAC} over the eIDAS provider's ephemeral public key $\widetilde{PK_{PR}}$ and sends r_{TO} together with T_{TO} to to eIDAS provider.

6. After receiving the random nonce r_{TO} the eIDAS provider computes the session keys $K_{Enc} = KDF_{Enc}(K, r_{TO})$ and $K_{MAC} = KDF_{MAC}(K, r_{TO})$, and verifies the authentication token $VERIFY(K_{MAC}, T_{TO}, \widetilde{PK_{PR}})$.

Author Index